The Book of

ISLAMIC DYNASTIES

A CELEBRATION OF ISLAMIC HISTORY AND CULTURE

WRITTEN AND ILLUSTRATED BY
LUQMAN NAGY

TA-HA PUBLISHERS LTD.

Published May 2008

Published by
Ta-Ha Publishers Ltd.
Unit 4, The Windsor Centre
Windsor Grove
London, SE27 9NT
www.taha.co.uk

Written and Illustrated by: Luqman Nagy
Edited by: Dr. Abia Afsar-Siddiqui
Typeset by: Planman Technologies India Pvt. Ltd

ISBN-10: 1 842 000 91 8 (Hardback)
ISBN-13: 978 1 84200 091 5 (Hardback)

ISBN-10: 1 842 000 93 4 (Paperback)
ISBN-13: 978 1 84200 094 6 (Paperback)

Printed and bound by: Mega Basim, Turkey

This book is dedicated to its first three readers: my children 'Abd al-Haq, Meryem and 'Abd al-Hay.

Front cover illustration: This shallow bowl decorated in the 'Kufi' style of Arabic writing is an example of Samanid pottery. It was made in Samarqand in 912.

Back cover illustration: This is an example of stucco and ceramic tile used by the Nasrids in the Alhambra, Spain.

Title page illustration: This beautiful *bismillah* is an example of the superb tile work found throughout the Mosque of Gawhar Shad, Mashhad, Iran, dated 1418.

CONTENTS

INTRODUCTION

Over the years, history and its importance have been very cleverly and concisely commented on by Western scholars. The American philosopher, George Santayana (1863–1952), for example, stated that, "Those who ignore [cannot learn from] history are doomed to repeat it." And, according to the British playwright George Bernard Shaw (1856–1950), "We learn from history that we learn nothing from history." But what did the great Arab social historian, Ibn Khaldun of Tunis (1332–1406), have to say about history? In his *Muqaddimah* (the Introduction to his *Universal History*), Ibn Khaldun, surely the greatest historian of the Middle Ages, offers us a definition of history without parallel:

> History is the record of human society, or world civilisation; of the changes that take place in the nature of that society, such as slavery, sociability, and group solidarity; of revolutions and uprisings by one set of people against another with the resulting kingdoms and states, with their various ranks; of different activities, and occupations of men, whether for gaining their livelihood or in the various sciences and crafts; and, in general, of all the transformations that society undergoes by its various nature ...[1]

Our history – the history of the varied Muslim peoples living across wide areas of the African and Asian continents – began fourteen centuries ago with the revelation of the Qur'an to the Prophet Muhammad ﷺ and the perfection of the true religion of Islam. Once it became clear that *Din al-Haq al-Islam* was not solely a religion of the Arabs, but truly a religion for all peoples and for all time, *Dar al-Islam* quickly expanded to the east and west of its original Arabian birthplace.

This book is an attempt to present in one concise volume an introduction to the many great Islamic dynasties that have arisen, shone and faded – like stars in the firmament – but have left the Muslim world all the richer. It attempts to record the history of some of the changes that took place in these varied societies and to note, in the words of Ibn Khaldun, the "revolutions and uprisings by one set of people against another with the resulting kingdoms and states".

The subtitle, *A Celebration of Islamic History and Culture*, reflects the importance of the great cultural legacy left behind by each of the dynasties discussed. In the globalised world of the twenty-first century in which we live, Western culture has invaded many Muslim minds. As an antidote to this, the present work also aims to enlighten its readers as to some of the enormous contributions made by Muslims to world civilisation. Each Islamic dynasty had its periods of strength which led to the social stability that encouraged the blossoming of Islamic culture.

This book is primarily intended as a reference work for anyone – young or old – interested in acquiring a basic knowledge of the major Islamic dynasties. Annotated illustrations reinforce many of the salient features discussed in each chapter. As old coins are one source of Islamic art and history readily available, many unique examples are presented here from the author's own coin collection.

---

[1] Ibn Khaldun. *The Muqaddimah* (trans. Franz Rosenthal). Vol. 1. London: Routledge and Kegan Paul, 1967:56.

The dynasties selected for inclusion in this book are ones well-recognised for their importance in the history of Islam. The list is incomplete, however. It is my sincere wish that readers of this book will be encouraged to study the history of these dynasties in greater detail and may even want to research ones not included here. For example, the study of the Islamic dynasties of sub-Saharan Africa and those of South-East Asia will also prove to be rewarding.

To fully understand events happening today in the Islamic world and elsewhere, Muslims must know their history. History does tend to repeat itself, but I am of the belief that lessons can be learned and that mistakes made in the past do not necessarily have to be repeated. As the former American president, Harry S. Truman (1884–1972) once said, "There is nothing new in the world except the history you do not know."

Lastly, I hope that readers will enjoy this book. The patient reader will certainly be rewarded, *insha'Allah*. To you all my warmest salaams.

Luqman Nagy
Holy Makkah
Saudi Arabia
June 20, 2004

NOTES

1. The following abbreviations have been used throughout the book:

- *sallalahu 'alayhi wa sallam* (may the peace and blessings of Allah be upon him). This is only used after the name of the Prophet Muhammad ﷺ.
- *radhiallahu 'anhu* (may Allah be pleased with him). This is used after the names of the Companions of the Prophet Muhammad ﷺ.
- *radhiallahu 'anha* (may Allah be pleased with her). This is used after the names of the female Companions of the Prophet Muhammad ﷺ.
- *radhiallahu 'anhum* (may Allah be pleased with them). This is used after the names of the Companions of the Prophet Muhammad ﷺ.
- *'alayhi as-salaam* (may peace be upon him). This is used after the names of the Prophets of Allah - other than Muhammad ﷺ - mentioned in the Holy Qur'an.

2. All dates in this book are Gregorian dates according to the Christian calendar.

CHAPTER ONE

THE UMAYYADS OF SYRIA (661–750)

With the death of the Prophet Muhammad ﷺ in 632, the rapidly growing *ummah* (Muslim community) was left without a delegated leader. The four Companions of the Prophet ﷺ who became successive rulers of the fledgling Islamic world were simple, sincerely pious men. Known as *Al-Khulafa' ar-Rashidun* (The Rightly Guided Khalifahs or successors), they were

1. Abu Bakr as-Siddiq ﷺ (632–634)
2. 'Umar ibn al-Khattab ﷺ (634–644)
3. 'Uthman ibn 'Affan ﷺ (644–656)
4. 'Ali ibn Abi Talib ﷺ (656–661)

They all ruled from the city of the Prophet ﷺ, *Al-Madinah al-Munawwarah*, guided in their conduct by the Holy Qur'an and *Sunnah*. It was Abu Bakr ﷺ who first suggested that he should be given the title *Khalifat Rasul Allah* (Successor of the Messenger of Allah). During the reign of 'Umar ﷺ, this title was shortened to *Khalifah* (Caliph) and a second title, *Amir al-Mu'minin* (Commander of the Faithful), was introduced.

'Ali ﷺ, the fourth caliph, was brutally assassinated in Kufa following years of bitter conflict with the governor of Syria, Mu'awiyah ibn Abu Sufyan. Mu'awiyah was the nephew of 'Uthman ﷺ and a member of the Umayyad clan of the Quraysh tribe. With the death of 'Ali ﷺ, he became the new caliph in 661 and the new capital of the Muslim Empire was then moved to Damascus, in Syria. Thus began the Umayyad Dynasty.

MU'AWIYAH IBN ABU SUFYAN (661–680)

The first Umayyad ruler, Mu'awiyah ibn Abu Sufyan, is remembered for establishing a well-trained army of Syrian soldiers and the first Muslim navy. During his reign, *Dar al-Islam* expanded in the West to almost reach Asia Minor and in the East reached the borders of Central Asia. Mu'awiyah used the intact structures of the former Byzantine state to help build his new government. He ruled with *hilm* (civilised restraint) and reportedly described his manner of governing in the following words:

> I apply not the sword where my lash suffices, nor my lash where my tongue is enough. And even if there be one hair binding me to my fellow men, I do not let it break: when they pull, I loosen, and if they loosen, I pull.

Mu'awiyah encouraged support for his son Yazid, who in 680 replaced his father as the second Umayyad ruler. The practice of hereditary succession (the title of *khalifah* automatically being transferred to another member of the family such as a son or brother) was thus established, eliminating the need for the election of a leader. However, not all Muslims approved of hereditary succession. Islamic historians, therefore, often refer to the Umayyad dynasty as a kingdom (*mamlakah*) and not a caliphate (*khalifat*) and to the rulers, with the exception of 'Umar ibn 'Abd al-'Aziz, as kings rather than caliphs. Unlike their predecessors, *Al-Khulafa' ar-Rashidun*, the new Umayyad monarchs, living in their luxurious palaces, became increasingly separated from and less able to identify with the Muslim community they led.

YAZID IBN MU'AWIYAH (680–683)

During his short rule, Yazid struggled with several rebellions. In the south of Iraq, in the new city of Kufa, the Shi'ites wanted Hussain ﷺ, the second son of 'Ali ﷺ and the grandson of the Prophet ﷺ, to be caliph. Hussain ﷺ and a small number of supporters, therefore, left Madinah and proceeded to Kufa, but before reaching the city, they were tragically murdered by the forces of Yazid on the plain of Karbala. This one event alone helped to permanently divide the Muslim *ummah* into two distinct factions: *Sunni* (followers of Prophet Muhammad ﷺ and his *sunnah*) and *Shi'a* (*Shi'at 'Ali*, the Party of 'Ali, who were the supporters of 'Ali ﷺ as caliph).

Yazid died in 683, passing his title to his only son, also named Mu'awiyah. However, Mu'awiyah II died in early 684, and with his death, the rule of the descendants of Abu Sufyan came to an end. Mu'awiyah II was succeeded by Marwan ibn Hakam, the then oldest member of the Umayyad clan, who ruled until his death in 685. He was succeeded by his son, 'Abd al-Malik.

'ABD AL-MALIK IBN MARWAN (685–705)

By this time the Islamic Empire was deeply divided and when 'Abd al-Malik ibn Marwan assumed his position, he set about the task of reunifying and expanding the Empire. During his long rule, political unrest in Iraq and Arabia was controlled. The Islamic Empire expanded to include parts of Central Asia and all of North Africa. The ethnic make-up of the *ummah* now included two very important groups. Arabs were brought into contact with the Berbers in North Africa and the Turks in Central Asia. Both Berbers and Turks were to play crucially significant roles in the later history of Islam.

Up until this time, the two pre-Islamic superpowers – the Greek Byzantine and Persian Sasanian Empires – had continued to use their own currency and languages in Muslim-dominated regions of the empire. During the rule of 'Abd al-Malik ibn Marwan, however, Arabic became the official language of the Umayyad state replacing the Byzantine Greek and Persian Pahlavi languages. The Byzantine gold *solidus* and the Sasanian silver *drachm* were replaced by a truly Islamic coinage depicting verses from the Qur'an instead of a human image (see illustration 1-1). 'Abd al-Malik also established an effective model for how government agencies should be organised and run. An elaborate system of communication links was set up which enabled messages to be sent from Damascus to all corners of the vast Islamic Empire.

As well as controlling political unrest and streamlining civil administration, he oversaw a number of major construction projects. The famous irrigation canals of the Tigris and Euphrates Valley of Iraq were cleared and re-opened. The construction of *Al-Qubbat as-Sakhra* (Dome of the Rock) is attributed to 'Abd al-Malik ibn Marwan who built it in 691 to cover the site of the *Mi'raj* (Ascension) of the Prophet Muhammad ﷺ to the Seven Heavens (see illustration 1-2).

'Abd al-Malik died in 705 leaving a stable and prosperous Islamic Empire to his successor, his son, Al-Walid.

AL-WALID IBN 'ABD AL-MALIK (705–715)

Al-Walid continued much of the good work begun by his father. During his rule, the Islamic Empire stretched, for the first time, from the Iberian Peninsula (present-day Spain and Portugal) in the West right across to the borders of India and China in the East.

1-1   THE FIRST TRUE ISLAMIC COINAGE: This is a silver *dirham* from the time of 'Abd al-Malik ibn Marwan, the fifth Umayyad caliph. Before this time, Islamic coins bore pictures of the ruling caliph. This beautiful example of an early Islamic coin bears the *shahadah* and *Surah al-Ikhlas*, but no human image. It was minted in the Umayyad capital, Damascus, in the year 700. Such coins were meant to be missionaries of the faith – calling all who held them in their hands to *Din al-Haq al-Islam*, the true religion of Islam.

1-2 THE DOME OF THE ROCK: The Dome of the Rock (*Al-Qubbat as-Sakhra*) in Jerusalem, along with the Al-Aqsa' Mosque, comprise *Al-Bayt al-Maqdas*, the third holiest site in Islam. 'Abd al-Malik ibn Marwan, the Umayyad caliph, built the Dome of the Rock in 691 to cover the site of *Al-Mi'raj* (the ascension of the Prophet ﷺ). This is the first great example of Islamic architecture and despite past earthquakes which have damaged or destroyed the Al-Aqsa' Mosque, the Dome of the Rock remains in excellent condition after more than thirteen centuries.

The reign of Al-Walid also saw much construction work ranging from schools, hospitals and other buildings of public service. However, his enduring legacies to Islamic architecture must be the building of *Al-Masjid al-Aqsa'* (The Al-Aqsa' Mosque) close to the Dome of the Rock built by his father in Jerusalem, and the Great Mosque (The Umayyad Mosque) in Damascus, which is now considered to be one of the great classical mosques.

Al-Walid was succeeded upon his death by his brother, Sulayman, who ruled for two and a half years. Although Sulayman had brothers and sons who could have succeeded him, he nominated his cousin and governor of Arabia, 'Umar ibn 'Abd al-'Aziz, as the next caliph, because of the latter's piety and ability. This was the first time in Umayyad history that a ruler had been elected according to Islamic principles and was thus a *khalifah* in the true sense of the word.

'UMAR IBN 'ABD AL-'AZIZ (717–720)

Of all the Umayyad rulers, the most respected and truly exceptional one was undoubtedly 'Umar ibn 'Abd al-'Aziz, often referred to as *Al-Khalifah as-Salih* (The Pious Caliph). 'Umar's mother was the granddaughter of 'Umar ibn al-Khattab ﷺ, the second Rightly Guided caliph. 'Umar ibn 'Abd al-'Aziz was born and brought up in Madinah, where early contact with religious scholars had made a profound impression on him. 'Umar refused to live in the royal palace in Damascus when he assumed the position of caliph, preferring instead that the family of the former ruler, Sulayman ibn 'Abd al-Malik, remain there while he chose to reside in a modest tent.

'Umar took his responsibilities as head of state very seriously and told his people that they could reject his leadership if he ever diverted from the Path of Allah. He envisioned a caliphate similar to the one under the leadership of *Al-Khulafa' ar-Rashidun*, based on true Islamic principles. As a result, he carried out a number of social reforms by following Islamic Law.

As the Islamic world expanded east and west, there was never a policy of forced conversion to Islam. In time, however, many non-Arabs converted to Islam so that by the end of the first Islamic century, there were many more non-Arab than Arab Muslims. These new non-Arab Muslims were called *mawali*. Up until the time of 'Umar ibn 'Abd al-'Aziz, the *mawali* had had to pay higher taxes than the Arabs in order to pay for the luxurious lifestyle of the Umayyad rulers. However, there was growing discontent among the *mawali*, along with Shi'ite groups, that they were not being accepted as true brothers-in-faith of the Arabs. Khalifah 'Umar realised that this unjust system of taxation was harming the sense of unity within the Muslim *ummah* and, therefore, reformed the tax system so that all Muslims were taxed equally. In addition, he ensured that the civil rights of both Arabs and non-Arabs were equal. This had the effect of not only unifying the Muslim population, but also encouraging non-Muslims to accept Islam.

Many important prison reforms were also carried out. Prisoners were educated and given a stipend (regular payment), while their human rights were also respected.

Khalifah 'Umar tried to adhere to the Islamic principles of equality and justice throughout his rule and was thus able to achieve unity, fairness and prosperity within the Islamic Empire during his rule of less than two and a half years. Gold *dinars* and silver *dirhams* were both minted in his name, yet when Khalifah 'Umar ibn 'Abd al-'Aziz died at the young age of thirty-six, he left behind only seventeen *dinars* to his name! He requested in his will that this money be spent for the rent of the house in which he had died and for the plot of land for his burial. The brightest period of the ninety-year long rule of the Umayyads had suddenly ended. It is indeed rare in the history of mankind for a ruler to be universally praised by even his most ardent enemies, but such was the case of 'Umar bin 'Abd al-'Aziz ⌖.

Khalifah 'Umar was succeeded by Yazid, another son of 'Abd al-Malik. Sadly, under the rule of Yazid II (720–724), the important social reforms of Khalifah 'Umar were all reversed and the Islamic Empire became as divided and discontented as before. Yazid II was succeeded in 724 by his brother, Hisham.

HISHAM IBN 'ABD AL-MALIK (724–743)

By the time that Hisham came to rule, the Islamic Empire was in great trouble with widespread disunity and discontent among the Muslims. 'Ali ibn Abi Talib ⌖, who was the son of one the Prophet's uncles, had been a caliph. Now the descendants of another of the Prophet's uncles, 'Abbas, felt that they had equal claim to be the new rulers of the Islamic Empire. The resultant 'Abbasid movement threatened the very existence of the Umayyads. Leading this movement was the head of the 'Abbas family, Muhammad ibn 'Ali, the great-grandson of 'Abbas. He exploited the dissatisfaction of the *mawali* and Shi'ites in Khorasan province (in present-day northeastern Iran) and Iraq to gain support for his cause. At this stage, the movement was still a clandestine one.

Despite these internal divisions, Hisham was a wise statesman and was able to improve many aspects of life within the Islamic Empire. He constructed many new cisterns and reservoirs, helped to support indigenous manufacturing, such as the silk industry, and had many works of literature and science translated into the Arabic language.

At the time of Hisham's death, the Islamic Empire stretched for 4,500 miles over three continents; from the south of France in the West to the borders of China in the East. The age of the Umayyads had reached its peak and would rapidly decline thereafter.

Over the next two years, there were three incompetent caliphs who were more interested in worldly affairs than in the proper governing of the state. By the time that Marwan II (nephew of 'Abd al-Malik) came to rule, the Empire was in steep decline. There was nothing that he could do stop the political instability. The leader of the 'Abbasid movement, Muhammad ibn 'Ali, had died but the movement gathered momentum under the leadership of Abu Muslim. In 747, the rebellion spread and the Umayyad governor of Khorasan was overthrown and replaced by an 'Abbasid. The slogan shouted in the streets was *Al-Sa'dah aal Muhammad* ⌖ - "Happiness is from the family of Muhammad ⌖".

Over the next couple of years, 'Abbasid forces continued to overthrow the Umayyads, taking over cities in Persia and Iraq. Finally, in 750, the 'Abbasid forces met the Umayyad army in Mosul, Iraq, and the latter was defeated. This signified the death of the Umayyads of Damascus and the birth of the new 'Abbasid dynasty.

The 'Abbasids were ruthless in killing all members of the Umayyad family, both young and old. However, one young Umayyad prince, 'Abd ar-Rahman, the grandson of Hisham, did manage to escape from Syria and fled to Spain where he established an Umayyad state in exile.

CHAPTER TWO

THE UMAYYADS OF SPAIN (756–1031)

The Iberian Peninsula (Spain and Portugal) is the only part of Western Europe that was occupied by Muslims for any length of time and whose culture still exhibits traces of its Islamic past. Islam first came to Spain, under the rule of the Umayyad caliph Al-Walid ibn 'Abd al-Malik, when in the year 711, the famous Berber commander, Tariq ibn Ziyad, landed on Spanish soil near the small mountain that still bears his name: Gibraltar (from the Arabic *Jabal Tariq* or Tariq's Mountain).

Spain quickly became known as the Muslim land of *Al-Andalus*, an Arabic word perhaps derived from the older Berber name for southern Spain: *Tamurt Wandalus* (Land of the Vandals). Within a hundred years of the death of the Prophet ﷺ, *Din al-Haq al-Islam* had spread from the deserts of Arabia east to the borders of China and India and to the land of the "Farthest West" (*Al-Maghreb al-Aqsa'*). The first dynasty of Islamic caliphs, the Umayyads, had been ruling this vast empire from their capital of Damascus in Syria, since its conquest.

However, the Umayyads were overthrown by the 'Abbasids in 750, who began to rule from their new capital of Baghdad in Iraq. Once in power, the 'Abbasids decided to kill all members of the Umayyad royal family. The only member of the family who escaped this massacre was the grandson of Hisham, 'Abd ar-Rahman. Together with a servant, he slowly proceeded to travel on foot across North Africa. Eventually, he reached Morocco in 755. From there, he crossed over into Spain, or Al-Andalus, where he found supporters in some South Arabian tribes who had settled there.

'Abd ar-Rahman was the founder of the new Umayyad dynasty and became the first Umayyad *amir* (prince) of Spain. Spain was now an independent state, separate from the 'Abbasid caliphate. The history of the Umayyads of Spain can be divided into two distinct periods: the independent Emirate (756–929) and the Caliphate (929–1031).

'ABD AR-RAHMAN I (756–788)

'Abd ar-Rahman soon replaced the ruling governor of Al-Andalus and made the city of Cordoba the capital of the new Umayyad state in Spain. When news of the newly-founded state reached the people of Syria, men who had once worked for the Umayyads in Damascus came to Spain to work for the new government.

However, the 'Abbasids of Baghdad tried to cause trouble for the new Umayyad *amir* of Spain, and the 'Abbasid caliph, Al-Mansur, even sent his army to invade and regain Spain in 763. Later in 778, the Holy Roman Emperor Charlemagne and his Christian army of Franks from the north also invaded Spain with the aim of capturing it from the Muslims. In addition, 'Abd ar-Rahman also had to deal with internal rebellions from the diverse and often discontented members of the population.

'Abd ar-Rahman successfully defended his state from both invading armies as well as controlling the rebellions within. Consequently, he soon became known as the *Saqr al-Quraysh* (Falcon of the Quraysh) even by his enemies in Baghdad. He had a fair complexion and red hair and also preferred to dress in white, the traditional colour of the Umayyads.

He set about establishing a system of justice and encouraged knowledge and learning. He took a keen interest in constructing buildings and mosques, and is best known for starting the construction of the Great Mosque in Cordoba in 785.

Despite the tragic events that led to his coming to Spain, 'Abd ar-Rahman always retained a fondness for his homeland of Syria. A story tells of 'Abd ar-Rahman bringing a date stone from Syria which he planted in his palace garden in Spain. He then wrote a poem in Arabic in which he praised this date tree. As an "immigrant stranger", 'Abd ar-Rahman likened himself to the lone date palm growing in his garden. Many other fruits and vegetables were also introduced into Spain by the Arabs. For example, rice, oranges and pomegranates (French for Granada apple) were all new crops brought from the East and cultivated in the rich, fertile soil of Al-Andalus, where they thrived.

Upon his death, 'Abd ar-Rahman I was succeeded by his son, Hisham I (788–796). During his reign, he was able to capture some areas of southern France. He was in turn succeeded by Al-Hakam I (796–822), who continued to encourage knowledge and learning as had his predecessors. He established the first university in Cordoba, which in time, became the centre of learning for the whole of Europe. He was succeeded by his son, 'Abd ar-Rahman II.

'ABD AR-RAHMAN II (822–852)

By the time of 'Abd ar-Rahman II, Al-Andalus had become the cultural capital of Islam in the West. Grand mosques and *madrasahs* were built throughout Spain and the Great Mosque of Cordoba, founded by 'Abd ar-Rahman I, was expanded. 'Abd ar-Rahman II wanted Cordoba to be as great a city as the 'Abbasid capital, Baghdad. A famous courtier named Ziryab was brought from Baghdad to teach the Muslims of Spain good taste in music, poetry, fashion and manners.

When 'Abd ar-Rahman II allowed regional governors more power, the Christian kingdoms in the north of Spain seized the opportunity to re-conquer Muslim territory. It was a feature of Muslim Spain that since its establishment in 711 until its collapse in 1492, groups of Christian monarchs repeatedly attempted a *reconquesta*, a total re-conquering of Spain.

'Abd ar-Rahman II was succeeded upon his death by a succession of his sons and grandsons.

'ABD AR-RAHMAN III (912–961)

'Abd ar-Rahman III became *amir* of Al-Andalus at the young age of twenty-one. The Arab conquerors of Spain had brought old tribal feuds with them to their new home. There was now a serious rebellion amongst the Arabs, Berbers, Spanish Muslims and Christians in Spain. Territory had been lost to the Christian kingdoms, but 'Abd ar-Rahman III soon took full control and his absolute power eventually resulted in a period of good government that brought peace and prosperity to the region.

'Abd ar-Rahman III used an enormous army of bodyguards for protection. These were the *saqaliba* (Slavs), or captives from many different non-Muslim lands, who were brought up and educated as Muslims in the court of the *amir*.

A new threat now came from abroad. To the south, the Shi'ite Fatimid dynasty had taken control of all of North Africa and, of course, had its eye on Al-Andalus. The Fatimids totally rejected the authority of the first three Rightfully Guided *Khalifahs*. They believed that 'Ali ﷺ alone was worthy of leading the community of Muslims after the Prophet's ﷺ death. The founder of the Fatimid dynasty, 'Ubayd Allah, proclaimed himself the *Mahdi* (Guided One) in 909. He believed he was the direct descendant of Isma'il, one of the sons of the sixth Shi'ite imam, Ja'far Sadiq, who was in turn a grandson of Hussain ﷺ, the grandson of the Prophet ﷺ and son of 'Ali and Fatima ﷺ. It is because of this lineage that 'Ubayd Allah coined himself and his successors Fatimids.

The Fatimids' version of Islamic theology was based on unorthodox Isma'ili doctrines. Isma'ili *da'is*, or missionaries, were being sent to spread their deviant creed throughout *Dar al-Islam*, even in the Umayyad caliphate of Al-Andalus. 'Abd ar-Rahman III and his navy were able to extend Umayyad control as far south as Morocco and were thus able to thwart any Fatimid incursion into Umayyad Spain.

'Abd ar-Rahman III and all previous Spanish Umayyad *amirs* had believed that the Muslim leader holding the title of *khalifah* should have authority over the Holy Cities of Makkah and Madinah. By 929, the weak 'Abbasid caliphs of Baghdad had little or no control over the birthplace of Islam, so in the same year, 'Abd ar-Rahman III took the opportunity of proclaiming himself *khalifah* and *Al-Nasir li Din Allah* (Defender of the Faith of Allah). He was also *Amir al-Mu'minin* (Commander of the Faithful). There were now three caliphs in *Dar al-Islam* – one in the West, in Umayyad Al-Andalus, one in Fatimid Cairo in Egypt and the third in the East, in 'Abbasid Baghdad, Iraq.

During his fifty years as ruler, 'Abd ar-Rahman III saw Cordoba, the capital city of the Spanish Umayyads, become the most cultured city in all of Europe – almost rivalling the great Byzantine capital of Constantinople (present-day Istanbul) at the other end of the Mediterranean Sea. While the population of the rest of Europe lived in crude, filthy towns and villages, the inhabitants of Cordoba enjoyed fine cobblestone streets lit at night, indoor plumbing and public baths and libraries on almost every street corner.

Cordoba during the time of 'Abd ar-Rahman III must have been a sight to see! The city of some 500,000 inhabitants was certainly the largest in Europe at the time. Magnificent marble palaces (such as the palace-city outside Cordoba of *Madinat az-Zahrah*, the City of Zahrah, one of the wives of 'Abd ar-Rahman III) and villas lined the banks of the *Wadi al-Kabir* (The Great River, or Guadalquivir in modern Spanish). Unfortunately, of all these buildings, only a few traces remain. One monument, however, and certainly the most important of its kind ever built in Europe, has survived from the time of the Umayyad caliphs of Spain. *Alhamdulillah*, the Great Mosque of Cordoba, although not used as a mosque today, is the one building that still captivates all who visit it.

Islamic Spain had experienced its first glorious flowering during the reign of 'Abd ar-Rahman III. His reign was an exceptional time of peace in all of Al-Andalus. The concept of ghettos did not exist. Jews, Christians and Muslims literally rubbed shoulders as they were neighbours residing on the same street and sharing the same public markets, baths, parks, libraries and centres of learning. In the world of the tenth century, Arabic was undoubtedly the language to know if one sought knowledge. Scholars from as far away as the British Isles gravitated towards the fabled city of Cordoba in order to study Arabic and thus partake of the rich font of knowledge available there. In fact, the extreme tolerance shown to non-Muslims during this time in history encouraged the transfer of vast amounts of knowledge from "enlightened" Spain to the impoverished "dark" towns of Europe. This was indeed the link – so often forgotten or not fully acknowledged by historians – between the Islamic and Christian worlds that eventually led to the Renaissance (or rebirth) in the West in the fifteenth century.

Following this long and fruitful rule, 'Abd ar-Rahman III was succeeded upon his death, by his son, Al-Hakam II.

AL-HAKAM II (961–976)

Al-Hakam II was ruler for fourteen years. He had made peace with most of his Christian neighbours so he had time to indulge in his two favourite pastimes, namely book collecting and constructing public works. Historians relate that he was an avid reader and at an early age began collecting books for his personal library. Al-Hakam II's representatives scoured the markets of all the world's great cities – Alexandria, Cairo, Damascus, Constantinople and Baghdad – for rare manuscripts (old or new) for his rapidly expanding library. By the time Al-Hakam II ascended the throne, his royal library contained no fewer than 400,000 volumes! All of these hand-copied manuscripts were carefully shelved and it is reported that Al-Hakam II himself had read and annotated all the books in his massive collection. He usually wrote at the beginning or end of each new book he acquired, the name of the author, his date of birth and death and also an interesting note about the author. These notes themselves became famous in the literary history of Al-Andalus. Al-Hakam II's palace also employed many librarians, bookbinders, copyists and artists. Unfortunately, Al-Hakam's famous library was destroyed by the invading Berbers in the early eleventh century.

While in other parts of Europe, where only the very privileged could even dream of learning how to read and write in any language, in Muslim Spain there was an extremely high rate of literacy amongst the general population. Al-Hakam II himself opened many new schools, specifically for the children of poorer families. As a true bibliophile (lover of books), it is even reported that the caliph opened his great royal library to the public (see illustration 2-1).

Al-Hakam II, not unlike his predecessors, was also interested in beautifying his capital city of Cordoba. The Great Mosque, for example, had been expanded several times since its first construction during the time of 'Abd ar-Rahman I. Centuries before, the Umayyads of Syria had used Byzantine craftsmen to help them construct the walls of intricate mosaic tiles in the Dome of the Rock and the Al-Aqsa' Mosque in Jerusalem and the Umayyad Mosque in Damascus. Therefore, Al-Hakam II, like his ancestors, requested the Byzantine Emperor in Constantinople, to send him a master craftsman along with glass mosaic tiles. The Byzantine Christian artist successfully taught the Spanish Muslim artisans the art of assembling a mosaic. The result was the astonishingly beautiful *mihrab* (prayer niche) of the Great Mosque of Cordoba that still amazes all who see it.

After the death of Al-Hakam in 976, and until 1031, a succession of weak caliphs led to the fall of the Spanish Umayyad caliphate. In 1031, the government of the last Umayyad ruler, Hisham III collapsed when the people of Cordoba rebelled. Al-Andalus soon became divided into twenty-three separate independent states (*Al-Muluk al-Tawa'if*) that used the political system of the caliphate as their model.

THE GREAT MOSQUE OF CORDOBA

The Great Mosque of Cordoba was begun by 'Abd ar-Rahman I soon after he became *amir*. As the city grew in size and beauty, so too did the mosque. Marble for its construction was brought from Tunis, Rome and even Constantinople, the Byzantine capital, which sent a gift of one hundred and forty marble columns. The interior of the mosque became a vast sea of columns that might have reminded some Arabs of a grove of date palms (see illustration 2-2). Every day, teachers would sit beneath a particular column and freely impart their knowledge to students who respectfully gathered around them.

Cordoba was re-conquered by the Christians in 1236, but for three hundred years, the Great Mosque of Cordoba was left unchanged. The Christian population of Cordoba used the mosque as a place

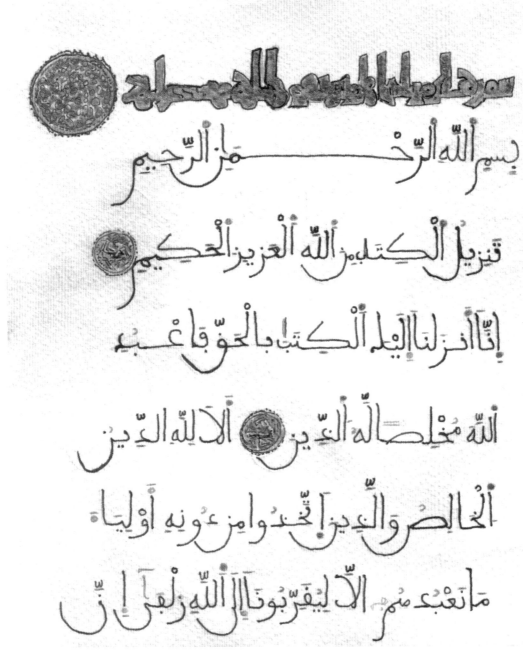

2-1 ANDALUSIAN CALLIGRAPHY: Over the eight centuries of Muslim rule in Spain and Portugal, countless handwritten copies of the Holy Qur'an were produced. A unique style of Arabic handwriting called *al-khat al-andalus* (Andalusian script) was soon developed in this part of the Islamic world. Here is a beautiful page from a Qur'an that might have been read in the Great Mosque of Cordoba; it shows the first two *ayahs* of *Surah al-Zumar*. Today, such copies of old Andalusian Qur'ans are rare because after the *reconquesta* (reconquest) of Muslim lands by the Spanish Christians in 1492, hundreds of thousands of priceless Arabic manuscripts were burned in bonfires all over Spain.

2-2   THE GREAT MOSQUE OF CORDOBA, SPAIN: This mosque, begun by 'Abd ar-Rahman I, grew larger as successive caliphs made additions. The interior, even today, resembles a vast forest of date palms with immense branches reaching high up to the ceiling. 'Abd ar-Rahman's architect wanted an interior with high ceilings, but the length of available marble columns was obviously limited. The problem was brilliantly solved by a two-tiered arrangement of arches, all resting on the same marble supports. Today, the interior of this enormous mosque exhibits the beauty of the unique arches of alternate red and yellow stone. The Great Mosque of Cordoba remains the largest mosque ever built in Europe and is still one of the most impressive Islamic monuments ever constructed.

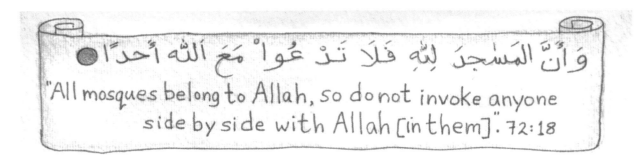

وَأَنَّ الْمَسَاجِدَ لِلَّهِ فَلَا تَدْعُوا مَعَ اللَّهِ أَحَدًا ۝

"All mosques belong to Allah, so do not invoke anyone side by side with Allah [in them]". 72:18

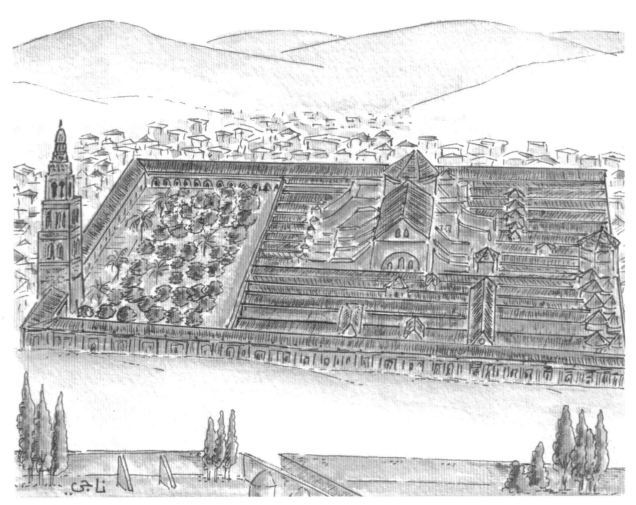

2-3 THE GREAT MOSQUE OF CORDOBA, SPAIN TODAY: Begun in 784, the Great Mosque of Cordoba, by the tenth century, had become the largest mosque in the world. For more than four centuries, the mosque was the centre of Islamic life for all the inhabitants of this historic city. But in 1236, Cordoba was retaken by the Christians. No changes were made to the mosque which was then used for Christian worship. In the sixteenth century, however, a cathedral was constructed in the middle of the mosque, thus destroying forever its unique architectural beauty.

The Spanish emperor Charles V (Holy Roman Emperor, 1516–1556), the grandson of Ferdinand and Isabella, was outraged at this example of Christian vandalism. He reportedly said that a Christian cathedral could be seen anywhere, but the *Masjid al-Kabir*, the Great Mosque of Cordoba, was unique in the world. Although permanently damaged by this desecration, the Mosque of Cordoba still stands along the Guadalquivir River as a testament to the Muslims of Al-Andalus, and their faith in *Din al-Haq al-Islam*.

of Christian worship without dramatically modifying the architecture of the spectacular building. But in the sixteenth century, the Spanish Emperor Charles V ordered that a cathedral be built in Cordoba. Unfortunately, it was constructed in the centre of the Great Mosque (see illustration 2-3). The Christian population was opposed to this clear defacement of such a beautiful building and even the Emperor himself regretted having ordered the construction of the cathedral when he saw how it had permanently destroyed the character of the Great Mosque.

Anyone who visits the Great Mosque of Cordoba today is shocked to see how this magnificent place of Muslim worship has been altered. The arches facing the courtyard are all walled in, making the interior much darker. In the past, there was open access to the mosque from the courtyard where Muslims could make their ablutions using the many public fountains found there.

The Christian kingdoms to the north would continue to re-conquer Muslim lands, valley by valley, town by town, and city by city until there remained only one Muslim kingdom in all of Spain. The final great flowering of culture in Islamic Spain was to occur in Granada under the Nasrid dynasty, in the thirteenth century.

CHAPTER THREE
THE 'ABBASIDS (749–1258 & 1261–1517)

With the arrival of the 'Abbasids in the year 749, the seat of power changed dramatically. Whereas the Umayyads residing in their capital of Damascus had been a distinctively Semitic Arab dynasty, the 'Abbasids of Baghdad, although indirect descendants of the Prophet Muhammad ﷺ through one of his uncles, Al-'Abbas ibn al-Muttalib, very soon became influenced by non-Arab Persians, and later by the Turks. The unrest among the *mawali* (non-Arab converts to Islam), especially in Iran, had helped the 'Abbasids to overthrow the Umayyads. The *mawali* now expected to be fully accepted as brothers-in-Islam. The caliphal capital was moved from Damascus in Arabian Syria to Persian Iraq – first to Kufa, and finally to the new city of Baghdad in 762. This resulted in a fusion of Semitic and Persian cultures that characterises this dynasty. One caliph was reported to have said, "The Persians have ruled themselves for a thousand years and didn't need our help [i.e. from the Arab nation] for even one day. We have been ruling for just one hundred or two hundred years and can't survive without them for even an hour!"

The 'Abbasids attempted to capitalise on their superior ancestry, being descended from the Prophet ﷺ. When the worldly Umayyads were deposed, the 'Abbasids promised an era of just Islamic rule. The white standard of the Umayyads was now replaced by the black one of the 'Abbasids. When a new 'Abbasid caliph took office, and on special occasions such as *'Eid* prayers, it became customary for him to wear the cloak or mantle (*Al-Khirqah al-Sharifah*) of the Prophet ﷺ. As a sign of his devotion to Allah and *Din al-Haq al-Islam*, each 'Abbasid ruler adopted a special religious *laqab* (title of honour). It is by these *alqab* that all of the fifty or so 'Abbasid caliphs are known. Examples include the caliphs *Al-Wathiq Billah* (the confiding in Allah) and *Al-Mutawakkil Billah* (the trusting in Allah). The first 'Abbasid caliph, Abu al-'Abbas, was an exception as his *laqab* was *As-Saffah* (the shedder of blood) due to his thirst for shedding Umayyad blood.

The history of the 'Abbasid dynasty can easily be divided into three distinct periods. The first begins with the establishment of the 'Abbasid state in 749 and ends with the occupation of Baghdad by the Persian-speaking Buyid leader Mu'izz ad-Dawla in 945. From this date until the Mongol invasion of Baghdad in 1258, the 'Abbasid state exerted little control over a series of many independent princedoms. Finally, a shadow 'Abbasid caliphate continued in Cairo from 1261 to 1517.

AL-MANSUR (754–775)

The short reign of the first 'Abbasid caliph, *As-Saffah* (750–754), was followed by that of his brother, Al-Mansur. Al-Mansur surrounded himself with administrators many of whom were non-Arab Persians. The Persian-speaking Barmakid family, for example, very quickly became a source of all the *wazirs* (chief ministers to the caliph) and thus were able to dominate the running of the 'Abbasid government. As the later caliphs became more and more isolated from their subjects, they adopted the pre-Islamic Sasanian (Persian) custom of holding elaborate ceremonies in luxurious palaces. In this way, the early 'Abbasid caliphs permitted their Barmakid *wazirs* to become the *de facto* rulers of the state until the latter were overthrown in 803.

BAGHDAD – THE NEW CAPITAL

In 762, after receiving advice from his *wazirs*, the caliph Al-Mansur chose the site of the small village of Baghdad to be the new 'Abbasid capital city. The city of Baghdad was built on the west side of the Tigris River not far from the ancient Sasanian winter capital of Ctesiphon (*Mada'in* in Arabic) which had fallen to the early Muslim victors after the famous Battle of Qadisiyyah in 636 (see illustration 3-1).

3-1   EMPIRES RISE AND FALL: In 637, the victorious Muslim Arabs entered Ctesiphon, the winter capital of the Persian Sasanian Empire. What surprised the Muslims most was the magnificent Palace of Khusraw (*Taq Kisra* in Arabic). Today, the palace is in ruins and lies thirty-two kilometres southeast of Baghdad. Here is the ruined vault of the great audience hall that contains the world's largest brick archway. The arrogant Khusraw II (590–628) likely received and read the letter of invitation to Islam from the Prophet Muhammad ﷺ under this very arch. He subsequently tore the letter up. On hearing this, the Prophet ﷺ simply replied, "May his kingdom be torn apart." In 628, Khusraw II was killed by his own son. After 637, *Taq Kisra* was used as a mosque by the Arabs, but later, the ruins of Ctesiphon provided building material for the new 'Abbasid capital of Baghdad.

Ibn Khaldun, the famous Arab social historian, writes eloquently of the decline and fall of empires:

> And when old age and weakness overtake a state, it begins to contract at the extremities, the centre remaining preserved until Allah decrees the total extinction of the state, whereupon the centre, too, is wiped out. ... Consider the Persian Empire, whose capital was Ctesiphon; once Ctesiphon had been captured by the Muslims, the total power of the Persians was wiped out; nor were the remaining outlying provinces of any use to Yazdagird [Yazdagird III, the last Sasanian monarch].*

* Ibn Khaldun. *The Muqaddimah* (trans. Franz Rosenthal). London: Routledge & Kegan Paul, 1967.

Al-Mansur thought that the site was ideal for a military base because it was situated on the Tigris and was also close to the Euphrates River. Baghdad was originally a circular city (first called *Dar as-Salam* and later *Madinat as-Salam*) surrounded by three thick concentric walls, the outermost one being about two-and-a-half kilometres in diameter. It was logical that the round city wall would not only be cheaper to construct but also easier to defend. Four main gates permitted entry into the city; from Syria (north), Basra (south), Khorasan (east), and Kufa (west). Baghdad was ideally situated on the great trade routes from China, Persia and India to the Mediterranean.

In the centre of Al-Mansur's "Round City" were the large caliphal palace, mosque and gardens. Lively shops and markets lined the four streets leading to the heart of the city. Soon after its construction, a similar settlement was built on the east bank of the Tigris River. The city grew so rapidly that by the ninth century, it measured about twenty-five square miles and had a population approaching half a million. Baghdad was a multi-ethnic, multi-lingual and multi-religious capital which truly reflected the varied inhabitants of the extensive 'Abbasid Empire.

As the Islamic Empire grew, so too did its new capital city, Baghdad, which soon became the largest cosmopolitan centre on earth, outside of China. Besides the wealth of agricultural crops taken from the fertile soil of Mesopotamia (the farmland between the Tigris and Euphrates Rivers), Baghdad quickly developed important textile and leather industries. Chinese papermakers were captured after the Battle of Talas in 751 and were subsequently taken to Samarqand where the secret of paper-making was revealed to Muslims for the first time. Within fifty years, a thriving paper industry in Baghdad provided the city's *suq al-warraqin* (paper sellers' market) with reams (from the Arabic *rizmah* meaning bundle) of inexpensive writing material.

Some Islamic scholars now began to copy the Qur'an on paper instead of the more traditional and much more expensive parchment (dried, stretched animal skin). The wide availability of such affordable paper initiated one of the most important "information explosions" in history. Countless scientific and philosophical manuscripts written in ancient Greek, Pahlavi (old Persian) and even Sanskrit (ancient language of India) could now be translated into Arabic by learned Christian, Jewish and Muslim scholars. Much of this translation work was done in the *Bayt al-Hikmah* (House of Knowledge), the academy founded for this purpose by Al-Mansur's grandson, Harun al-Rashid, and great-grandson, Al-Ma'mun.

The historical importance of this astonishing period of creative activity cannot be overestimated. The goal of these translators was clear: to translate into Arabic – and thus preserve – the entire scientific legacy of the Ancient Greeks. The thirst for knowledge in the Islamic world was such that this Greek learning gained a new life when it was transmitted through a new language, Arabic. The direct result of this enormous translation effort, begun in Baghdad in the eighth century, can be seen centuries later in different parts of the Islamic world where Muslim scholars had internalised this Greek learning and were now writing original scientific works of their own. For example, without the translations made in Baghdad, the great Muslim philosopher of Al-Andalus, Ibn Rushd (1126–1198), would never have been able to write his extremely detailed *Commentaries on Aristotle*.

Perhaps equally important, was the conversion of many non-Arabs to Islam under the rule of Al-Mansur. While the Umayyads had discouraged conversions to Islam, the more inclusive 'Abbasid regime meant that the number of Muslims in the caliphate doubled. At the beginning of Al-Mansur's rule, roughly eight percent of the residents in the caliphate were Muslim. By the end of his rule, this number had risen to fifteen percent.

Al-Mansur died in 775 on his way to Hajj and was succeeded by his son and grandsons, one of whom was Harun al-Rashid.

HARUN AL-RASHID (786–809)

The golden age of the 'Abbasid dynasty continued with the rule of Harun al-Rashid. Baghdad had become a flourishing trading centre on the Silk Road. Merchants from the East and West met there. With the secret of Chinese papermaking now known by the Arabs, inexpensive paper soon flooded the market. At the same time, "Arabic numerals" – the revolutionary Indian system of calculation that included the number zero, or *sifr* in Arabic – were adopted by the Islamic world.

By the end of the eighth century, the 'Abbasid state had reached its zenith. The state treasury was full and extensive trade links all across the Empire encouraged the expansion of commerce. Baghdad prospered. A very sophisticated system of banking enabled merchants to conduct business securely. Letters of credit (a type of cheque), for example, issued in Baghdad would be honoured even in North Africa or Central Asia. Inspectors, known as *muhtasibs*, would roam the markets ensuring the accuracy of weights and measures there. At this time, the ancient Persian postal system was reorganised and improved. Communication relay towers were built at regular intervals from the 'Abbasid capital to as far away as Morocco! Even carrier pigeons were used in this complex communications network.

Towards the end of the rule of Harun al-Rashid, the 'Abbasid empire began to shrink in size. In the West, Ibrahim ibn al-Aghlab, Harun's trusted governor in Tunisia, declared himself independent of Baghdad and subsequently established the Aghlabid dynasty. Revolts in various parts of Egypt, Arabia and Iran also helped to weaken the caliphate.

Harun al-Rashid left his empire to his two sons of different mothers. While Al-Amin was given Iraq to rule, Al-Ma'mun was given Iran. A brief but bloody civil war broke out between the two brothers with Al-Ma'mun finally becoming victorious and seizing the caliphate for himself in 813.

AL-MA'MUN IBN HARUN (813–833)

Al-Ma'mun, like his father, continued to encourage the translation of important works of classical learning in his *Bayt al-Hikmah*. Outstanding achievements in the fields of science and the fine arts also occurred during his reign. Al-Ma'mun could be considered the most intellectual and important of the 'Abbasid rulers despite making several serious blunders in his life. For example, he publicly declared the Qur'an to be "created". This official acceptance of the Mu'tazilite[2] school of philosophy was rejected by his subjects and many of the *'ulema*, or religious scholars of the day, who believed the Qur'an to be the "uncreated" word of Allah in its essence. The Mu'tazilites also attempted to analyse the *hadith* by logical reasoning.

After Al-Ma'mun adopted the revolutionary Mu'tazilite philosophy, the *'ulema* were questioned about many of their beliefs. Thus began the period in Islamic history called the *mihnah* (testing or trial), or the Islamic Inquisition. During the last four years of Al-Ma'mun's life, *qadis* (judges), *muhaddiths* (scholars of *ahadith*), and even *muadhdhins* (callers to prayer) from cities like Baghdad,

---

[2] "Those who have removed themselves", from the Arabic *a'tazala*, "to remove oneself".

Damascus, Makkah and Madinah were all given an *imtihan* (test) to determine their willingness to accept the Mu'tazilite doctrine. Anyone who disagreed with the Mu'tazilites was severely punished. The Muslim masses simply could not accept the doctrine of a "created" Qur'an. The famous jurist, Ahmad ibn Hanbal (780–855), for example, believed in the "Eternal" Qur'an that could be understood through the *sunnah* of the Prophet ﷺ. In 834, he, like many others, was flogged, enchained and imprisoned for rejecting Mu'tazilite beliefs.

The *mihnah* continued during the reign of Al-Ma'mun's brother and successor, Al-Mu'tasim, and lasted for twenty years. It was finally ended in 847 under the rule of the caliph, Al-Mutawakkil. Ahmad ibn Hanbal, now a free man, refused the new caliph's offer to take care of his affairs. Throughout his life he had always wanted to remain distant from those in power. In old age, however, Ibn Hanbal did forgive one of his torturers who had come to his bedside. The importance of this failed Islamic Inquisition was to show that the spiritual authority of the state rested with the *'ulema* and caliphs could no longer attempt to interfere in religious matters.

Al-Ma'mun made yet another mistake. He had entrusted the remote Iranian province of Khorasan to his general, Tahir ibn al-Hussain. In 820, his descendants founded the independent Tahirid state and a year later ceased to mention the caliph's name in the Friday *khutbah* (sermon). This and similar renegade states clearly eroded the central control of the 'Abbasids in the provinces of the Empire.

AL-MU'TASIM IBN HARUN (833–842)

With the death of Al-Ma'mun in 833, his brother, Al-Mu'tasim, became the new caliph. He is noteworthy for importing and employing Turkish slave soldiers known as *mamluks* as a defence force. Al-Mu'tasim vacated Baghdad and built a new capital at Samarra', one hundred kilometres to the north. Samarra' remained the caliphal capital for almost sixty years (see illustration 3-2).

WEAKENING OF THE 'ABBASID STATE

The *mamluk* troops rose to positions of great power, eventually deposing the next caliph, Al-Mutawakkil, in 862. These Turkish soldiers were able to remove and install caliphs whenever they wanted. Caliphs were now mere puppets representing a weak dismembered 'Abbasid state and in 935, the title of *Amir al-'Umara'*, "Commander of Commanders", was given to the head of the *mamluk* troops.

The once vast and unified 'Abbasid Empire had disintegrated into a number of (semi-) independent states: the Aghlabids, Tulinids, Hamdanids, Tahirids, Saffarids and the Samanids, to name but a few. In 945, Baghdad fell to a Shi'ite family of *amirs*, the Buyids, from the northern part of Iran, who remained in power there for almost a century.

With the arrival of a new wave of invaders, the Great Seljuqs (a Turkic people from Central Asia), the old 'Abbasid state was partially reunified under Sunni rulers once again. The Seljuq commander, Tughril Beg, entered Baghdad in 1055. Caliphs were still appointed, but the real power lay in the hands of the Turkish Seljuq sultans. Within a century, the Seljuqs too had become a weak force and until the arrival of the first Mongol hordes in the middle of the thirteenth century, a string of incompetent caliphs ruled Baghdad.

3-2 SPIRAL MINARET: For almost sixty years, the 'Abbasid capital was centred in Samarra', a new city one hundred kilometres to the north of Baghdad. Whereas little or nothing is left of caliphal Baghdad which was totally destroyed by Hulagu Khan in 1258, the surviving ruins of Samarra' still impress the visitor. Here is one example of several "spiral" minarets that exist at Samarra'. This solid tower of sun-baked brick resembles the ancient Mesopotamian ziggurats (terraced step pyramid temples) in shape, but symbolises the Oneness of Allah and the strength of the new faith in the region.

THE MONGOL INVASION

The thirteenth century saw wave upon wave of Mongol horsemen invade most parts of Western Asia. Originally an illiterate nomadic people, whose homeland is present-day Mongolia, they swept westwards with the sole aim of destroying the sedentary "civilised" agrarian societies they encountered and at this, they were extremely successful. Just what caused these nomads to attempt to conquer the world?

Jenghiz Khan (1162–1227) was the first leader to unite the various Mongol tribes. In 1206 he was given the title of Great Khan. With extremely skilled and disciplined horsemen who could endure riding for weeks on end with little more than dried yoghurt or raw meat as sustenance, the Mongols soon overran the kingdoms of northern and western China. Once subdued, the Mongols would return to their home base of traditional *gers* (circular, portable felt tents) in Mongolia and wait to receive tribute from all their conquered territories. Any town or city refusing to immediately surrender to Mongol forces suffered a terrible fate. No mercy was ever shown in such instances. Some cities, such as Balkh, the magnificent centre of Islamic learning (in present-day northern Afghanistan), were so totally destroyed by the Mongol hordes, they never fully recovered. Even today Balkh is essentially just a pile of rubble. Farmers were also not spared. The Mongols loathed sedentary farmers who were usually automatically killed or enslaved. Their farmlands were ploughed under to provide pasture for the tens of thousands of Mongol horses, the real backbone of the Mongol war machine. With sufficient open grassland, the Mongol armies were able to traverse immense distances; from central Mongolia to the grasslands of southern Russia and even to central Hungary, thousands of kilometres away.

At the beginning of the fourteenth century, the Ilkhans of Iran – grandsons of the Great Khan Jenghiz – had all become Muslims and had given up the nomadic life and shamanic beliefs of their ancestors for the cultural life of the urban elite. Jenghiz Khan himself never accepted Islam even though not long before his death he showed an interest in it after his conquest of the Central Asian city of Bukhara. He equated Allah with his own shamanic deity, *tengri*, the god of the "Eternal Blue Sky".

Hulagu Khan, the grandson of Jenghiz Khan, invaded Iraq in the mid-thirteenth century and by this time, the 'Abbasids were powerless to stop the invasion. The last Iraqi 'Abbasid caliph, Al-Musta'sim (1242–1258), was unable to offer any resistance to the Mongols. Only the unified might of the Egyptian Mamluk state stopped the Mongols from continuing their destructive onslaught into North Africa.

DESTRUCTION OF BAGHDAD

The sophisticated culture of 'Abbasid Baghdad came to a very sad and sudden end with the total destruction of the city (see illustration 3-3) and the death of its last caliph, Al-Musta'sim in 1258. According to the *yasa*, the sacred law of the shamanic Mongols, animals were to be slaughtered by a blow to the head. Similarly, away from the battlefield, murder had to be bloodless. The *yasa* did not permit the shedding of blood as it would desecrate the earth. Since Baghdad had not surrendered to Hulagu Khan, the city experienced the full wrath of the Mongol leader. Al-Musta'sim, the pathetic last 'Abbasid caliph, who had not really believed the Mongols would attack his city, suffered a terrible death. In order not to shed the caliph's blood, it is reported that he was wrapped up in a palace carpet and trampled to death by Mongol horsemen. Al-Musta'sim might have held out some

3-3   THE DESTRUCTION OF BAGHDAD: Five centuries of civilisation came to a sudden end when the Mongol Hulagu Khan destroyed the city of Baghdad in 1258. The Mongol leader showed no mercy towards the Muslim inhabitants of the city. Libraries containing the accumulated knowledge of centuries were burned and their books thrown into the Tigris River. Greek, Pahlavi and Sanskrit manuscripts along with their Arabic translations were all lost. The ink of these valuable books mixed with the blood of the innocent inhabitants of Baghdad in the darkened waters of the Tigris River.

hope of being saved by neighbouring Islamic states, but it is another sad fact of history that the divisions in the Islamic world were so complete that no Muslim state, large or small, was willing to raise a hand in defence of the helpless 'Abbasid caliphate.

Re-Emergence of a Shadow 'Abbasid Caliphate

Relatives of Al-Musta'sim did survive the destruction of Baghdad and reappeared in Cairo, the capital of Mamluk Egypt, in 1261. Here a shadow caliphate continued until 1517. The Egyptian branch of the 'Abbasid dynasty ended with its last caliph, Al-Mutawakkil III (1508–1516 and 1517), being taken prisoner to Constantinople by the conquering Ottoman sultan, Selim I.

The caliphate was then passed on to the Ottoman Turks whose sultans held it for four hundred years, right up until 1924 when it was abolished by Kemal Atatürk, the president and founder of the modern Republic of Turkey.

Although the caliphate had survived the decimation of Baghdad in 1258 and had continued to exist right up to the twentieth century, it never regained the prestige it had once held in the early 'Abbasid period, the truly "golden age" of Islamic civilisation. Indeed, the legacy of the 'Abbasid dynasty must surely be the vast cultural diversity which enriched the Islamic civilisation that thrived under its rule. Despite the many violent political upheavals, Islamic culture – the study of the natural sciences along with medicine, philosophy, literature, the Islamic sciences and all the fine arts – reached unparalleled levels of achievement during 'Abbasid times.

CHAPTER FOUR

THE SAMANIDS (819–1005)

We have seen how, in the middle of the ninth century, the 'Abbasid Empire had disintegrated into a series of provincial states such as the Aghlabids of Tunisia, the Hamdanids of northern Iraq, the Tahirids of Khorasan, and the Saffarids of eastern Iran, all of whom were ruled by former 'Abbasid governors. Of these many breakaway principalities that weakened the central authority of the 'Abbasid state, the Samanids of Central Asia, were certainly the most famous.

ORIGINS OF THE DYNASTY

The Samanid dynasty is named after its founder, Saman-Khoda (819–864), a Persian-speaking descendant of a ruling family of Zoroastrian priests born near the city of Balkh in northern Afghanistan. During the reign of the 'Abbasid caliph, Al-Ma'mun, he rejected the ancient Zoroastrian faith of his ancestors and embraced Islam. The Samanids were Persian speakers of ethnic Tajik origin and, therefore, could not fabricate an Arab or any other royal ancestral connection. In later times, however, a legend popularised the belief that they were descended from Bahram, the great Sasanian war hero.

Four grandsons of Saman-Khoda faithfully served Al-Ma'mun and as payment each received a separate province to govern. Nuh was given Samarqand while Ahmad got Ferghana; Shash was given to Yahya and Herat to Ilyas. Nasr, Ahmad's son, successfully overthrew the Tahirid dynasty in eastern Iran and was thus able to establish a new capital for his family of rulers in Bukhara.

In 875, Nasr I (864–892) became the *amir* of Transoxiana.[3] The Samanids quickly became rulers of much more territory under Nasr's brother, Isma'il I (892–907), who defeated the Saffarids in Khorasan in 900. Much of Central Asia, Afghanistan and eastern Iran were now part of the Samanid Empire. Isma'il I, indeed, can be considered the true founder of the Samanid dynasty. Even though Samanid rulers were quite independent of the Baghdad caliph, they continued to refer to themselves as *amirs*, and to regularly pay respect to the 'Abbasid caliph in the Friday *khutbah*.

IMPORTANCE OF THE SAMANIDS

The Samanids were an important dynasty for several reasons. They were one of the first regional dynasties to take power after the Arab conquest of Persian territory. During the reign of the greatest Samanid ruler, Nasr II (914–943), the grandson of Isma'il I, Samanid domains extended from Iraq in the west, to the borders of India in the east and from Turkistan in the north, to the Persian Gulf in the south. During the long reign of Nasr II, Isma'ili missionary activity (originating in Fatimid Egypt) was rampant in Samanid lands. It was revealed that even in Nasr II's court in Bukhara, converts to the heretical Isma'ili doctrine had been made. Even Nasr II himself, is reported to have converted to

---

[3] Transoxiana is called *ma wara' an-nahr* in Arabic, meaning "that which is beyond the river", i.e. the territory north of the Oxus River or *Amu Darya*; the land comprising parts of present-day Uzbekistan, Tajikistan and southwest Kazakhstan.

Isma'ilism. Only when the Sunni *'ulema* and Samanid military forces revolted was the court purged of all Isma'ili heretics. Nasr II once again accepted orthodox Sunni Islam.

Bukhara, the Samanid capital, and Samarqand quickly became thriving centres of Persian language and culture. During this short period of peace and prosperity, Bukhara attracted many important scholars and artists. The Samanids, not unlike other Muslim rulers elsewhere, were tolerant of other religions. Jewish merchants, for example, were permitted to work in the profitable Silk Road trade. Silk and other luxury items were regularly exported to Europe by camel caravan from China. Nestorian (Syriac) Christians, Buddhists and Manicheans were also to be found in the thriving Samanid trading towns.

Bukhara is still a famous city today in the Central Asian nation of Uzbekistan. But one thousand years ago, it had a much larger population of some 300,000 inhabitants. Its numerous religious colleges or *madrasahs* attracted students from as far away as Al-Andalus. During the reign of Nasr II, Persian language poets, such as Rudaki (the first important poet of the "New Persian" language), were welcomed at the Samanid court. This was truly the "golden age" of the Samanids. Two important court *wazirs* were themselves gifted scholars; 'Abdallah al-Jayhani wrote geographical works and Al-Bal'ami translated the famous *Universal History* of Al-Tabari from Arabic into Persian for the first time. Exemplary and efficient government administrators ensured enormous tax revenues from the extensive farmlands in Samanid territories. Low taxes and market places overflowing with commodities helped make life very pleasant for the average citizen.

IMPORTANCE OF THE PERSIAN LANGUAGE

The Persian language was undergoing changes in the ninth century. Pahlavi (see illustration 4-1), the old form of the Persian language spoken during pre-Islamic Sasanian times, was now absorbing new words and grammatical structures from Arabic which continued to be used for administrative purposes alongside the New Persian. The old Pahlavi alphabet was also being replaced by a slightly modified Arabic one. This new Persian became the official language of the Samanid Empire and was a very important development. *Dar al-Islam* had grown in a very short period of time to cover an enormous geographical expanse. Non-Arab Muslim peoples, like the Persians and later the Turks, showed that Arabic could be a flexible vehicle in the Islamisation of other languages.

Two very important writers appeared at the court of the Samanids just at the time when the dynasty was losing power in the region. One of the last Samanid rulers, Nuh II (976–997) asked a court poet called Daqiqi to write a history of pre-Islamic Iran in rhyming verse. Unfortunately, Daqiqi died before finishing his poem, so the great Persian poet Firdawsi (935[?]–1020) began to compose his version of the Persian national poem, the *Shahnameh*, the "Book of Kings" (see illustration 4-2). According to legend, Firdawsi completed his poetic masterpiece (originally some 60,000 rhyming couplets) after more than thirty years of great sacrifice. He presented it to the new ruler in the region, the Ghaznavid sultan Mahmud, who had promised him a gold *dinar* for each verse written. Firdawsi was, therefore, heart-broken when he was given silver *dirhams* instead. The reason Mahmud reneged on his promise is disputed. Some say he wanted to spend more on his Indian campaigns; others say he was a miser by nature. Nevertheless, the *Shahnameh*, after one thousand years, remains the most widely read and memorised poem in the Persian language.

Ibn Sina (980–1037), one of the greatest intellects of all time, was born during the reign of Nuh II. Ibn Sina's father, employed by the Samanids, gave his son the best education money could buy in

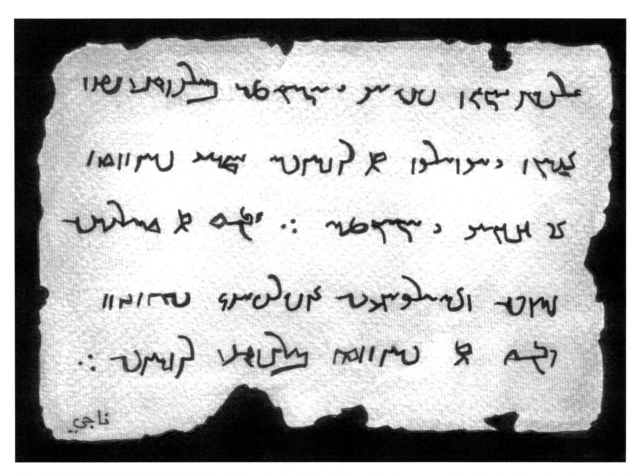

4-1 THE PAHLAVI LANGUAGE: For centuries before Islam, the language of the Persian Sasanian Empire had been Pahlavi, an old form of the Persian language. Pahlavi was written in a unique alphabet and was read from right to left. Here is a rare example of a Pahlavi text written on dried animal skin called parchment. The written form of this language survived into the tenth century. Eventually, most Zoroastrian (follower of the ancient religion of pre-Islamic Iran) Persians embraced Islam and the old Pahlavi writing system was then abandoned. The Persian-speaking Muslims started using a modified form of the Arabic alphabet that they continue to use today.

the capital city of Bukhara. By the age of sixteen, the precocious Ibn Sina was already practising medicine when he successfully cured the Samanid *amir* of a very serious ailment. As a reward for this, Ibn Sina was permitted to use the extensive Samanid royal library. Ibn Sina died relatively young, but wrote over two hundred books on a variety of subjects. He had once said, "I prefer to live a short life with width than to live a narrow one with length."

Ibn Sina's most well-known work, *Al-Qanun fi al-Tibb* (The Canon of Medicine) is undoubtedly the most famous book in the history of medicine. This one monumental work is over one million words in length! It became the basic medical textbook in Christian Europe for almost six hundred years while the Islamic world continued to use it as a reference work until the nineteenth century. Even today, medical doctors can discover in it effective herbal remedies for illnesses that Ibn Sina had successfully diagnosed and treated. *Al-Qanun fi al-Tibb* is a veritable medical encyclopaedia like no other. Ibn Sina was able to synthesise the total medical knowledge of his day using ancient Greek, Indian and Islamic sources. He supplemented all this with meticulous notes on his own careful observation of patients and suggested many original treatments as cures for diseases.

4-2 THE NEW PERSIAN WRITING: The pre-Islamic Pahlavi form of the Persian language changed greatly when the Persian-speaking peoples of Iran and Central Asia became Muslims. The "new Persian" was now written using the Arabic alphabet; many Arabic words and grammatical structures were absorbed by it. Persian literature has its origin during this time. Firdawsi, the great Persian poet, wrote his *Shahnameh*, or "Book of Kings", using the Persian language and script. This page comes from an old handwritten copy of the *Shahnameh*. Persian speakers today still read this one thousand year-old epic poem with immense joy.

SAMANID ART

The Samanids were Sunni Muslims who encouraged the spread of Islam in the territories to the north and east of their realm. Samanid traders brought *Din al-Haq al-Islam* to many tribes belonging to the Western Turks. Samanid textiles and metalwork were of high quality and the many silver *dirhams* minted by Samanid rulers were of extremely high purity. Consequently, such coins were widely used all over Southern Asia as common currency. Huge hoards, or stockpiles, of Samanid silver *dirhams* have been unearthed in recent times in Sweden, Finland and northern Russia (see illustration 4-3). This clearly shows that the Vikings of Northern Europe ventured south to Samanid lands to trade their furs and slaves in the markets of Central Asia. Samanid coins have even been found as far west as Britain and Iceland.

Samanid coins themselves are superb miniature works of Islamic art. Samanid pottery, however, was an even more important contribution to Islamic art and culture. Many beautiful pieces of Samanid pottery have survived to this day. These works of art are quite often multi-coloured ceramic pieces with extremely fine Arabic calligraphy (see illustration 4-4). Many art historians believe these Samanid plates and bowls exhibit the most beautiful Arabic calligraphy painted on any pottery. Beautifully woven Samanid textiles – soft cotton fabrics and shiny silks – were produced locally and often exported.

4-3 WELL-TRAVELLED SAMANID COINS: Samanid traders ventured north from their Central Asian homeland into non-Muslim lands and traded with Russians and Vikings who prized the high quality silver contained in Samanid coins. Beautiful silver *dirhams* like this one from the time of Nuh II (980) were an extremely popular currency. Hoards (hidden supplies for future use) of such coins are frequently found today in northern Europe, thus proving the extent of Samanid commercial links a thousand years ago.

Very little has survived of the grand palaces and public buildings of the Samanid era. One building, however, the mausoleum of Isma'il Saman in Bukhara, has been preserved and it clearly shows the great originality of Samanid architects (see illustration 4-5). The entire building is made of traditional, unglazed, kiln-dried bricks placed in such a way as to create the most exquisite "basket weave" patterns. This monumental tomb which houses the remains of several Samanid rulers is one of the first examples of its kind in the history of Islamic architecture.

4-4 SAMANID POTTERY: A thousand years ago, the Samanids ruled large parts of Central Asia from their capital of Bukhara. Few buildings remain from this distant time, but many beautiful pieces of Samanid pottery have survived. This is an example of a shallow bowl decorated in an extremely beautiful "Kufi" style of Arabic writing. The inscription is from the Holy Qur'an, *Surah al-Qalam, ayah* 52: *Wa ma huwa 'illa dhikrul-lil'alameen.* "[Be patient] for it is nothing less than the Message [from Allah] to all mankind." This beautiful work of Islamic art was made in Samarqand in 912.

ناجي

4-5   TOMB OF ISMA'IL SAMAN: The most important building from the Samanid period is the Mausoleum of Isma'il Saman in Bukhara, Uzbekistan. The building is made of unglazed baked bricks which are placed in such a way as to create highly decorative "basket weave" patterns. This work of Islamic art dates from the tenth century.

Beginning with the Samanids in the ninth century, the city of Bukhara became an important cultural, economic and political centre that survived for a thousand years – right up until the early 1920s when the Russian Bolsheviks deposed the last ruling *amir*.[4]

DECLINE OF THE SAMANIDS

As so often happened in this part of the world, once a dynasty showed any signs of weakness, another was ready to take its place. During the reign of Nuh II, the wealthy noble class united in opposition against the ruling family. Turkish officers in the government had also allied themselves with the new Muslim Turkish tribes from the mountainous region of Western China. Nuh II, in order to maintain at least some control of his realm, invited the Turkish army of Sebuktigin and his son Mahmud to help him ward off the threat. As a reward for this aid, Nuh II was forced to give Sebuktigin almost total control of Ghazna, a provincial area of Afghanistan. Both Nuh II and Sebuktigin died in 997, leaving the struggle to their sons: the last real Samanid ruler, Mansur II (997–999) and Mahmud of Ghazna, respectively. In 999, Mahmud declared himself an independent *amir* controlling all Samanid lands south of the Oxus River and took the title of *sultan* as well. Mansur II was succeeded by his brothers, 'Abd al-Malik II (999–1000) and Isma'il II (1000–1005). However, the Samanid era finally ended with the assassination of Isma'il II in the year 1005. The Ghaznavids were now the undisputed power in Southern Asia.

The importance of the Samanid dynasty had been to act as a buffer state between the non-Muslim Turkish tribes of Western China and the inhabited regions of Iran. The Oxus River was considered the border between the civilised and uncivilised worlds of Western Asia. After the collapse of the Samanid dynasty, Turkish nomadic armies poured westwards down into Persian and Arab lands.

---

[4] The last ruling *amir* was Mohammed Alim Khan (1880–1944), a direct descendant of Jenghiz Khan and last ruler of the Manghits, the last of the Bukharan dynasties.

CHAPTER FIVE
THE FATIMIDS (909–1171)

In the early tenth century, a large part of northwest Africa, centred around present-day Tunisia, was under the control of the Aghlabid dynasty. This dynasty had come about when the 'Abbasid governor, Ibrahim ibn al-Aghlab, had cut ties with the Baghdad government and proclaimed independence. At this time, an Isma'ili *da'i* (missionary) named Abu 'Abdallah al-Shi'i amassed followers among the Kutama Berbers of eastern Algeria. He was also undermining the regional Aghlabid dynasty. Abu 'Abdallah later persuaded the same Berber tribe to accept 'Ubayd Allah (another Isma'ili *da'i*) as their spiritual and temporal leader. Many of these early events in Fatimid history are shrouded in mystery and even among Isma'ili historians there is some confusion. But, clearly by the year 909, 'Ubayd Allah was able to replace the Aghlabid dynasty with his own one, the Fatimids.

'UBAYD ALLAH (909–934)

'Ubayd Allah being a Shi'ite, believed that 'Ali ؓ should have been chosen as the first of the *Khulafa' ar-Rashidun* upon the death of the Prophet Muhammad ﷺ. 'Ubayd Allah in all probability fabricated a lineage that showed he was descended from the Prophet ﷺ through his daughter Fatima az-Zahra ؓ. Although the genealogy is considered a weak one, 'Ubayd Allah still maintained his kinship with the Prophet ﷺ and, therefore, called his dynasty the Fatimids. 'Ubayd Allah, as an Isma'ili Shi'ite, believed that the line of righteous rulers (*imams*) had ended with the death of the Seventh Imam, Isma'il, hence, the name "Isma'ili". The Fatimids were the first powerful Shi'ite dynasty in Islamic history (see illustration 5-1).

Fatimid history can be neatly divided into two distinct periods: the North African and the Egyptian.

NORTH AFRICAN PERIOD (909–973)

'Ubayd Allah proclaimed himself the *Mahdi* (Guided One) and in 920 proceeded to establish the first Fatimid capital, *Al-Mahdiyyah*, in Ifriqiyah (Tunisia). The imposing ruins of this coastal capital with its grand mosque and palace can still be seen today. Once all the former Aghlabid territories in northwest Africa and Sicily had been conquered, the Fatimids turned their attention to the east. Their real goal was not only to be a thorn in the side of the 'Abbasids, but they also aimed at eventually replacing the Sunni 'Abbasid state with their own deviant form of Shi'ism.

The first four Fatimid caliphs were based in North Africa. 'Ubayd Allah al-Mahdi (909–934), the founder of the dynasty, Al-Qa'im (934–946) and Al-Mansur (946–953) never left the region. Al-Mu'izz (953–975) proceeded to Egypt in 973 only after his general, Jawhar, had established a Fatimid stronghold there, namely the new city of Cairo. During this period of Fatimid history, these four caliphs all had to deal with consolidating their power in the region. The Berber tribes were not united in their support of the Fatimids and there was also constant Sunni opposition to contend with.

5-1 FATIMID COIN - A MINIATURE WORK OF ART: The Fatimids of Egypt were the first important Shi'ite dynasty to have any real power in Islamic history. For two and a half centuries, their political aim was to overthrow the *sunni* 'Abbasid state and impose their own form of Shi'ism. It is not surprising, therefore, that even Fatimid coins became a form of religious propaganda. This gold *dinar* is typically Fatimid with the inscriptions running around three concentric circles. "'Ali is the Friend of Allah" is found on all such coins and often the Fatimid caliph refers to himself as "Allah's Slave and His Friend".

The Fatimids developed a powerful army and navy which they used effectively in expanding and protecting their empire. Some semblance of peace was finally brought to the region by Al-Mu'izz's able general, Jawhar, who marched as far as the Atlantic coast quelling any resistance.

From the outset, the Fatimids had their sights set on Egypt. 'Ubayd Allah had tried on two occasions to conquer "The Gift of the Nile": once in 913 and again in 919. Both campaigns, which were led by his son, Al-Qa'im, proved unsuccessful. In 925, after Al-Qa'im had become caliph, yet another abortive attempt was made to capture Egypt.

CONQUEST OF EGYPT (969)

Because of Al-Mu'izz's pacification of the North African territories, he was able to plan a careful, methodical conquest of Egypt, which at the time was suffering from a severe famine. In July 969, Jawhar and his army entered *Al-Fustat* (the city founded by 'Amr ibn al-'As ﷺ in the very early days of Islam) and thus Egypt became part of the Fatimid Empire and remained so for two hundred years. The city of *Al-Qahirah* (present-day Cairo) was established immediately in order to house the Fatimid army. This city soon replaced *Al-Mahdiyyah* (in Tunisia) as the Fatimid capital.

As the Fatimids never recognised the 'Abbasid caliph in Baghdad, they used the term *khalifah* for themselves. Devout followers of the Fatimid caliphs believed them to be infallible and sinless – the "living imams" of the Isma'ili faith. In order to spread their beliefs, the Fatimids established training centres for their missionaries (*da'is*). The large *Dar al-'Ilm* (House of Knowledge) and *Dar al-Hikmah* (House of Wisdom) in Cairo were just such centres which competed with the Nizamiyyah College of Sunni learning in Baghdad. In 980, Jawhar laid the foundation of the Al-Azhar Mosque, one of the oldest universities in the world, for a similar purpose, namely to propagate the Isma'ili faith. Fatimid missionaries were active in Umayyad Spain, in 'Abbasid territory, and as far away as Central Asia and India. While the very foreign Isma'ili doctrine was practised by the Fatimid caliphs within their courts, the vast majority of the Egyptian population remained Sunni. Isma'ilism was simply too strange a doctrine for the majority of Muslims to accept.

EXTENT OF THE FATIMID EMPIRE

Attempts were made to extend the Fatimid Empire further east immediately after the capture of Egypt. By the time of the caliph Al-'Aziz (975–996), Fatimid lands extended from the Atlantic shores to the Red Sea and included Yemen, and for brief periods, the Hijaz, Syria and Palestine. The Fatimids were great propagandists and made no secret of the fact that they believed Allah had decreed that they govern the world. This of course meant the elimination of the three regional powers: the Umayyads of Spain, the Christian Byzantines based in Constantinople, and the 'Abbasids of Baghdad. However, neither potent Isma'ili propaganda nor the force of arms was able to achieve these goals.

ISMA'ILI DOCTRINE

The Fatimids attempted to make Isma'ilism a state religion, but failed. There was a constant battle between Sunni loyalists who were still in the overwhelming majority in Egypt and throughout the Empire. While a *muadhdhin* in Ifriqiyah was killed for not reciting, "Come to the best of works" in the Isma'ili form of the *adhan*, greater tolerance was often shown to Christians and Jews.

Central to Isma'ili doctrine was the distinction between *zahir* or exterior, visible aspects of the religion and *batin*, or esoteric inner, unchangeable truths. Secretive initiation rites, the mystical interpretation of letters of the Arabic alphabet, complex hierarchies and ranks of *da'is* and the concept of *taqiyyah* (or concealment of one's true religious beliefs) all further complicated the understanding and acceptance of Isma'ilism by the Sunni masses.

Popular riots throughout the Fatimid Empire in the early eleventh century wiped out most Isma'ili communities in North Africa. A century later, Isma'ilism was rarely practised in Egypt outside court circles. The famous Isma'ili "Assassins" of northern Iran, notorious for their political assassinations of many important Sunni Muslims from the eleventh to thirteenth centuries, kept the doctrines alive for another century until their remote mountain strongholds such as Alamut in northern Iran were systematically destroyed by Hulagu Khan and his Mongol army in 1256. This branch of Isma'ilism was never revived. Isma'ilis do, however, survive today as minority communities in parts of Syria, India, East Africa, Britain and North America.

AL-HAKIM (996–1021)

The strangest of all Fatimid caliphs and one of the most eccentric rulers in all Islamic history must certainly be Al-Hakim. In 996, he was proclaimed caliph at the age of eleven upon the death of his father, Al-'Aziz. Al-Hakim began his rule by building the mosque which bears his name located in the heart of Old Cairo. The two enormous minarets of the Mosque of Al-Hakim were as unique as their builder (see illustration 5-2). During the twenty-five years of his reign, Al-Hakim became progressively more insane. He is remembered for his despotic and cruel decrees which were often abolished and later re-introduced. But he was also remarkably liberal on other occasions. For example, at times he

5-2   THE MOSQUE OF AL-HAKIM: Perhaps the most eccentric ruler in all of Islamic history was the Fatimid caliph, Al-Hakim. He progressively grew insane as he reigned as *imam*, or spiritual head of the Isma'ili faith. Despite his bizarre behaviour, he offered aid to many scientists and scholars who resided at his court in Cairo. The Mosque of Al-Hakim was built on a massive scale. Two huge minarets stand at corners of the courtyard. The one you see here is unique, like its builder; it resembles no other minaret in all of Cairo.

permitted Jews and Christians who had embraced Islam to return to their respective faiths. Unlike most rulers, who stayed secluded in their opulent palaces, Al-Hakim broke with tradition and riding a donkey (named *Al-Qamr* meaning moon), would often leave his palace at night and roam the city. He wanted to spy on his subjects and inspect the marketplace. At that time he had made night-time into daytime by prohibiting sleeping at night! No one was permitted to work during the day; all business was to be conducted at night. Furthermore, to keep women indoors, he even forbade the manufacture of women's shoes!

Despite the very peculiar behaviour of Al-Hakim, he reportedly had a personal library of some 200,000 books and many great scholars, artists and poets worked at his court. The renowned Muslim astronomer, 'Ali ibn Yunus, for example, wrote his important astronomical tables during this time. Al-Hakim personally supplied Ibn Yunus with an observatory to conduct his scientific observations of the heavens. Ibn al-Haytham, the greatest Arab physicist, wrote his important work on optics during his stay at Al-Hakim's court.

Towards the end of his life, certain fanatic Isma'ili supporters proclaimed Al-Hakim's "divinity". Al-Hakim apparently encouraged these supporters in this ultimate form of *shirk* (the most detested sin of polytheism). His life had been one of incredible excesses and contradictions. Al-Hakim's death, not unlike his life, was mysterious. In 1021, he was last seen riding his donkey on a road leading to the hills surrounding Cairo. For some of his followers, his strange and unexplained disappearance was even more proof of his "divinity". Today, these followers are known as the Druzes, a non-Muslim people who live mainly in certain mountainous regions of Syria and Lebanon. In truth, however, several days after his disappearance, Al-Hakim's bloodied clothes were found – a likely indication that he had been murdered.

DECLINE OF THE FATIMIDS

Much of what we know about life in Fatimid Egypt comes from the written accounts of an Iranian Isma'ili missionary named Nasr al-Khusraw, who visited Egypt from 1046–1049. The many *suqs* or markets he saw there were overflowing with fruits and vegetables of all kinds. The extremely fertile soil along the banks of the River Nile enabled farmers to grow two or even three crops in a year. Perhaps one of the most surprising comments Nasr made concerned the buying and selling of mosques. As a rule, the grand old mosques of Cairo belonged to the descendants of the rulers who had built them and could be sold to the highest bidder. During the reign of Al-Hakim, for example, there were two very important mosques in Cairo: the Ibn Tulun Mosque (see illustration 5-3) and the Mosque of 'Amr ibn al-'As ﷺ. Al-Hakim bought both mosques for many thousands of gold *dinars*.

The Fatimid Empire at its zenith stretched across all of North Africa and into Palestine, Arabia and Yemen. But, by the year 1060, this once vast empire had been reduced to only Egypt. A series of weak caliphs and internal dissension over succession hastened the decline of this dynasty. In 1071, the Seljuq Turkish occupation of Jerusalem (*Al-Quds*) was one of several events that initiated the Crusades, a period in which hundreds of thousands of European Christians invaded Muslim lands in the Middle East. The destruction of the Church of the Holy Sepulchre in Jerusalem by Al-Hakim, just before his death, was another event never forgotten in Europe.

5-3   THE IBN TULUN MOSQUE: A Turkish slave soldier, named Ahmed ibn Tulun, was sent by the 'Abbasid caliph to be governor of Egypt in the ninth century. Eventually, Ibn Tulun established his own dynasty – the Tulunid – and built one of the greatest mosques in all of Egypt. The "spiral" minaret (with its winding exterior staircase) of the Mosque of Ibn Tulun resembles similar minarets Ibn Tulun might have seen while growing up in Samarra', outside of Baghdad. Nasr Khusraw, the Iranian traveller, tells us that in Fatimid times, mosques were sold by the descendants of the rulers who built them. The Fatimid caliph Al-Hakim, we are told, purchased the Mosque of Ibn Tulun – along with another important mosque in old Cairo: the Mosque of 'Amr ibn al-'As ﷺ – for thousands of gold *dinars*.

Fearing that the Crusaders might attempt to occupy Egypt, the Fatimid rulers asked for help from Nur ad-Din al-Zangi, the independent ruler of northern Syria. This eventually led to Salah ad-Din al-Ayyubi taking control of Egypt when the last Fatimid caliph Al-'Adid died in 1171.

Salah ad-Din now recognised the 'Abbasid caliph in Baghdad, and Egypt was once again ruled by Sunni leaders. Isma'ilism had never taken root among the Egyptian people and with the death of Al-'Adid, Isma'ilism was never seen again in Egypt. It is noteworthy that the late Aga Khan III, Prince Sultan Mohammed (1877–1957), grandfather of the present leader of the world's Isma'ili community, chose to be buried in a large mausoleum overlooking the River Nile in Egypt, the ancestral homeland of the first and only Isma'ili Shi'ite dynasty.

LEGACY OF THE FATIMIDS

The most enduring legacy of the Fatimid dynasty must surely be the Mosque of Al-Azhar, begun in 970. Initially built as the first congregational mosque for the new capital of *Al-Qahirah*, it soon became the training centre for Isma'ili *da'is*. Today, the Al-Azhar University has become the foremost seat of Islamic learning in the world and is now a vibrant training centre for Sunni Muslims.

CHAPTER SIX
THE GHAZNAVIDS (977–1186)

We have seen how Sebuktigin, a Turkish slave, had become an independent ruler after the Samanid dynasty collapsed. As governor of Ghazna (the present-day Afghan city of Ghazni), he became the founder of a new dynasty, the Ghaznavids. From 977 until his death in 997, Sebuktigin continued to expand his kingdom east towards the Indian border. Although the Ghaznavids extended their empire to include all of Afghanistan and parts of Iran and Central Asia, they are most remembered for their conquest of northwest India.

MAHMUD IBN SEBUKTIGIN (998–1030)

In 998, the most famous Ghaznavid ruler, Abu'l-Qasim Mahmud ibn Sebuktigin, usurped the throne from his younger brother Isma'il, who had been their father's chosen successor as sultan. Mahmud consolidated his control of the area around Ghazna and once in full control, proceeded west to defeat his opponents in Khorasan, in northeast Iran. Being a staunch Sunni like his father, he still showed nominal allegiance to the 'Abbasid caliph in far-off Baghdad. The 'Abbasid caliph, Al-Qadir, presented Mahmud with the governorship of two provinces: Khorasan and Ghazna and he was also given the *laqab* of *Yamin ad-Dawla* (Right Hand of the State), which soon came to be applied to the whole dynasty. Mahmud extended his empire by seizing parts of Shi'ite Iran and then, always acting as a *ghazi*, or frontier warrior, he brought Sunni Islam to regions still outside of *Dar al-Islam*.

Mahmud very soon looked eastward to India and in 1001 vowed to invade that vast land once a year and to invite the many Hindu kingdoms there to Islam. Travelling with a large army, Mahmud kept his word. He made a total of seventeen raids into India and as a result of the great riches he brought back, his capital of Ghazna became one of the most thriving centres of Islamic culture in all of Asia. Mahmud also used his new-found wealth to fund his large professional army which was a constant drain on his resources.

During his raids, Mahmud had many Indian temples destroyed. In 1026, for example, during his last Indian campaign, the temple dedicated to Shiva[5] in the city of Somnath (in the present-day Indian state of Gujarat), was left in ruins. Even an Arab ruler of Multan (in Sindh province in present-day Pakistan) was attacked and deposed for being Isma'ili and supporting the Fatimid caliphs of Egypt.

While critics argue that Mahmud was only concerned with stealing the great wealth housed in the Hindu temples throughout India, the truth is that Mahmud was a *ghazi*, but did not impose Islam on his Indian subjects. Indeed, his own army included Hindu troops that travelled alongside Muslim ones. In 712, Islam had first been introduced into the Sindh province of northwest India by Muhammad ibn Qasim, the young Umayyad governor of Persia, but for several centuries this remained the frontier between *Dar al-Islam* and *Dar al-Harb*. Mahmud was the first Muslim to bring the message of Islam right into the heart of Hindu India (see illustration 6-1). Mahmud most probably never thought

---

[5] One of the principal Hindu gods worshipped as "the destroyer and restorer".

6-1 AN INVITATION TO ISLAM: The most important Ghaznavid ruler was unquestionably Mahmud (998–1030). His military raids into the heartland of India have often been criticised. Mahmud did destroy non-Muslim temples and shrines, but he also tried to spread the message of Islam. This extraordinary silver *dirham* is dated 1028 and was minted (struck) in "Mahmudpur", Mahmud's second capital of Lahore, in present-day Pakistan. On the left, the *kalimah* is clearly inscribed in Arabic; on the right, Mahmud attempted to translate the *kalimah* into Sanskrit, the sacred language of the majority Hindus. For Hindus, who worship literally hundreds of tangible idols, "Allah" is very aptly rendered "the Invisible" in Sanskrit. This bilingual coin and its sincere attempt at *da'wah* (inviting to Islam) is unique in the history of Islam.

it possible for him to convert the Hindu population of India to Islam – the numbers were simply too huge and there was, of course, great opposition to his raids by some Hindu principalities. In the past, invaders like Alexander the Great would leave their newly conquered lands to the mercy of their soldiers. Mahmud, however, chose to govern his new territories and to bring law and order to them. While most Muslim rulers of the day held the lofty titles of *khalifah* (caliph), *malik* (king) or *amir* (prince), Mahmud became the first important Muslim ruler to be known as *sultan* (authority).

AL-BIRUNI (973–1048)

In 973, one of the greatest and most original of all Muslim scholars, Abu Rayhan al-Biruni, was born in a suburb of the capital of Khwarizm in Central Asia. It was here that he received his education in the sciences from the learned masters of his day.

Scholars, artists, poets and scientists commonly sought out princely courts where they could be patronised. In one of his many books, Al-Biruni laments the difficulties of scholars in search of suitable patrons.

> Once a sage was asked why scholars always flock to the doors of the rich, while the rich are not inclined to call at the doors of scholars. "The scholars" he answered, "are well aware of the use of money, but the rich are ignorant of the nobility of science."[6]

---

[6] *India by Al-Biruni* (ed. Qeyamuddin Ahmad). Delhi: National Book Trust, India, 1988: 90.

We recall that Firdawsi and Ibn Sina were welcomed at the Samanid court in Bukhara. Al-Biruni, likewise, offered his scholarly services first to Al-Mansur II, one of the last Samanid *amirs* and later to the Khwarizmshah prince, Abu'l-'Abbas Ma'mun. But, as is so often the case, rulers are deposed and their families and court attendants imprisoned, enslaved or even worse. Al-Biruni quickly lost his patron when Mahmud ibn Sebuktigin invaded the territories of Khwarizm on the southern shores of the Aral Sea. Al-Biruni along with other scholars who had been employed by the same Khwarizmshah prince were taken as prisoners back to Ghazna.

Mahmud immediately recognised Al-Biruni's exceptional abilities and likely employed him as his official court astrologer. As his empire grew wealthier, Mahmud welcomed scholars and artists of all kinds to his capital. It was fortuitous that Al-Biruni was present in Ghazna when Mahmud began his expeditions into northwest India.

Al-Biruni accompanied Mahmud on one of these expeditions to India and eventually settled there. Over a period of twenty years, Al-Biruni became very familiar with Hindu culture. He was a very gifted linguist and knew at least six languages. While in India, Al-Biruni learned Sanskrit, the ancient language of the Hindus, and from Hindu scholars learned Indian philosophy, mathematics and geography. Al-Biruni, likewise, taught the Hindus the science and philosophy of the Ancient Greeks and Muslim Arabs. Eventually, in 1030, he was able to write his most famous book, the *Kitab al-Hind* (The Book of India). In this superb encyclopaedic book, Al-Biruni discussed in detail the history, social structure and customs of Hindu society. Some scholars believe the *Kitab al-Hind* represents the first example in history of anyone attempting to understand a foreign culture in a totally objective and impersonal way. It is for this reason Al-Biruni is sometimes called "the father of anthropology".

Al-Biruni had mastered the Sanskrit language so well that he even translated a famous Sanskrit religious text, the *Patanjali Yoga*, into Arabic. He also translated a famous work on mathematics from Ancient Greek into Sanskrit. One thousand years ago, he observed the fossilised remains of marine life along the Indus River valley and accurately concluded that it must have once been an ancient sea basin. Al-Biruni was clearly a scientist far ahead of his time.

Al-Biruni returned to Ghazna when Mahmud's son, Mas'ud, became the new sultan after the death of his father. At the royal court, Al-Biruni completed his longest work, *Al-Qanun al-Mas'udi* (The Encyclopedia of Astronomy), an extremely important work on astronomy which he dedicated to his new patron, Sultan Mas'ud. In this monumental work, Al-Biruni listed more than one thousand stars and gave accurate calculations of latitude and longitude. Incredibly, he also calculated the radius of the Earth to within fifteen kilometres of the estimate given today! Sceptics, who still believed the Earth was flat, were told to observe the curved shadow of the Earth on the Moon's surface during a lunar eclipse.

FIRDAWSI'S *SHAHNAMEH*

Poets were welcomed at the royal court at Ghazna. The great national epic poem of Iran, the *Shahnameh* (The Book of Kings), had been started by the Persian poet Daqiqi in the court of the Samanids in Bukhara. Firdawsi, another Persian poet, continued the massive task of writing the pre-Islamic history of the Iranian people in rhyming verse. In 1010, he finally completed his *Shahnameh* consisting of 60,000 couplets. Historians tell us that Mahmud had promised Firdawsi a gold *dinar* for every line of poetry written; however, Firdawsi was paid in silver *dirhams* instead. Several reasons have been suggested for such a deliberate affront to one of the greatest poets the world has ever known. Some say Mahmud was by nature a spendthrift and would only pay large sums for poems that honoured him. Others say Mahmud's own court poets might have been jealous of Firdawsi's amazing accomplishment. Firdawsi refused Mahmud's silver *dirhams* and not long after died a pauper in Tus, his birthplace, just before Mahmud had decided to finally give the poet his due payment in gold *dinars*. Firdawsi rightly predicted on the last page of his poem that his epic would be read forever by the Persian people. After a thousand years, the *Shahnameh* is read, understood and respected by all Persian speakers, so perhaps this is the better reward.

Mas'ud ibn Mahmud (1031–1041)

During the reign of Mas'ud, Turkish nomadic tribes had been permitted to roam on Ghaznavid land. In 1038, these nomads united under a leader named Tughril Beg who claimed the land as his own. Two years later, in 1040, the Seljuq Turks led by Tughril Beg defeated Mas'ud's army at the Battle of Dandanqan. With this decisive defeat, Mas'ud had lost the western half of his father's empire, which comprised all the Persian territories.

The Ghaznavid dynasty continued to survive, but played a much smaller role in the history of the region. For the next century and a half, the Ghaznavids maintained a strong presence in the city of Lahore (in present-day Pakistan), often called "small Ghazna". Over time, lands in Central Asia were lost to various Turkish tribes and by the later years of the twelfth century, the Ghaznavid Empire had been reduced to parts of eastern Afghanistan and northern India.

In 1186, a new and more powerful group of invaders from central Afghanistan, the Ghurids, entered Lahore and deposed the last Ghaznavid sultan, Khusraw Malik (1160–1186).

Legacy of the Ghaznavids

The history of the Ghaznavids and its greatest leader, Sultan Mahmud, will always be associated with the conquest of India. Despite Mahmud's many shortcomings, he was a valiant Muslim who, during his time, believed in spreading the message of his religion, *Din al-Haq al-Islam*, to the farthest corners of his realm. The Ghaznavid presence in the Punjab lasted for two centuries during which time part of the Indian subcontinent became thoroughly Islamised. It was no surprise, therefore, that one thousand years later, this region formed part of the new independent Muslim state of Pakistan.

With his generosity to poets and scholars alike, Mahmud enabled the Islamic world of his day – for the first time in history – to become enriched by an exchange of ideas and trade between the vast subcontinent of India and *Dar al-Islam*. Al-Biruni could be considered the first Muslim anthropologist and, because of his enormous contribution to human knowledge, many other Muslims would undertake similar research in later centuries. The true legacy of the Ghaznavids must certainly be this cross-fertilisation of cultures. India became aware of the Islamic world, while Indian culture, along with many amazing Indian discoveries, spread beyond the borders of the Hindu world. India, over the next several hundred years, would witness the emergence of two powerful Islamic dynasties: the Delhi Sultanate and the Mughals.

CHAPTER SEVEN

THE GREAT SELJUQS (1040–1194)

The origin of the Seljuq Turks lies on the grassy Central Asian steppes. Like all Turkish tribes, they were shamanists who worshipped the natural world. A nomadic band of Turkish-speaking shepherds, led by Seljuq, embraced Islam in about the year 960 (see illustration 7-1). Two grandsons of Seljuq, Chaghri Beg and Tughril Beg, moved south from the area of present-day Kazakhstan with their tribe to seek better pasture for their animals. Eventually, they settled in Ghaznavid territory in Khorasan. Here, as we have already seen, the Battle of Dandanqan took place in 1040. The battle resulted in the loss of all Ghaznavid land in the western half of Sultan Mahmud's Empire. Tughril Beg now became ruler of the western region of the new Great Seljuq Empire. He controlled parts of Iran, Iraq and parts of eastern Anatolia (Turkey). Chaghri Beg, on the other hand, governed the eastern half of the Empire in Central Asia.

In their westward push, the Seljuqs removed the Shi'ite Buyid rulers from Isfahan, which became the new Seljuq capital. By 1055, the Seljuqs, under the command of Tughril Beg, had reached Baghdad where they unseated the Buyids who had controlled the Sunni caliphate for more than a century. Once again, northern Syria, Iraq and parts of Iran were all unified under a Sunni commander. In gratitude, Tughril Beg was given the title *sultan* by the 'Abbasid caliph, Al-Qa'im.

BATTLE OF MALAZGIRT (AUGUST 26, 1071)

As rulers, the Great Seljuqs were impressive. They brought order and public security to the territory they governed. With the death of Tughril Beg in 1063, Alp Arslan (1063–1072), the son of Chaghri Beg, became the new Seljuq sultan. Perhaps the most important event in the history of the Great Seljuqs was their victory on the plains of Malazgirt (formerly Manzikert), to the north of Lake Van, in eastern Turkey. There, Alp Arslan (Turkish for "valiant lion") and his Seljuq army faced the leader of the Eastern Roman Empire, the Greek Byzantine Emperor Romanus Diogenes IV. The Battle of Malazgirt was fought on August 26, 1071 and proved to be one of the most important battles in the history of Western Asia.

The Byzantine Emperor Romanus had led two previous campaigns against the invading nomadic Turks on his eastern frontier. This time, however, because of his superior manpower, he felt confident he could decisively defeat Alp Arslan. Historical accounts give differing estimates as to the size of the Byzantine army, but it was likely to have been between 60,000 and 100,000 soldiers which included Arab, Russian, Georgian, Armenian and even some Turkish mercenaries. Alp Arslan's forces, however, numbered no more than 15,000, but as the battle took place on a Friday, they felt their prayers would give them an advantage. Despite the desertion of some of his foreign mercenaries to the enemy, Romanus rejected the peace treaty offered to him. He still believed his army vastly outnumbered that of the Seljuqs, so his victory was assured. At sunset, there was a disorderly retreat of some Byzantine troops to their camp and the Seljuqs were able to ambush them. This resulted in the capture of the Byzantine Emperor. Alp Arslan's agile mounted archers, though far fewer in number than those of his enemy, had proved to be far superior.

7-1 CIRCULAR TOMBS: The Seljuq Turks were originally nomads who roamed Central Asia in search of pasture. Turkic nomads still exist today in many parts of the region and still live in round, semi-circular tents. Tomb towers such as the one here – dating from the early fourteenth century – were built as burial chambers for important Seljuq officials and their families. The shape of these buildings, called *kumbets* in Turkish, resemble the nomadic tents, or *yurts*, that Seljuq nomads once lived in. Today, *kumbets* can be seen dotting the landscape in many parts of Turkey and Iran.

History tells us that the Byzantine Emperor was brought before the victorious Alp Arslan who asked him what he thought would be a just punishment. Romanus replied that if he had captured Alp Arslan in battle, he would have either killed him or led him off to be exhibited in the streets of Constantinople. Alp Arslan said he forgave the Emperor and set him free! Romanus' Byzantine subjects were not so forgiving; they blinded their Emperor, who later died of his injury.

Unfortunately, several months after his victory, Alp Arslan was slain in a senseless skirmish with a prisoner on the eastern frontiers of his empire. He had not permitted his bodyguards to do their job and while dying of a stab wound, believed that vanity had killed him. Before he died, he told his son, Malik Shah, "I had been warned against protecting myself and letting my courage get in the way of my good sense. I forgot these warnings and here I lie, dying in agony. Remember well the lessons learned and do not allow your vanity to overreach your good sense…"

The importance of the Battle of Malazgirt cannot be exaggerated. The Muslim victory at this battle led directly to the Islamisation of the lands which now comprise present-day Turkey. The Seljuqs had extended *Dar al-Islam* into the very heart of Byzantine Christian territory in Asia Minor. Seljuq nomads, farmers and *ghazis* began to move across all of Anatolia until they reached the Aegean Sea (off the coast of western Turkey). Very little territory was left to the Byzantines in this part of the world. In an extremely short period of time, vast tracts of former Greek-speaking land became forever Turkish.

From their newly-conquered territories, the Seljuqs were able to use resources there to support a huge expanding army. In 1071, the Seljuqs also occupied Jerusalem (*Al-Quds*), replacing the Fatimids. This event, along with the expansion into Byzantine lands, greatly alarmed Christian Europe and was certainly one cause of the First Crusade in 1095.

NIZAM AL-MULK (1063–1092) AND MALIK SHAH (1072–1092)

That Seljuq rule was so stable and efficient was mainly due to one man. For a period of thirty years, Nizam al-Mulk proved to be a very wise, imaginative, and successful *wazir* of the Seljuq state. He lived in the Seljuq capital of Isfahan and worked for both Alp Arslan and his son, the new ruler, Malik Shah. During the latter's twenty-year reign, the Great Seljuq Empire stretched from Syria to Khorasan. Although the Seljuqs had annexed the western half of the Ghaznavid Empire, they still managed to co-exist with this Turkish dynasty. A more important task now lay in securing the western frontiers from incursions by Arab and Kurdish neighbours or from the Christian Byzantines and Georgians. A particular concern was to prevent any encroachment of the Isma'ili Fatimids from Palestine.

On many occasions, the Seljuqs confronted the Christian world on the battlefield, but the real enemy of the Seljuq state was always Isma'ili terror. Ever since the Fatimid dynasty established themselves in their new capital of Cairo, their caliphs had been active in spreading Isma'ili religious propaganda. They were considered the infallible "imams" of Isma'ili doctrine. To counteract the influence of the Isma'ili propaganda being delivered from the Fatimid centre at the Al-Azhar in Cairo, Nizam al-Mulk established the Nizamiyyah University in Baghdad in 1067. It soon became the most important Sunni training centre in the region. The great theologian, Imam al-Ghazali (1058–1111) spent a part of his early teaching life at the Nizamiyyah University in Baghdad.

Many other Nizamiyyah colleges were established in other parts of the vast Seljuq Empire, such as at Herat and Balkh in Afghanistan, and Nishapur in Khorasan. They were all extremely well run and offered the highest possible education available anywhere. The Nizamiyyah colleges not only defended Sunni Islam against Isma'ili propaganda, but also trained able administrators for the Seljuq state which now stretched from Central Anatolia (Turkey) to the Oxus River (*Amu Darya*) in Central Asia.

Nizam al-Mulk, a Persian by birth, was one of the most gifted administrators in all of Islamic history. He had the ability to educate the rough, nomadic Turkish rulers in the finer cultural traditions of the Persians. He is remembered for his famous book of advice to rulers, the *Siyaset Nameh* (The Book of Good Government), which is still read with interest today. Nizam al-Mulk begins his book with the following illuminating words:

> In every age and time, God (be He exalted) chooses one member of the human race and, having endowed him with goodly and kingly virtues, entrusts him with the interests of the world and the well-being of His servants; He charges that person to close the doors of corruption, confusion and discord, and He imparts to him such dignity and majesty in the eyes and hearts of men, that under his just rule they may live their lives in constant security and ever wish for his reign to continue.[7]

Nizam al-Mulk travelled with the sultan Alp Arslan on all his campaigns and became so trusted and respected by the Seljuq sultans that he soon controlled all decision-making in the court. As *wazir*, or minister of state, he oversaw the prosperity of the Great Seljuq state and was, therefore, the *de facto* ruler of the Seljuq Empire for thirty years. Nizam al-Mulk had grown up during the Ghaznavid era and successfully used their rulers as a model for governing the Seljuq state.

During this period, Isma'ili *da'is* were very active all over the Middle East. One group of Isma'ilis was called the "Assassins" because they conducted political assassinations of important individuals who publicly disagreed with Isma'ili beliefs; the name was given to them by the Christian crusaders. Nizam al-Mulk was very outspoken in his denouncements of the Isma'ilis. It was, therefore, not surprising that in 1092, on his way from Isfahan to Baghdad, Nizam al-Mulk was murdered by a group of Isma'ili "terrorists". Later, his brother and son were also killed. Even Salah ad-Din al-Ayyubi was targeted by the Isma'ilis. (You may recall that Salah ad-Din had deposed Al-'Adid, the last Isma'ili Fatimid calpih in Cairo.)

Among the scholars and artists attracted to Malik Shah's court in Isfahan was 'Umar Khayyam (1048–1131), the famous Persian mathematician and poet. While there, he helped reform the calendar and establish an observatory.

The Great Seljuq state was much weakened when Malik Shah was poisoned in a suspected assassination in 1092 at the age of fifty-eight. No one Seljuq leader could now hold the Empire together. Kilij Arslan I fled to Anatolia where he established a new dynasty of "Rum" Seljuqs. The once unified Seljuq Empire was forever divided when Malik Shah's brother, Tutush I, and four sons fought over supremacy. Military commanders and *atabegs*[8] ensured the dynasty's survival – albeit in a fragmented form – for another century.

While Mahmud I ibn Malik Shah (1092–1094) now ruled Iran, Tutush I and his line of Seljuq rulers governed Aleppo and Damascus in Syria (1092–1117) and another line ruled in Kirman in southeast

---

[7] Darke, Hubert. *The Book of Government of Rules for Kings: The Siyar Muluk or Siyasat-nama of Nizam al-Mulk.* London: Curzon, 2002: 9.

[8] The title *atabeg*, from the Turkish *ata* (father) and *beg* (chief), was first given to the guardians or proxy fathers of young Seljuq princes. These *atabegs*, as military advisers, frequently overthrew their rulers and took control for themselves.

Iran (1092–1187). The longest surviving branch of the Great Seljuqs contolled Khorasan in northeast Iran (1092–1194). The dismembered Seljuq state could offer little resistance to the Khwarizm-Shahis, who had once been governors of Seljuq territories. The last of the Great Seljuqs, Tughril III of Khorasan, died in 1194 during a battle against the Khwarizm-Shahi leader, 'Ala' ad-Din Tekish. Some historians maintain that the much weakened Seljuq state directly enabled the First Crusaders (of the First Crusade launched in 1095) to succeed in occupying Jerusalem in July 1099.

LEGACY OF THE GREAT SELJUQS

The Great Seljuqs left two very important legacies. Firstly, they helped stop Shi'ite and Isma'ili Islam from dominating in the region and initiated the Islamisation of all present-day Turkey; and secondly, the system of Islamic *madrasah* education was also greatly improved by the establishment of the Nizamiyyah colleges throughout their domains.

CHAPTER EIGHT
THE SELJUQS OF RUM (1077–1307)

After the death of Malik Shah in 1092, the Seljuq world broke apart into a number of independent principalities ruled by *atabegs*. The Great Seljuqs had made the mistake of dividing up the state into provinces ruled by the sultans' sons or other relatives.

One branch of the Seljuq family established its own dynasty on the high plateau of Central Anatolia. These were the Seljuqs of *Rum* – the lands of the East Romans or Byzantines – who became the longest-lasting of all the Seljuq states. Qonya (the ancient Iconium or present-day Konya in Central Turkey) eventually became their new capital. Turkish nomads began to flood into Anatolia and settle in all corners, slowly replacing the old Greek and Armenian Christian culture with a new Turkish and Muslim one.

AFTER MALAZGIRT (1071)

We recall that at the Battle of Malazgirt in August 1071, the Seljuq sultan Alp Arslan defeated the Byzantine Emperor Diogenes Romanus. By the following year, both leaders were dead. The new Byzantine emperor in Constantinople needed help to suppress a rebellion in his territory. He asked Sulayman ibn Qutlumish, the son of Alp Arslan's brother, for help and when the Seljuqs assisted the Byzantines, they decided to move their capital west to Nicaea (present-day İznik in northwestern Turkey) in 1077. It was here that Sulayman declared himself sultan of a new dynasty. Sulayman ibn Qutlumish was now very close to the Byzantine capital, but it would take another four hundred years before it fell to the Muslims in 1453.

THE CRUSADES

Kilij Arslan I (1092–1107), the son of Sulayman, at the young age of seventeen, broke off all ties with his Great Seljuq family members centred in Isfahan. He proclaimed himself the first "Sultan of Rum". In Europe, meanwhile, the Catholic Pope Urban II encouraged a crusade to capture Jerusalem (*Al-Quds*) from Muslim control and in 1096, the first crusaders left Europe on foot for the long march to the Holy Land. This was the "People's Crusade", an army comprised mainly of peasants, that was utterly defeated outside of the city of Constantinople. The following year, another army of Christians comprising the "First Crusade" arrived in the Byzantine capital on their way to recapture Jerusalem.

In 1097, the crusaders along with the combined might of the Byzantines occupied Kilij Arslan's capital of Nicaea. He immediately transferred his capital to Konya, a much safer location in Central Anatolia. The fledgling Seljuq principality of Konya was just one of many Turkish *beyliks* (small princedoms or provinces). The First Crusade then proceeded south, crossing Seljuq territory until finally reaching the Holy Land.

Once again, Jerusalem was re-occupied by the Christians in 1099. In later years, Kilij Arslan I was able to destroy several crusader armies passing though Seljuq lands and bring a degree of stability and prosperity to Anatolia.

KONYA – THE SELJUQ CAPITAL

The remarkably beautiful Turkish city of Konya, known in classical times as Iconium, lies to the south of present-day Ankara, on the edge of the Anatolian plateau. The wealth of Seljuq monuments that have survived there attests to the importance of the city when it was the capital of the Seljuqs of Rum.

Konya lies to the north of the Taurus Mountains on a flat plain well-irrigated by underground springs. Historical records frequently cite the town's many orchards and gardens of which passing crusaders would avail themselves. Even today, Konya's many gardens make it a green oasis on an often dusty barren plain.

Konya really began to resemble a capital city during the reign of Mas'ud I (1116–1156), the son of Kilij Arslan I. A large congregational Friday mosque and palace were built on the one hill overlooking the town. Later, many important *madrasahs*, *khanaqahs* (Sufi dervish lodges) and *bedestans* (covered, domed market places) were also constructed.

The city was a multi-ethnic mix of Byzantine Greeks and Armenians, along with a small Jewish community, newly arrived Seljuq Turks and some Iranians. *Khans*, or caravanserais were built inside the city and along all roads leading in and out. The role of these "way stations" was indispensable in the safe transport of people and merchandise across Asia.

KILIJ ARSLAN II (1156–1192)

Kilij Arslan II, who succeeded his father, Mas'ud, as sultan in 1156, is recognised as being one of the most important sultans of Rum. In his long reign he was able to finally bring all of Anatolia – from the shores of the Aegean Sea to the furthest reaches of eastern Turkey – under Seljuq control. This achievement was only possible, however, once Byzantine claims to Seljuq lands ceased.

There had always been a tenuous peace between Kilij Arslan II and Manual I Comnenus, the Byzantine emperor. While the Seljuqs of Rum wanted to expand westwards towards the sea, the Byzantines coveted Seljuq territory in the east that had been lost to them after their defeat at Malazgirt in 1071. The two powerful armies met again to determine, once and for all, the suzerainty of Anatolia.

BATTLE OF MYRIOCEPHALON (SEPTEMBER 17, 1176)

The large Byzantine army, supported by the crusader King Baldwin of Antioch and his forces, confronted Kilij Arslan II's equally impressive Seljuq one at Myriocephalon. This battlefield was located immediately to the west of Konya, near Lake Eğirdir. On September 17, 1176, the Seljuqs cleverly ambushed the Byzantine forces resulting in their total defeat. Baldwin was killed in battle and the outright victory of the Seljuqs at Myriocephalon reminded the Emperor Manual I Comnenus of his ancestors' defeat at Malazgirt a century before.

The Byzantines had no longer the means to attack Konya and had seemingly lost any hope of expelling the Seljuq Turks from Anatolia. This had been a great psychological victory for the Muslims as it showed the former power in the region, the Greek Byzantines, that there was a new power to contend with. After the Battle of Myriocephalon, no serious attempt was ever made again to recover Anatolian land. Essentially, the Byzantine Empire in Asia had now been reduced to small areas around Constantinople and along some coastal regions of the Black Sea.

Mongol Invasion (1243)

In 1207, the new sultan Kai Khusraw I (1192–1196 and 1205–1211), captured the Mediterranean port city of Antalya. For the first time in their history, the Seljuqs of Rum had a trading outlet on the south coast.

The greatest Seljuq ruler of Rum was 'Ala' ad-Din Kai-Qubad I. During his reign (1220–1237), a brief "golden age" of relative peace ensued. Anatolia became prosperous with farmland generating large amounts of agricultural produce that could be exported. A shipyard was built on the Mediterranean coast and many large Seljuq cities and towns such as Konya had massive defensive walls built around them. The royal court of Sultan 'Ala' ad-Din Kai-Qubad I received many scholars and artists who had fled from the Mongols in the East.

The peaceful years ended abruptly when, during the reign of Kai-Khusraw II (1237–1246), the westward moving Mongol army of Hulagu Khan invaded the Seljuq world. No nation had yet been able to defeat the Mongols; their seemingly unquenchable desire for conquest had now led them to the borders of Anatolia. In 1243, the Seljuq sultan Kai-Khusraw II confronted the Mongols for the first time.

The Battle of Kose Dagh (June 26, 1243)

On an open plain in eastern Anatolia (near Sivas), the Mongol commander Baiju and his army faced the Seljuqs of Rum. In 1241, Baiju had been commissioned by the Great Khan to expand the Mongol Empire in the west. One of Baiju's objectives, therefore, was to defeat the forces of the Seljuqs of Rum and make them vassals of the Mongols. The Battle of Kose Dagh took place on June 26, 1243. Even though Kai-Khusraw II had a large army (including vassal Greeks and Armenians), victory belonged to the Mongols. Their success lay in being able to quickly leave a battle then return when the enemy was in disarray. By fleeing the battlefield and leaving his army to the mercy of the Mongols, Kai-Khusraw II had essentially offered the Mongols free access to all of Anatolia and the Seljuq sultanate of Rum. The Mongols' success at Kose Dagh sealed the fate of the once independent Seljuq state.

Until the year 1307, the former heartland of the Seljuqs of Rum, Central Anatolia, remained a Mongol province governed by the Ilkhan Mongols of Iran, a dynasty descended from Hulagu Khan. The last Seljuq ruler of any importance, Kai-Khusraw III (1265–1284), gave the title "Protector of the Border" to Osman, one of his nobles who had supported him. The descendants of this Osman – the Ottoman Turks – would, in a short time, become rulers of an empire as vast as that of ancient Rome.

In 1302, the Seljuq sultan, 'Ala' ad-Din Kai-Qubad III (1298–1302), was removed from power by the Ilkhanid sultan, Ghazan Khan. Finally, another Seljuq vassal of the Ilkhanid Mongols, Mas'ud II (1284–1296 and 1303–1307/8), who had previously been involved in a plot against the Ilkhans – but not executed – was returned to the Seljuq throne in 1303. By 1307, however, the last vestiges of the Seljuq Rum sultanate had disappeared. Anatolia now disintegrated into many small principalities or *beyliks*, resembling the *Muluk al-Tawa'if* of post-caliphate Al-Andalus.

Seljuq Art

Despite the constant warring with crusader armies and infighting amongst the Seljuq family itself, the Seljuqs of Rum, during their two centuries of power, became a very artistic and creative people. They created some of the most remarkable art in all of Islamic history. Of particular importance is

8-1   TURQUOISE TILE WORK: The Seljuqs of Rum occupied most parts of Anatolia (present-day Asian Turkey) for two centuries. Today, many mosques, *madrasahs*, tombs and palaces built by their gifted craftsmen can still be seen in the principal former Seljuq towns of Turkey. The Seljuqs of Rum developed a complex technique of cut tile work and used this very effectively in most of their building projects. Extremely complicated geometric patterns combined with elaborate Arabic inscriptions were produced using the preferred colours of turquoise and black.

The example here is a section of tile work from the Great Karatay Madrasah in Konya, the Seljuq capital. Although many Seljuq buildings in Turkey have been rebuilt over the years, the original *mihrab* and wall tile work usually has remained intact. These shiny black and turquoise tiles with their complex designs and delicate Qur'anic inscriptions in the *thuluth* script, are truly some of the finest ever made in *Dar al-Islam*.

8.2   GEOMETRIC GENIUS: A beautiful example of Seljuq tilework from an old *madrasah* in Konya, Turkey.

the splendour of Seljuq tile work. From a very early date, Seljuq craftsmen developed techniques for the manufacture of a wide variety of ceramic tiles. The most common colours were a bright cobalt blue, several shades of turquoise, and a shiny black. Seljuq artists used this stunning, bold tile work as both exterior decoration on minarets and interior decoration in *mihrab* (prayer niche) construction (see illustrations 8-1 and 8-2). The Seljuqs' love of Arabic calligraphy can be seen not only on their *mihrab* walls, but also on many of their exquisitely crafted silver and gold coins (see illustration 8-3).

Large numbers of Muslim Turkish nomads sought refuge in Anatolia during Seljuq times, fleeing the Mongol hordes of Hulagu Khan. While some of these Turkish Muslims were *ghazis*, who fought to extend the borders of *Dar al-Islam*, others were Turkish nomads who became settled farmers and helped make Anatolia a fertile "bread basket" in later centuries.

MEVLANA JALAL AD-DIN RUMI (1207–1273)

In the early thirteenth century, great cities of the Islamic East, one by one, were being invaded and totally destroyed by Mongol armies. Many such cities never recovered from the onslaught and have remained in ruins that can be seen to this day. One such city is Balkh, which was an important trading centre and cultural capital in the north of present-day Afghanistan. Before this city fell to the Mongols, a famous scholar who had been born there decided to escape west. Baha ad-Din Waled left Balkh with his young son, Jalal ad-Din, and in 1228, after several years of wandering, reached the welcoming safety of the Seljuq capital of Konya. Sultan 'Ala' ad-Din Kai-Qubad I invited this scholar and his family to stay in Konya permanently. Jalal ad-Din, like his father, was a native speaker of Persian. He received an excellent education and soon became a religious teacher. Later

8-3 SELJUQ SILVER: The Seljuqs of Rum, once settled in their new capital of Konya, in central Turkey, became patrons of Islamic art. Seljuq sultans had a great fondness for Arabic calligraphy. Beautiful monumental inscriptions in Arabic can be seen in Seljuq monuments all over the city of Konya. These are carved into stone, marble, wood and are also painted in black on the famous Seljuq tile work. Even Seljuq coins were covered in beautifully designed Arabic calligraphy. This coin is a silver *dirham* and dates from the time of Kilij Arslan IV (1248–1265). It bears the *kalimah* in a bold, distinctively Seljuq style of writing.

in his life, Jalal ad-Din Rumi wrote several very long books of religious poetry in the Persian language. The *Mathnawi* is the most famous of these books. His poetry is read and appreciated by both Muslims and non-Muslims alike to this day. One of his most well-known verses in Persian reads:

az muhhabat, kharha gul mishavad,
vaz muhhabat, nar nur mishavad.

From Divine Grace, thorns become roses,
And from the same kindness,
[the] fire (*nar*) [of Hell] becomes
[the] light (*nur*) [of Paradise].[9]

Today the city of Konya in Central Turkey, welcomes many tourists. They visit the tomb of Mevlana Jalal ad-Din Rumi, and the many mosques and *madrasahs* left from the time when Konya was the capital of the Seljuqs of Rum.

[9] Author's translation.

CHAPTER NINE

THE BERBER DYNASTIES:
THE ALMORAVIDS (1056–1147)

Ever since 'Uqba ibn Nafi's arrival at the Moroccan shores of the Atlantic Ocean in 681, wave after wave of Arab immigrants from Yemen, Arabia and Syria had come to *Al-Maghreb al-Aqsa'* ("The Farthest West" of the Islamic world), as Northwest Africa was called. We have seen how the last Umayyad prince, 'Abd ar-Rahman I, fled Syria and seeking safety in *Al-Maghreb al-Aqsa'*, eventually established the Spanish Umayyad dynasty. In 788, yet another refugee, Idris ibn 'Abdallah, a relative of 'Ali ﷺ, sought shelter in Morocco and quickly established the first Arab dynasty (the Idrisids) there. Before the Arabs arrived in Northwest Africa, however, the region was inhabited by local Berber tribes. The Berbers quickly embraced Islam and later helped in the conquest of Al-Andalus in 711. Tariq ibn Ziyad, the leader of the invasion, was himself a Berber.

BERBER ORIGINS

The Berbers are one of the most interesting of Africa's indigenous peoples. They predominantly inhabit the areas of North Africa stretching from the Siwa oasis in western Egypt to the shores of the Atlantic Ocean in Morocco and south to the edges of the Sahara Desert and the Niger River in West Africa. The term "Berber" derives from the ancient Greek *barbaroi* (uncivilised non-Greek peoples). The Berbers, however, have always used the term *Imazighen* (freemen) to identify themselves.

Today, several dialects of their unique language, *Tamazight*, are spoken across North Africa. The precise origin of the Berber people also remains a mystery. It is supposed that in the very distant past they entered North Africa and then, over thousands of years, received admixtures of black African, Asian and European genetic pools. This perhaps explains the racial mix amongst the Berbers who can have very differing skin colours. Rock paintings in many parts of the Sahara clearly indicate the presence of Berbers there in very ancient times.

ISLAMISATION OF THE BERBERS

Before the arrival of Islam to North Africa (first between 642 and 669), there were communities of Christian and Jewish Berbers throughout the region. In the remoter areas, a traditional form of nature worship was practised.

In 670, 'Uqba ibn Nafi' founded his military base camp of Qayrawan (in present-day Tunisia). A more systematic movement of Arab Muslims into the western regions of the *Maghreb* (Morocco and Algeria) was now possible. Initially, Berber tribes were quite willing to embrace Islam; they saw the religion of the Arabs as being fair and just. But, unfortunately, the Berbers were forced to pay heavy taxes and, even as Muslims, were made to feel like second-class citizens in their own homeland. Later, when the Berbers entered Al-Andalus with Arab commanders, a similar discrimination was experienced. We recall that the Umayyads of Syria had made this same mistake in their Iranian territories where the non-Arab *mawali* Muslims rose up in opposition to the state. Therefore, not all newly-converted Berbers of Northwest Africa necessarily supported the caliphs in Damascus or later, Baghdad. Some Berbers even became Kharijites.[10]

The appearance of indigenous Berber dynasties in Northwest Africa, beginning in the eleventh century, was a direct result of the need to reinvigorate the waning Islamic spirit of many Berber communities.

ORIGINS OF THE DYNASTY

In the eleventh century, the Sanhaja group of nomadic Berber tribes occupied the area in the far south of present-day Morocco. A Sanhaja chief, Yahya ibn Ibrahim, had made the pilgrimage to Holy Makkah and on his way back home, passed through the city of Qayrawan, a major centre of Islamic learning. Yahya was told by a teacher of Maliki law to visit Wajjaj al-Lamti at his monastic retreat in Sus in southern Morocco. Yahya, upon reaching Sus, was persuaded to travel further south into the desert with a learned *da'i* named 'Abdallah ibn Yasin.

'Abdallah ibn Yasin's aim was to further educate the Berbers in their Islamic faith. On an island in the Niger River, in present-day Senegal, a religious fortress or *ribat* was built. From this *ribat* grew a powerful religious movement that soon controlled vast areas of Northwest Africa. The dynasty thus created became known as *Al-Murabitun* (the inhabitants of the *ribat*), or the Almoravids.

The Muslims inhabiting the *ribat* of 'Abdallah ibn Yasin were indoctrinated into an extremely disciplined way of life. They were obliged to memorise all of 'Abdallah's *fatwas* or legal opinions and 'Abdallah himself led all the congregational prayers. From this remote religious centre, the *Murabitun* eventually spread out to all Saharan towns and villages carrying their puritanical Islamic teachings. It must be remembered that there were still some Berber tribes in Morocco that had not accepted Islam; and the ones that had, had often not fully learned its tenets.

YUSUF IBN TASHFIN (1061–1106)

'Abdallah ibn Yasin died on a campaign with the *Murabitun* in the mountainous tribal regions of Morocco in 1059. He had several spiritual successors, the most important being Yusuf ibn Tashfin. From his newly-founded capital of Marrakesh, at the foothills of the Atlas Mountains, he conquered most of the *Maghreb* and later, even Spain. The Sanhaja Berbers were related to the Tuaregs, the famous "blue men of the Sahara". While many Berbers in the northern mountainous regions of Morocco were traditionally farmers, the Tuaregs were desert nomads. The Tuareg men always wore a very long turban (*litham*) that was dyed indigo blue. It was wrapped around the head, covering the face except the eyes. As the turban was never removed, over time, the indigo dye slowly coloured the skin blue. Because the Almoravids also adopted the wearing of

---

[10] A term derived from the Arabic meaning "those who split off or go out". Kharijites were those Muslims from 'Ali's ⁂ camp who opposed both 'Ali ⁂ and Mu'awiyah as caliph after the Battle of Siffin in 658. As all Muslims were equal, they believed their *jihad* against the aristocracy of the Quraysh to be justified. Kharijites were extremists who followed an absolute literal interpretation of the Qur'an and *Sunnah*. Any good Muslim - regardless of race or lineage - could be elected caliph as long as he had the full support of the *ummah* (Islamic community). Pockets of Muslims whose ancestors were Kharijites survive to this day in Oman, the Mzab of Algeria, in remote parts of Tunisia and Libya, and on the island of Zanzibar.

the *litham*, or "turban veil", the Arabs correctly called these Berbers "the people of the veil" or *Al-Mulaththamun*.

After the collapse of the Umayyad caliphate in Spain in 1031, Al-Andalus, or Muslim Spain, reverted to an assortment of weak kingdoms and principalities known as *Al-Muluk al-Tawa'if*. The Christian armies of Northern Spain had been successful in recapturing Muslim territory. In 1085, for example, the former Visigothic capital of Toledo fell to Christian forces. The leaders of *Al-Muluk al-Tawa'if* asked for help from Yusuf ibn Tashfin in Morocco, who responded by sending a large army of Moroccans and Africans. This combined force was able to successfully defeat King Alfonso VI of Castile and Leon at the Battle of Zallaqah in 1086. For almost four centuries, conflicts in Muslim Spain had been between Spanish Muslim rulers and Spanish Christian rulers. Now that foreign African troops were on Spanish soil, the struggle was seen as being between the forces of Christian Europe and *Din al-Haq al-Islam*.

Yusuf ibn Tashfin held the title of *Amir al-Muslimin* (Commander of the Muslims), but still accepted the 'Abbasid caliph in Baghdad as *Amir al-Mu'minin* (Commander of the Faithful). He saw himself as the protector of the purity, sincerity and decency of the Islamic faith. He believed that many of the habits and practices of the Muslim princedoms in Spain had become non-Islamic in many ways. Therefore, in 1091, Yusuf ibn Tashfin returned to Spain with the honest intention of re-educating and bringing the Muslims there back to traditional Islamic practices. This time, however, the Almoravids stayed in Spain which became part of their empire in Northwest Africa. This first Berber dynasty to occupy Al-Andalus was much less tolerant of the multi-faith society they found there. The Almoravids never really became "Andalusian" and certainly did not understand the concept of *convivencia*, the peaceful co-existence of religious communities on Spanish soil.

The Almoravid dynasty was born in the desert. Muslims during this period lived a simple life according to the Qur'an and *Sunnah* of the Prophet Muhammad ﷺ. The architecture of the Almoravid period was, therefore, quite stark and plain. However, one important architectural feature, the horseshoe arch, was used to great effect by Almoravid architects. The horseshoe arch can be seen prominently in many public gateways, mosques and other Almoravid buildings which have survived in both Spain and North Africa (see illustration 9-1).

The Almoravids lost control of their empire when they realised they could not fight on two fronts: the Masmuda Berbers in southern Morocco and the Christian forces in Al-Andalus. Within forty years of Yusuf ibn Tashfin's death, the Almoravid Empire was being replaced by another, the Almohads.

Ibn Khaldun (1332–1406)

Ibn Khaldun, the great Muslim social historian and father of sociology, was born in Tunis, but was of Andalusian lineage. He lived and worked in Morocco, Tunisia and Egypt in the fourteenth century. Ibn Khaldun was a very keen and accurate observer of the political life of his day. He noted, as a rule, that political dynasties usually degenerate – both mentally and morally – after three generations, or approximately one hundred years. According to Ibn Khaldun's theory, a wave of nomadic invaders from the desert, bringing new blood, then moves into the urban areas and replaces the degenerate dynasty of rulers. The Almoravids had ruled for just one hundred years, but they too, in time, had become degenerate, succumbed by the beauty and luxury

9-1 THE MOROCCAN MOSQUE: The Almoravids were the first Berber dynasty to gain control of Northwest Africa and later, parts of Al-Andalus (Spain). Because they were a traditional, religious movement, their buildings appear quite plain. The one architectural feature they used to great effect was the horseshoe arch. Here one can see horseshoe arches in the courtyard of the *Masjid Qarawiyyin*, one of the most important mosques in Morocco. In the Qarawiyyin Mosque in Fez, one can see some of the finest use of wood, tile and stucco in any Islamic building. Even the interior floors and the bases of columns are covered with multi-coloured hand-woven reed matting. Fez is the religious and cultural capital of Morocco. This mosque lies in the centre of the old city and has been used as a place of worship and as a traditional Islamic university for one thousand years. The Mosque of Qarawayyin is a masterpiece of Islamic art, both inside and out.

of Al-Andalus, some say, and had grown accustomed to extravagant living. So, according to Ibn Khaldun, they were necessarily replaced by a stronger, more disciplined and religious group of desert nomads.

LEGACY OF THE ALMORAVIDS

Historians have often labelled the Almoravids as fanatical and uncivilised. The desert-dwelling *Al-Murabitun* Berbers were simply unfamiliar with the refined urban lifestyle of the towns and cities of Al-Andalus. In the short century that they were in power, the Almoravids were able to unite the various desert and mountain tribes of Morocco for the first time in history, which was no mean feat. We can, therefore, conclude that the true origins of the present-day kingdom of Morocco lie in the establishment of the unified Almoravid state.

CHAPTER TEN
THE ALMOHADS (1130–1269)

Just as the Almoravids were a Berber dynasty founded on a strict, religious doctrine, the Almohads were also a fundamentalist religious movement. The Almohads (from the Arabic *Al-Muwahhidun*, "Unitarians" or "Supporters of the Unity of Allah", i.e. *tawhid*) intended to re-educate the Berber peoples – and all others in the *Maghreb* – in the true practice of Islam.

MUHAMMAD IBN TUMART (1121–1130)

The most influential leader of the Almohad dynasty was the founder himself, Muhammad ibn Tumart. He belonged to the Berber Masmuda tribe living in the High Atlas Mountains of Morocco. Like the Almoravid spiritual leader, Yusuf ibn Tashfin, Ibn Tumart made the Pilgrimage to Holy Makkah and before returning home, studied in the Islamic cultural capitals of Baghdad and Damascus. When he did return to Morocco, he established a missionary centre in a *ribat* where he converted and reformed the Berber people of the Atlas Mountains. Ibn Tumart preached a return to the original teachings of Islam, namely the Holy Qur'an and the *Sunnah* of the Prophet ﷺ. The central theme of Ibn Tumart's reformist message is reflected the following *hadith* of the Prophet ﷺ:

> The one who sees anything wrong should act to change it by hand. If he cannot do it with his hand, he should do it with his tongue. If he cannot do it with his tongue, he should do it with his heart. This is what the religion demands you to do. (Narrated by Abu Sa'id al-Khudri ﷺ in *Sahih Muslim*)

Ibn Tumart opposed the literal, word-for-word interpretation of the Holy Qur'an. He believed that the concept of *tawhid* (the Unity of Allah) could only be understood if one accepted that Allah had no human characteristics. Later, from this same *ribat* at Tinmal (a town located in the High Atlas Mountains, approximately one hundred kilometres south of Marrakesh), Ibn Tumart proclaimed himself the *Mahdi* and initiated a *jihad* against the ruling Almoravid state and anyone else who disagreed with him. Brute military force was used to achieve his position of power. For example, it is said that Ibn Tumart once had the entire population of a Berber town massacred.

His new reformist movement had succeeded in coalescing large segments of the Moroccan Berber society. Ibn Tumart preached in the Berber tongue and offered his Berber followers an *'aqida* (doctrine of belief) in their own language. Berbers were admonished to follow Almohad *imams* who were able to recite the *tawhid* in the Berber language. It has been suggested that the importance given to the Berber language in Almohad theology could have been in direct opposition to that of Arabic in the traditional Maliki *fiqh*.

Ibn Tumart's message was a simple and fundamentalist one. He spearheaded the founding of a second Berber dynasty which attempted to reform the morals of the Moroccan masses. His story is one of a charismatic Berber leader who, with fiery rhetoric, was able to empower the disparate tribes of Morocco to unite under one banner for a brief moment in history.

Ibn Tumart died before he saw his followers replace the embattled Almoravids. Ibn Tumart's trusted lieutenant and first disciple, 'Abd al-Mu'min (1130–1163), became the new Almohad ruler on the death of Ibn Tumart in 1130. The *Mahdi*'s death was concealed from the masses though and only after two years was 'Abd al-Mu'min proclaimed his successor.

The *jihad* waged against the Almoravids was successful when all of North Africa was finally taken by Almohad forces led by 'Abd al-Mu'min. This was made possible due to the massive army and navy the Almohads had created. By 1147, the resultant unified Almohad Empire, which included all of Morocco, Algeria and even Ifriqiyah (Tunisia), became one of the largest in the history of North Africa. The new Almohad capital became Marrakesh, the city founded by the Almoravids a century before.

'ABD AL-MU'MIN (1130–1163)

Ibn Tumart had been a very wise, but impatient and extremely austere ruler. His traditional view of Islam and how Muslims should live was very soon forgotten once he died. 'Abd al-Mu'min began to build beautiful and expensive monuments in his capital city (see illustration 10-2). The Kutubiyah Mosque (see illustration 10-1) is one such extravagant building that he constructed. Marrakesh quickly became a centre of Islamic culture where several important Arab scientists and philosophers were attracted to the court of 'Abd al-Mu'min and his successors. But besides the scholars and artists, many capable administrators were also brought over from Al-Andalus who proved to be indispensable in the running of the Almohad state.

The Almohad Empire was most prosperous during the reigns of the three sons of 'Abd al-Mu'min: Abu Ya'qub Yusuf (1163–1184), Abu Yusuf Ya'qub al-Mansur (1184–1199), and Muhammad an-Nasir (1199–1213).

Like the Almoravids, the Almohads were a pure Berber dynasty. All leaders and administrators in the Almohad government came from a ruling class of Berber nobles. When the Almohads took over the administration of the Almoravid territory in Spain in 1170, a Spanish form of central government modified the traditional Berber way of governing.

IBN TUFAYL (C.1105–1185)

One illustrious Muslim philosopher and physician invited to the Almohad court in Marrakesh was the great Andalusian, Abu Bakr ibn Tufayl. Because of his medical skills, Ibn Tufayl was asked by Sultan Abu Ya'qub Yusuf to settle in his capital. It was here in Marrakesh that he wrote his amazing book, *Hayy ibn Yaqdhan* (The Living Son of the Awake) – one of the most important books ever written in the Arabic language. This philosophical tale about the development of a human soul became an instant bestseller. The hero of the story, Hayy ibn Yaqdhan, grows up on a remote, uninhabited tropical island off the coast of India. In the following excerpt, Ibn Tufayl describes the wonder Hayy felt at realising all creation was the work of *Al-Khaliq*.

> When he [Hayy] realised that all creation was God's work, he looked at it then from the viewpoint of this power which the Creator had: the wonder of His craftsmanship, the subtleness of His wisdom and the precision of His knowledge. As he contemplated the wonders of creation, from the smallest to the greatest, he realised all this could derive only from a Creator of complete perfection - 'From whom is not hidden the least little atom in the Heavens or on earth: nor is there anything less than that, or greater.' [Qur'an: *Surah Saba'*, *ayah* 3][11]

---

[11] Ibn Tufail, Abu Bakr Muhammad. *The Journey of the Soul [The Story of Hai bin Yaqzan]* (trans. by Dr. Riad Kocache). London: The Octagon Press, 1982: 31-32.

10-1 MARRAKESH MINARET: The Almohad Berber ruler, ʻAbd al-Muʼmin (1130–1163) constructed this impressive minaret in Marrakesh, his capital city in southern Morocco. After almost nine centuries, this minaret still stands by the famous Kutubiyah Mosque and can be seen from many parts of the city. An old Islamic custom is to hang lanterns atop minarets on special events like *Laylat al-Qadr* in Ramadan. Today, of course, electric light bulbs are more commonly used. Minarets such as this were also constructed by the Almohads in Al-Andalus. In the Spanish city of Seville, for example, a huge minaret resembling that of the Kutubiyah still dominates the old part of the city.

10-2   MOROCCAN GOLD: The Almohads were a Berber dynasty whose leaders came from the tribes of non-Arab Berbers who lived in the remote areas of the High Atlas Mountains of Morocco. Once the Berbers had embraced Islam in the eighth century, they became ardent followers of *Din al-Haq al-Islam*. A unique form of Arabic handwriting soon developed in the *maghreb* (Northwest Africa) regions of the Islamic world. This style of writing is still taught in Morocco today. On this beautiful gold *dinar*, from the time of the Almohad ruler, 'Abd al-Mu'min (mid-twelfth century), the *kalimah* is written in the distinctive *maghrebi* style. Many numismatists (coin experts) agree that this one Islamic coin is perhaps the most beautiful ever minted in *Dar al-Islam*.

The book identifies seven developmental stages, each of seven years duration. Childhood frustration gives way to practical reasoning, wonderment, and by the age of thirty-five, wisdom produces a passionate love of God. Allah has given *'aql* (wisdom or reason) to man alone. Hayy, therefore, uses both observation and reasoning to try to comprehend his world and universe. As a result, he successfully arrives at knowing the Truth. Ibn Tufayl concludes that one needs philosophy to fully understand religion. In the seventeenth century, *Hayy ibn Yaqdhan* was translated into several European languages, including English for the first time in 1710. It became as popular in translation as it had been in Arabic throughout the Islamic world. Because of these new translations, Ibn Tufayl's story reached the famous English writer, Daniel Defoe, author of *Robinson Crusoe* (first published in 1717). Defoe had obviously been inspired by *Hayy ibn Yaqdhan* when writing his own novel about a shipwrecked sailor.

IMPORTANT BATTLES

Two important battles marked the Almohad period of the history of Spain. In 1195, the Almohads were victorious at the Battle of Alarcos, defeating a coalition of Christian armies. But, just a few years later, the Muslims suffered their most important defeat in the eight century-long history of Islamic Spain. At the Battle of Las Navas de Tolosa, in 1212, a united force of Spanish, Portuguese, and other European knights defeated the Almohad army and encouraged the Christians to continue their *reconquesta*, the process of taking over, or re-conquering all the Muslim lands of Spain. After this devastating defeat, the remaining Almohads returned to their North African territories, but by the middle of the thirteenth century, they had lost their empire to yet other groups of Berbers.

Comparisons can easily be made between the Almohads and the Fatimids. While the strange Fatimid Isma'ili doctrines were never understood or accepted by the Egyptian masses, the "Almohadism" of Ibn Tumart was welcomed by large numbers of his own people, the Berbers, in Morocco. However, in Spain, the Almohads were always seen as uncouth, foreign occupiers. Their imposed Almohadism could never replace the Maliki *fiqh* engrained in the hearts of most Muslims in Al-Andalus.

The Almohads had wanted to bring a simpler, purer, more traditional form of Islam to the peoples of North Africa and Spain. In the end, the Almohads resembled their Berber predecessors, the Almoravids. The Almohads mirrored Ibn Khaldun's theory of history: a group of nomadic people moves from the countryside into settled urban areas and within three generations loses its religious fervour and subsequently becomes accustomed to a luxurious lifestyle. And this, in turn, leads to yet further invasions of nomads out of the desert to replace them.

CHAPTER ELEVEN

THE AYYUBIDS (1169–1260)

We have learned of the reasons that initiated the Crusades, the military expeditions by European Christians to occupy the Holy Land. Jerusalem (*Al-Quds*), a holy city for Jews, Christians and Muslims, had been occupied by the Seljuq Turks since 1071. In Europe, many criminals and opportunists along with ignorant country folk joined the call to wage a war of liberation of the Holy Land from Muslim control. The truth is that many European Christians saw the crusades not as a religious, spiritual duty, but simply as a means to get wealthy. For example, Catholic Europe regarded the Byzantine (Greek) Orthodox Christians of the East Roman Empire with contempt. So, it was not surprising, therefore, that in April 1204, crusading Christians (of the Fourth Crusade) attacked, looted, desecrated and torched Constantinople, the ancient capital city of the Byzantine Empire. These crusaders never reached the Holy Land, but after butchering the population of Constantinople, did establish a hated Latin kingdom there that ruled over the Greek city for half a century.

ORIGINS OF THE DYNASTY

In the late twelfth century, the Seljuqs of Rum were in control of Central Anatolia, but the Byzantines still controlled western regions and thus permitted the crusaders coming from Europe to reach seaports on the Mediterranean coast. At the same time, the Christian city of Edessa (present-day Urfa) in southern Turkey had been seized by a powerful new Muslim ruler in the area. Zangi was the *atabeg* (Turkish guardian/tutor of a prince) in northern Syria. One of Zangi's sons, Nur ad-Din, however, was to become renowned for his continuous attacks on the crusaders who passed through his land. Nur ad-Din united the Muslims of Syria against a common enemy and by the middle of the twelfth century, had even attracted the attention of the Fatimid caliph in Cairo. By this time, the Fatimid caliphs were weak, being mere puppets of their much stronger generals. When the young Fatimid caliph, Al-'Adid, felt a threat from the "crusader kings" of Jerusalem, he asked for assistance from Nur ad-Din who sent him a Kurdish general, Shirkuh, to help out. Within a short time, Shirkuh had become the *wazir* of the Fatimid court. When Shirkuh died, the power entrusted to him was passed on to Salah ad-Din, the son of Shirkuh's brother, Ayyub. Within two years, Salah ad-Din had taken full control of the government and by 1171, the Fatimid dynasty was no more. Egypt once again became a stronghold for Sunni Islam and has remained so to this day. The fact that Sunni Egypt once again paid allegiance to the 'Abbasid caliph in Baghdad is clear from the title conferred on Salah ad-Din at this time: *Muhyi Dawlat Amir al-Mu'minin* (Reviver of the Empire of the Commander of the Faithful). With the death of Nur ad-Din in 1174, Egypt and the Ayyubid dynasty became the new regional power.

SALAH AD-DIN (1169–1193)

The Ayyubid dynasty was established by Yusuf, the son of Ayyub, known by both Muslims and Europeans as *Salah ad-Din* (Righteousness of the Faith). Although the family had its origins in a small town in Armenia, Salah ad-Din was born in the Iraqi town of Tikrit, not far from Baghdad.

His father, Ayyub, and his uncle, Shirkuh, were employed there by the ruling Seljuqs. Salah ad-Din was not an Arab, but a Kurd, a member of a non-Semitic ethnic minority that has inhabited various parts of the Middle East for thousands of years. One's ethnicity or cultural background might be interesting, but what matters most in Islam is one's faith and adherence to the Qur'an and *Sunnah*. Salah ad-Din united the *ummah* at a time of great danger, minimising the importance of the ethnic origin, native language and skin colour of individuals. Indeed, some Kurds today actually criticise Salah ad-Din for not having encouraged Kurdish nationalism! Salah ad-Din had been brought up in towns and cities and had learned how to wage war and make peace honourably. He was learned in matters of religion – he was a scholar of *hadith* – and chose an extremely simple lifestyle even though he had become master of a great empire.

On the death of Nur ad-Din al-Zangi in 1174, the 'Abbasid caliph, Al-Mustadi, granted Salah ad-Din the title of *sultan*. He was clearly the most obvious successor of Nur ad-Din. Territories once controlled by Nur ad-Din, namely Damascus and Aleppo (Halab), had to be won before they could become part of the Ayyubid realm. Moreover, in order to defeat the large numbers of crusaders who had permanently settled in the region, Salah ad-Din needed to win the support of all former Zangid forces. It was during this period (c. 1176) of consolidating his power in Aleppo that two attempts were made on his life. The Isma'ili Assassins, who had murdered Nizam al-Mulk in 1092, were, however, unsuccessful in eliminating the would-be liberator of Jerusalem.

Later, even parts of Yemen and, for a time, Holy Makkah, were ruled by Salah ad-Din and his family. It was Palestine, though, that really preoccupied him. His strength lay in his army which consisted mainly of Kurds and Turks. The economic wealth generated from the Nile River valley enabled Salah ad-Din to develop and improve his army, a pre-requisite if he was to confront the ever-increasing number of crusading armies in Syria and Palestine.

BATTLE OF HITTIN (JULY 4, 1187)

Salah ad-Din had recovered much territory from the crusaders in Palestine. However, the one remaining area still under crusader control was Jerusalem.

By the spring of 1187, Salah ad-Din had amassed sufficient forces – estimated at some 7,000 cavalry – to begin the campaign to liberate Jerusalem and all surrounding areas. Salah ad-Din awaited the enemy on a plain overlooking Lake Tiberius, the only source of fresh drinking water at the time. The site was near a small village called Hittin.

The crusaders, led by Raymond III of Tripoli (in present-day Lebanon) and numbering about 12,000, had travelled all day along a waterless plateau to reach Tiberius; understandably, they were exhausted and thirsty. Salah ad-Din had blocked access to the fresh water of the lake. As nightfall approached, the crusaders camped on the parched, barren plain contemplated the battle that would ensue the next morning. Salah ad-Din spent the night in prayer and in consultation with his generals. He ordered that some of his troops move in the stealth of night to surround the enemy, thus preventing any possible retreat.

Early the next morning, on July 4, 1187, the weakened crusader army, almost dying from thirst, attempted to move down from their position to reach the waters of Lake Tiberius. The crusaders fought valiantly but were doomed from the start. Being surrounded on all sides, they were totally routed. Salah ad-Din's generals in the midst of battle permitted Raymond of Tripoli to escape.

Finally, the crusaders, now leaderless, and having suffered heavy losses, capitulated. What remained of the vast army was taken prisoner. A part of the True Cross (on which Christians believe 'Isa ﷺ was crucified) had been taken into battle by the crusading king. The relic fell into the hands of Salah ad-Din who carried it off to Damascus.

Salah ad-Din had dealt the crusaders a serious blow. The Battle of Hittin had resulted in the greatest defeat of any crusading army. After the battle, Salah ad-Din's victories continued as many crusader towns were too inadequately garrisoned to withstand a siege. By the end of September 1187, *Al-Malik al-Nasir Salah ad-Dunya wa'd-Din* (The Defending King, Honour of the World and of the Faith), was prepared to move onto Jerusalem, the ultimate goal of his *jihad*.

Salah ad-Din's exemplary behaviour, on the battlefield and off, had an impact on his non-Muslim enemies. He showed respect for those around him and mercy on those he conquered. Many non-Muslim Europeans began to examine their own religion more objectively. Until they had actually come into contact with Muslims, many Europeans had believed the only culture and civilisation of any value was that of the Christian West. Now, they saw the truth for themselves: Islam not only produced honourable leaders such as Salah ad-Din, but also scientific geniuses such as Ibn Sina and Al-Biruni. Islam was now seen by some as a religion as great as any other. It is also true that many crusaders, once settled in the Holy Land, began to learn Arabic and even dress and eat like Muslims. Many never wanted to return to Europe and a number of them actually embraced *Al-Din al-Haq al-Islam*.

LIBERATION OF *AL-QUDS* (OCTOBER 2, 1187)

Historical accounts provide very accurate details of the liberation of Jerusalem from Christian control. The Christian takeover of the city back in 1099 had resulted in the slaughter of its inhabitants; the streets, we are told, ran deep with the blood of Muslims, both young and old.

Very different events occurred when Salah ad-Din finally entered the city on Friday, October 2, 1187, the very day Muslims were to celebrate *Laylat al-Mi'raj*. Before the liberation of the holy city, Salah ad-Din is reported to have said:

> If Allah blesses us by enabling us to drive His enemies out of Jerusalem, how fortunate and happy we would be! For Jerusalem has been controlled by the enemy for ninety-one (*hijrah*) years, during which time Allah has received nothing from us here in the way of adoration.

During the peaceful takeover of *Al-Quds*, Salah ad-Din forbade the ill-treatment of anyone, saying that such behaviour was unbecoming of a Muslim. He ensured there was no massacre of Christians or pillaging of the city. Thousands of Christians were permitted to leave Jerusalem and were safely escorted to the coastal city of Tyre. Those not able to pay the exit tax were often exempted and widows and orphans even received gifts before departing.

Masha'Allah, Salah ad-Din's generosity, sincerity, honesty and decency are all remembered, even today – not only by Muslims, but by many nations who once opposed him.

FRIDAY *KHUTBAH* (OCTOBER 9, 1187)

In one short week, Salah ad-Din and his followers transformed *Al-Masjid al-Aqsa'* (The Al-Aqsa' Mosque) and *Al-Qubbat as-Sakhra* (The Dome of the Rock) to their original character. All parts of *Al-Bayt al-Maqdas* (the *Haram al-Sharif* on Mount Moriah) were purified with huge quantities of rose water and, of course, the first to be cleansed was the *mihrab* of *Al-Masjid al-Aqsa'* which had been desecrated by the crusaders. An exquisitely carved wooden *minbar*, which had been commissioned by Nur ad-Din al-Zangi, was transported from Aleppo in Syria to be placed in *Al-Masjid al-Aqsa'*. With *Al-Bayt al-Maqdas* cleared of all debris, the first *Salat al-Jum'ah* (Friday prayer) in almost one hundred years was performed on Friday October 9, 1187. Many religious leaders vied for the honour of delivering the sermon. The *khutbah* delivered that day by Muhi ad-Din ibn Zaki, the *qadi* of Damascus, perfectly captured its great historical importance.

> Jerusalem is the residence of your father Ibrahim ﷺ, the place of ascension of your Prophet ﷺ, the burial ground of Messengers, and the place of descent of revelations. …Glory to Allah who bestowed this victory upon Islam and who has returned the city to the fold of Islam after a century of perdition! Honour to His army which He has chosen to complete the conquest! And may salvation be upon you, Salah ad-Din, son of 'Ayyub; you have restored the spurned dignity of this nation.

Salah ad-Din's victory was justifiably compared to that of 'Umar ibn Khattab's ﷺ, years before, as he had accomplished what so many others had failed to do.

Ibn Jubayr (1145–1217)

Salah ad-Din ruled as sultan for twenty-four years. Eight of these were spent in Cairo. He introduced the *madrasah* system of education and built hospitals that were advanced for their time. A first-hand witness to the fair and just government of Salah ad-Din was the famous Spanish traveller, Ibn Jubayr. In 1183, he set off from Al-Andalus to make the Pilgrimage to Holy Makkah. His two year-long journey is described in detail in his amazing travelogue (*rihlah*) that can still be read today in Arabic, English and other foreign language translations. Ibn Jubayr speaks very highly of Salah ad-Din. In one passage, he recounts the generosity of the sultan to foreign students living in Cairo (see illustration 11-1).

> One of the sultan's most generous acts was the allotting of two loaves of bread daily for each of the Moroccan *ibna' as-sabil* ["sons of the road" – people entitled to the funds from the *bayt al-mal* (public treasury)], whatever their number; and for the daily distribution he appointed a person he trusted. Every day two thousand loaves or more …were regularly distributed.[12]

And of the hospitals in Cairo, Ibn Jubayr writes:

> Another of the many things we saw, doing honour to the Sultan, was the *maristan* [hospital] in the city of Cairo. It is a palace, goodly for its beauty and spaciousness. This benefaction he made so that he might deserve a heavenly reward, and to acquire merit. He appointed as intendant a man of science with whom he placed a store of drugs. … In the rooms of this palace were placed beds, fully appointed, for lying patients. At the disposal of the intendant are servants whose duty it is, morning and evening, to examine the conditions of the sick, and to bring them the food and potions that befit them.[13]

Although the Ayyubid dynasty was short-lived, many important scholars and scientists found their way to the court of Salah ad-Din. Spanish Muslims and Jews, in particular, seemed attracted to Cairo under Ayyubid rule. Musa ibn Maymun (d.1204), for example, the greatest Jewish writer of the Middle Ages, was Salah ad-Din's private physician and also treated his son. The great botanist, Ibn Baytar (d.1248), settled in Cairo, working for the Ayyubid sultan, Al-Malik al-Kamil, a nephew

---

[12] Ibn Jubayr. *The Travels of Ibn Jubayr* (trans. Roland Broadhurst), New Delhi: Goodword Books, 2001: 34.

[13] Ibid., 43-44.

11-1 SALAH AD-DIN SILVER: Although the great Salah ad-Din, liberator of *al-Quds* (Jerusalem), issued silver *dirhams* and gold *dinars* during his lifetime, he himself, died poor. This beautiful silver *dirham* was minted in Damascus during the time of Salah ad-Din. The *kalimah* is inscribed around the margin. In the square is written *Sultan al-Islam wa'l-Muslimun* (Sultan of Islam and the Muslims). On the left, the following is inscribed: *al-Nasir Salah al-Dunya wa'd-Din* (the Defending King, Honour of the World and of the Faith).

of Salah ad-Din. Another Spanish Muslim, Ibn 'Arabi (d.1240), the mystic, resided in Cairo briefly during this period and is said to have written some of his poems there.

DECLINE OF THE AYYUBIDS

The Ayyubid state had been unified under the powerful leadership of Salah ad-Din. But, on his death in 1193, the state was permanently divided amongst the Ayyubid family with branches in Cairo, Damascus, Aleppo, Hamah and Hims. Salah ad-Din's three sons proved very ineffective rulers. Salah ad-Din's brother, Al-Malik al-'Adil, became sultan in Egypt and was followed by Al-Malik al-Kamil whose death in 1238 marks the true end of the unified Ayyubid state. In order to avoid another crusade, these last two rulers tried to preserve the peaceful relations with the Christian enemy. Sadly, the Third Crusade (1189-1192), erased most of what Salah ad-Din had achieved.

With the death of Al-Malik al-Kamil, his two sons, Al-Adil II and Al-Salih Ayyub, succeeded him in Egypt and Syria respectively. But, even though branches of the dynasty survived in various parts of Syria and Palestine, the Ayyubid Empire was forever wracked by civil war.

By the year 1250, the Mamluks – the slave soldiers of Turkish origin who, ironically, had been introduced into Egypt by Salah ad-Din – had taken power in Cairo. In that year, the Mamluk slave general, Aybak, the founder of the Mamluk dynasty, deposed Turan Shah, the last Ayyubid sultan of Egypt. By 1334, the last Ayyubid rulers of Syria and Palestine had all been deposed and their realms incorporated into the powerful new Mamluk state.

Amazing as it may seem, Salah ad-Din and his illustrious life, were forgotten soon after his death. All his initial successes, crowned with the recovery of Jerusalem, were relegated to history books

11-2 THE LIBERATOR OF JERUSALEM: Salah ad-Din al-Ayyubi was born in Tikrit, Iraq, but lived in various parts of Syria, Palestine and Egypt. History has recorded his achievements and Muslims and non-Muslims alike respect the honour and justice with which he led his life. The Muslim world honoured him in his lifetime during the first Friday *khutbah* delivered after the liberation of Jerusalem in 1187. Salah ad-Din died on March 4, 1193 at the age of fifty-six. His tomb lies in a quiet garden of jasmine and orange trees, next to the Great Umayyad Mosque in old Damascus. The Arabic inscription on the carved wooden coffin of Salah ad-Din asks Allah to receive his soul and grant him *Jannah*.

when the Ayyubids began to lose territory once again to the crusaders. In Europe, however, the legend of Salah ad-Din and his exemplary behaviour on the battlefield and off had been spread by crusaders – both kings and commoners – who returned to Europe. The legend only grew over time. Seven hundred years after the death of Salah ad-Din, in 1899, his neglected tomb was visited by the German Emperor Kaiser Wilhelm II. The domed mausoleum one sees today behind the Umayyad Mosque in Damascus was built by this foreign leader (see illustration 11-2). An inscription on the tomb reads: "From one great emperor to another."

There is no doubt that Salah ad-Din and his life will remain a cherished memory for Muslims for centuries to come.

CHAPTER TWELVE
THE DELHI SULTANATE (1206–1556)

In 711, just as Tariq ibn Ziyad in the West was about to cross over the Straits of Gibraltar and seize Spain in the name of *Din al-Haq al-Islam*, in the East, Muhammad ibn Qasim captured Sindh province in western India (present-day Pakistan) and initiated the Umayyad – and later the 'Abbasid – influence in the area.

The Islamic settlements in India during the Umayyad period were established mainly along the Indus River in present-day Pakistan. It was several centuries later, during the reign of Mahmud of Ghazna (998–1030), that Islam penetrated into the Hindu heartland of India. The Ghaznavids made successive raids into India over a period of some twenty years. Al-Biruni, the great Persian scholar, accompanied Mahmud on one of his campaigns, eventually remaining in India to write his masterful account (*Kitab al-Hind*) of the habits, customs and religion of Hindu India. This was the first time in Islamic history that a learned Muslim had objectively studied a non-Muslim culture in any real detail. The Ghaznavids were still based in Ghazna (in present-day Afghanistan), but later moved to Lahore (in present-day Pakistan). The successors to the Ghaznavids, the Afghan sultans of Ghur, were the first Muslims to permanently settle in India proper.

THE GHURIDS

The Ghurids are a little known dynasty who had their capital in an extremely remote and mountainous region of Central Afghanistan. In the middle of the eleventh century, they succeeded in taking over Ghaznavid territory after the death of Sultan Mas'ud ibn Mahmud in 1040. Within a century, the Ghurids had occupied Ghazna and in 1186, with the conquest of Lahore, had brought the Ghaznavid dynasty to an end.

Mu'izz ad-Din Muhammad Ghuri (1162–1206) was perhaps the most important Ghurid ruler. In 1192, he defeated Prithvi Raja Chauhan in a battle in northwestern India. With the defeat and subsequent death of this last Hindu ruler of Delhi, the Ghurids were able to seize more Indian territory.

When Muhammad Ghuri died in 1206, Qutb ad-Din Aybak, his most trusted Turkish general, continued the conquest of India, eventually establishing his own independent state with Delhi as its capital. The Delhi Sultanate had been born.

The Delhi Sultanate is the name given to a series of five Delhi-based Islamic dynasties that ruled over northern India and present-day Pakistan from 1210 (the year in which Qutb ad-Din Aybak died) until 1526 (the year in which Babur Shah became the first Great Mughal Emperor). These were

a) The Mamluk or Slave Dynasty (1206–1290)
b) The Khaljis (1290–1321)
c) The Tughluqids (1321–1414)
d) The Sayyids (1414–1451)
e) The Lodis (1451–1526).

QUTB AD-DIN AYBAK (1206–1210)

Qutub ad-Din Aybak was the founder of the first of these dynasties. Because he himself and several later sultans – all his descendants – had been Turkish military slaves (*mamluks*), this period is known as the "Slave" or "Mamluk" dynasty of Delhi sultans.

In his four short years as the first "slave" sultan, Qutb ad-Din Aybak succeeded in establishing a sound system of administration for his new sultanate. He began his rule in Lahore, the second capital of the old Ghaznavid Empire, and then made Delhi his capital. Because of this move further east into India, Qutb ad-Din Aybak is considered the first Muslim ruler of South Asia. In 1210, he died accidentally while playing a game of polo.

Qutb ad-Din Aybak is remembered for constructing the first Islamic monuments of the Delhi Sultanate. The *Quwwat al-Islam* (The Might of Islam) Mosque was built on the site of the fortress city of Qila Rai Pithora, renamed by Prithvi Raja Chauhan, the last Hindu ruler of Delhi. This was India's first great mosque. Twenty-seven Hindu and Jain[14] temples were demolished, and from the rubble, Hindu artisans used piles of masonry to build this extraordinary mosque. Ancient columns from Hindu temples, for example, were used to construct the arcades of the courtyard which can still be seen today.

QUTB MINAR

Qutb ad-Din Aybak also began the construction of the famous minaret which stands next to the *Quwwat al-Islam* Mosque, but it took the efforts of two more slave rulers to complete it. The *Qutb Minar* is truly monumental and at 72.5 metres in height is easily the tallest minaret of its kind in the world (see illustration 12-1). At this time in Islamic history, many very tall minarets of this sort had been built in Iran, Afghanistan and parts of Central Asia and served as powerful, visual symbols of the might of Islam and the principle of *tawhid*.

The *Qutb Minar* resembles another victory tower, namely the Minaret of Djam in Central Afghanistan, which was only rediscovered in 1957 (see illustration 12-2)! The Ghurid sultan, Ghiyath ad-Din Muhammad (1163–1203), built it just before Qutb ad-Din Aybak began to build his tower in Delhi. While the Minaret of Djam is made completely of brick with some ceramic decoration, the *Qutb Minar* uses massive, carved red sandstone blocks. Great monumental bands of exquisite Arabic calligraphy contrast with the equally beautiful bands of floral patterns which come from Hindu tradition (see illustration 12-3). Even today, this tower is as awe-inspiring as it was eight hundred years ago when it proclaimed the permanent arrival of Islam in South Asia.

This is what the famous fourteenth century "traveller of Islam", Ibn Battutah, had to say about the *Quwwat al-Islam* Mosque and its magnificent minaret:

> The site was formerly occupied by an idol temple and was converted into a mosque on the conquest of the city. In the northern court is the minaret, which has no parallel in the lands of Islam. It is built of red stone, unlike the rest of the edifice, ornamented with sculptures, and of great height. The ball on top is of glistening white marble and its "apples" [small balls surmounting a minaret] are of pure gold. The passage is so wide that elephants could go up by it. A person in whom I have confidence, told me that when it was being built, he saw an elephant

---

[14] A follower of an ancient Indian religion (Jainism) who believes in the transmigration of souls and denies the existence of a supreme being.

12-1 THE QUTB MINAR: The Turkish general, Qutb ad-Din Aybak, had worked for the Ghurid sultan Muhammad. It is not surprising, therefore, that Qutb ad-Din Aybak built this "victory tower" after the likeness of the Minaret of Djam (see illustration 12-2). The Qutb Minar celebrates the arrival of *Din al-Haq al-Islam* in northern India. This great stone minaret is an important attraction to all who visit India today.

climbing with stones to the top. The sultan Qutb ad-Din Aybak wished to build one in the western court even larger, but was cut off by death when only a third of it had been completed. This minaret is one of the wonders of the world for size, and the width of its passages is such that three elephants could mount it abreast.[15]

---

[15] Ibn Battutah. *The Travels of Ibn Battutah*. (trans. H.A.R. Gibb), New Delhi: Goodword Books, 2001: 195-196.

12-2 A HIDDEN TREASURE: This magnificent minaret, belonging to a mosque that no longer exists, had been hidden from the outside world for almost eight hundred years until it was rediscovered in 1957! The little known Ghurid dynasty, centred in the remote, high mountains of central Afghanistan, played a short, but important role in Islamic history. In 1186, the Ghurids entered Lahore and deposed the last Ghaznavid sultan. This outstanding example of brick construction, known as the Minaret of Djam, was built by the Ghurid sultan Muhammad in about the year 1190. The minaret rises like a finger proclaiming the Oneness of Allah. At sixty-five metres in height, it is the second tallest brick minaret in the world. It resembles other such towers that were built in other parts of Central Asia. These minarets not only called the faithful to prayers, but were also used as landmarks for travellers on the Silk Road and as bold, powerful reminders of the permanent presence of *Din al-Haq al-Islam* in the region. The Minaret of Djam is covered with *ayahs* from *Surah al-Fath* and the complete *Surah Maryam*.

12-3 MASTERFUL CARVING: The Qutb Minar, at 72.5 metres, is one of the tallest*
minarets of its kind in the world. The minaret is built from massive red sandstone blocks.
In the carved decoration is a fusion of styles; the Arabic calligraphy contrasts with floral patterns coming from Hindu tradition. It is reported that twenty-seven Indian temples provided
the building material for this minaret and the adjoining Quwwat al-Islam Mosque. Arabic
inscriptions, like the ones seen here predominate, but Sanskrit texts were also carved into
the sandstone.

* The world's tallest is the 210-metre minaret of the Mosque of Hassan II (1993) in Casablanca,
Morocco.

In the same travel book (*rihlah*), Ibn Battutah mentioned that Delhi was a city comprised of four townships: Old Delhi; Siri – built by 'Ala ad-Din Khalji; Tughlaqabad – built by Ghiyath ad-Din Tughluq; and Jahanpanah – built by Muhammad Shah. The mosque and minaret of Qutb ad-Din Aybak are all that remain of the first Islamic city of Old Delhi.

Shams ad-Din Iltutmish (1211–1236)

Aram Shah, Qutb ad-Din Aybak's son, succeeded his father as second Delhi sultan in 1210, but was soon overthrown by Shams ad-Din Iltutmish, the son-in-law of Qutb ad-Din Aybak, who became the third ruler of the Delhi Sultanate.

In 1229, the 'Abbasid caliph, Al-Mustansir, recognised that an independent Muslim state had been formed in northern India and awarded Iltutmish the title of *Nasir Amir al-Mu'minin* (Helper of the Commander of the Faithful).

Iltutmish is most remembered for uniting regions of northern India – from Sindh in the West to Bengal in the East – into an Islamic state. By the middle of the thirteenth century, even parts of central India had been brought under the control of the Delhi Sultanate. Despite the fact that Hindus were offered positions in the running of the government, revolts in the conquered territories finally led to the collapse of the Slave Dynasty in 1290.

'Ala ad-Din Khalji (1296–1316)

Up until the end of the Slave Dynasty of Delhi sultans in 1290, the dynasty had been thoroughly Turkish in that all the sultans had a Central Asian Turkish origin.

During the reign of the Khalji sultans, the ethnic mix of Turks and Indians through intermarriage became more apparent. The Khalji Dynasty ruled the Delhi Sultanate for approximately thirty years from 1290 to 1320. For over half of this period, northern India was ruled by 'Ala ad-Din Khalji.

'Ala ad-Din had ambitions to expand his sultanate, but had to first deal with an incursion from the Chaghatai Mongols of Central Asia in 1299. Once this was successfully repulsed, 'Ala ad-Din Khalji extended the suzerainty of the Delhi Sultanate – and, therefore, the territory of *Dar al-Islam* – to include Gujarat and parts of Rajasthan in the west and the Deccan Plateau in central India. His army even reached as far as the Hindu kingdoms of southern India. The Khalji sultans agreed to receive an annual tribute from some of these kingdoms instead of ruling them directly. In 1311, 'Ala ad-Din's general, Malik Kafur, raided the city of Madurai, in the very far south of India. Madurai was a very important Hindu pilgrimage centre; however, the Hindu king there prevented the area from becoming a permanent part of *Dar al-Islam*.

Of 'Ala ad-Din Khalji's many sons, only Qutb ad-Din Mubarak Shah Khalji (1316–1320) reigned as sultan. His assassination prompted the takeover of the Delhi Sultanate by yet another family, the Tughluqs.

Muhammad ibn Tughluq (1325–1351)

Ghiyath ad-Din Tughluq (1320–1325) was the founding father of the Tughluq Dynasty of Delhi sultans. During his short reign, the Delhi sultanate extended to include many former Hindu kingdoms into the Islamic state, including the Deccan Plateau in the far south. However, his rule was cut short when he died in a freak hunting accident enabling his eldest son, Muhammad, to ascend the throne in 1325.

Muhammad ibn Tughluq is remembered for having poor judgement and making some decisions that undermined confidence in his government. In 1327, he attempted to forcibly move his government along with the population of Delhi to the southern territories. His new southern capital was named Dawlatabad, which for a time, shared power with Delhi. But due to an inadequate water supply there, the plan failed and after two years, Muhammad relocated his government back to Delhi. On the long march back, many former residents of Delhi died from the gruelling ordeal.

Although Muhammad ibn Tughluq showed great generosity to Muslims, he was often merciless towards his Hindu subjects. Revolts by the Hindus in southern India resulted in a loss of territory to an independent state there. With his shrinking empire, Muhammad ibn Tughluq began to look north and west for lands to conquer. His planned military campaigns to both Central Asia

12-4 WORTHLESS MONEY: Muhammad ibn Tughluq is remembered for spreading the message of Islam into the southernmost regions of India. But, he made some noteworthy mistakes in his life. For example, he replaced his silver coinage with inexpensive copper or brass tokens which were supposed to have the same value. The copper coinage was illegally copied and the market was soon flooded with fake coins, which soon lost all their value. Here is one of the small brass tokens Muhammad ibn Tughluq issued between 1329 and 1331 to replace the regular silver *tankas*. The Arabic inscription is bold and pompous, but accurately reflects the character of this sultan. It reads *man ata'a al-sultan fa-qad ata'a Ar-Rahman*, "Whoever obeys the sultan [Muhammad ibn Tughluq], obeys Allah, Ar-Rahman"!

and Tibet resulted in failure. It is said that before his death, Muhammad was even considering a possible invasion of Iran and China. In order to finance these military campaigns, Muhammad ibn Tughluq increased taxes to support the cost of his large army, but this led to a revolt among the peasants.

It was not for a lack of silver and gold that in 1329, Muhamamd ibn Tughluq decided to experiment with a copper and brass token coinage to replace the silver *tankas* in circulation; he had apparently gotten the idea from the Chinese (see illustration 12-4). Therefore, token coins were issued having the same value as regular silver *tankas*. However, the copper tokens were too easily copied and forgers ended up flooding the market with fake coins. Muhammad's token coins, of course, soon lost all their value. After only two years, he had to recall them (including the forgeries) and replace them with the traditional silver *tankas*.

Despite these errors of judgement, Muhammad ibn Tughluq was also known as a generous and hospitable ruler. Muslims from all over *Dar al-Islam* were welcomed to his court. The great Moroccan traveller, Ibn Battutah – sometimes called the Arab Marco Polo – accepted this invitation after performing the Hajj. He had also heard that the gifts Muhammad gave his guests always exceeded the value of those he received. Unable to find a ship sailing from Jeddah on the Red Sea to anywhere in India, Ibn Battutah decided to travel north, overland through the land of the Turks. Eventually, after many adventures, he did reach India and the court of Muhammad ibn Tughluq who was more than happy to offer the Moroccan a lucrative job as a *qadi*.

END OF THE TUGHLUQ DYNASTY

When Muhammad ibn Tughluq died in 1351 while campaigning in Sindh, he was succeeded by his cousin, Firuz Shah Tughluq. After his death in 1388, Firuz Tughluq's sons and grandsons fought amongst themselves for control of the dynasty. Infighting had weakened the Delhi Sultanate to the extent that Timur-i Lang was able to invade India in 1398 with his conquering Mongol army.

The Tughluq dynasty was severely weakened by Timur's looting of Delhi. The population of the Tughluq capital was massacred and the city destroyed. The Delhi Sultanate never fully recovered from this disaster. As was customary, Timur transported the most gifted craftsmen, engineers and artists from Delhi – as he did from all the cities he conquered – to Samarqand where they worked on grand projects to beautify Timur's Central Asian capital.

SAYYID DYNASTY (1414–1451)

In the year 1414, more than a decade after the catastrophic Timurid invasion of northern India, Delhi remained the capital of a vanished empire. With the death of Mahmud, the last Tughluq sultan, in 1414, Khidr Khan, the former governor of Multan seized power and with him began the very short-lived Sayyid dynasty of Delhi sultans. This family claimed descent from the Prophet Muhammad ﷺ, thus were called *sayyids*. Khidhr Khan, the first Sayyid sultan, and his three successors, were no more than weak provincial rulers. It was not surprising then that in 1451, the last Sayyid ruler, 'Ala ad- Din 'Alam Shah, submitted to a more powerful Afghan family of Pashtun leaders: the Lodis.

LODI DYNASTY (1451–1526)

The Delhi Sultanate fell into the hands of the Afghan Lodis in 1451. The Lodi dynasty neatly consisted of three generations of rulers: Bahlul Lodi, the founder (1451–1489); his son, Sikander Lodi (1489–1517); and Sikander's son, Ibrahim II, the last of the Lodis (1517–1526).

Bahlul Lodi had been the governor of the Punjab before ascending the throne of the Delhi Sultanate. As sultan, he pacified many provincial areas of the realm, restored Muslim prestige in India and also re-established the importance of Delhi. On his death, a council of Afghan chiefs elected one of his sons, Sikander, to succeed him. The latter is remembered as a strong and just ruler who further extended the influence of the Delhi Sultanate and who founded the city of Agra in 1504, as his capital.

The last of the Lodis, Ibrahim ibn Sikander, had a problematic reign. He had to contend with dissension in his family and with groups of Afghan nobles vying for power. He did not manage these situations well and as a result, he had no lack of enemies. As a direct consequence of the loathing many Afghans felt towards Ibrahim, the governor of Punjab, Dawlat Khan Lodi and 'Alam Khan, Ibrahim's uncle, invited Babur Shah, the Chaghatai Turk and last Timurid ruler of Central Asia, to intervene. Essentially, this was an open invitation to depose Ibrahim Lodi and establish a new dynasty in northern India to fill the vacuum. Ibrahim, the despised Lodi sultan, met his rival, Babur Shah, at Panipat in April 1526.

FIRST BATTLE OF PANIPAT (APRIL 21, 1526)

The two rival armies met at Panipat, a barren plain approximately eighty kilometres to the north of Delhi. Historians tell us that Ibrahim's forces outnumbered those of Babur by about ten to one. Ibrahim also made use of hundreds of Indian war elephants. Babur's strength lay not only in his superior weaponry, but also in the deep hatred felt in the ranks of Ibrahim's army. Babur's cannon power – the first ever seen in India – and expert bowmen certainly helped him in battle, but desertions from the Lodi side were also a crucial element leading to Babur's victory.

The First Battle of Panipat lasted only a few hours and by noon, the valiant, but vain, Ibrahim Lodi lay dead on the battlefield. His tomb can still be seen in Panipat. In Babur Shah's autobiography, the *Babur Nameh,* the victor of Panipat recollects that "the mighty army of Delhi was laid in the dust in the course of half a day".

The First Battle of Panipat was significant for several important reasons. Panipat heralded the first large-scale use of gun powder weaponry in South Asia. It also clearly marked the beginning of Turko-Mongol (Mughal) suzerainty in northern India and the subsequent founding of the Mughal dynasty which was to rule India for the next three hundred years.

END OF THE DELHI SULTANATE

After the First Battle of Panipat, the Delhi Sultanate survived only in name; its greatness had vanished. Its one strength had been to protect India from the invading Mongol hordes of Jenghiz Khan in the thirteenth century. But the first Panipat battle did not necessarily signal a complete end to the Delhi Sultanate. It was temporarily revived by another Afghan leader, Shir Shah Sur and his family members, the Suris. It was not until another battle at Panipat in 1556, that it became apparent to all that the Mughal presence in India would become permanent. After this date, the old Delhi Sultanate very naturally became part of the fabric of the much mightier Mughal Empire.

Chapter Thirteen
The Nasrids of Spain (1232–1492)

We return, once again, to Muslim Spain to read the final chapter in the eight hundred year-long history of Al-Andalus. After their tragic defeat at the Battle of Las Navas de Tolosa (*Al-'Iqab* or the punishment, in Arabic) in 1212, the last of the Berber dynasties to control Spain, the Almohads, returned to North Africa. Muslim Spain at this time was a disunited state consisting of many local rulers who governed their own small kingdoms (*Al-Muluk al-Tawa'if*). To survive, the Muslims very often joined forces with Christian armies in order to defeat this or that Muslim king. One member of the prominent Bani Nasr family, Muhammad I ibn Nasr, or Muhammad ibn al-Ahmar, gained control of the southern regions of Spain in 1232. The beautiful city of Granada became the capital of the Nasrid Kingdom of Granada and the stage upon which the final compelling act in the history of Islamic Spain was played out.

MUHAMMAD IBN AL-AHMAR (1232–1273)

The Nasrids, while a minor dynasty compared to others in Islamic history, are forever remembered as being the last Muslim monarchs to rule Spain. The Bani Nasr were descendants of Sa'd ibn 'Ubaydah ﷺ, one of the Companions of the Prophet ﷺ.[16]

Muhammad ibn al-Ahmar controlled the wild and mountainous region in the far south of the Iberian Peninsula from the Straits of Gibraltar to the Mediterranean coastal town of Almeria. The capital of Granada was situated in the centre of this region. For two and a half centuries, the Nasrids struggled to maintain their independence while all around them important Islamic kingdoms fell, one by one, into the hands of the Spanish Christians. Muhammad ibn al-Ahmar himself lost important towns in his kingdom to the Christians, but still held territory. In order to ensure Granada's survival, Muhammad ibn al-Ahmar made treaties with Christian monarchs such as Ferdinand III of Castile and León. As Muslim cities like Cordoba, Seville and Valencia were lost to the enemy, refugees from these and other cities and towns flooded into the Kingdom of Granada, the last Muslim stronghold on the Iberian Peninsula. In addition, another threat lay to the south of the Kingdom of Granada. The Merinids of Morocco were vying for control of the Straits of Gibraltar.

By carefully balancing his alliances with the Christian kings to the north and the Berber Merinid sultans in Morocco, Muhammad ibn al-Ahmar preserved the independence of Granada even though there were certainly many Islamic scholars of the day who denounced making treaties and alliances with non-Muslim rulers.

YUSUF I IBN ISMA'IL (1333–1354)

By the fourteenth century, the Nasrids had begun to prosper. The complex system of irrigation channels that had been developed by the Arabs over the centuries made the *vega* (Spanish for plain) an agricultural

---

[16] At the time of the Muslim conquest of Spain in the eighth century, several *Ansar* families left Arabia and settled in Al-Andalus.

paradise producing all kinds of fruits and vegetables. Granada was beautified and its court attracted many poets such as Abu 'Abdallah ibn Zamraq and historians like Abu 'Abdallah ibn al-Khatib.

There was increasing pressure on the Nasrid kingdom from the northern Christian kingdoms and, despite the Nasrid rivalry with the Merinids, the young Nasrid sultan Yusuf I invited the Moroccan Merinid sultan Abu'l-Hasan to help him recapture the town of Tarifa, near Gibraltar. The Christian king Alfonso XI of Castile had similarly asked for help from the kings of Portugal and Aragon; their forces even had militias from as far away as the Basque provinces. The ensuing Battle of the Rio Salado in 1340 ended in a defeat for the Muslims, despite their likely having superior numbers on the battlefield. The lightly armed Muslims were simply no match for the heavily armoured Christians who were fighting on familiar terrain. The Merinid forces from Morocco suffered a disastrous defeat and, once again, an African army had been repelled and made to return home. For this reason, the Battle of the Rio Salado resembled that of Las Navas de Tolosa a century earlier.

Ibn Battutah, the famous Moroccan traveller, visited Muslim Spain during the reign of Sultan Yusuf I. In his remarkable *rihlah* (travelogue), he writes:

> I went on to the city of Gharnata [Granada] the metropolis of Al-Andalus and the bride of its cities; its environs have not their equal in any country in the world. They extend for the space of forty miles, and are traversed by the celebrated river of Shannil [Xenil] and many other streams. Around it on every side are orchards, gardens, flowering meadows, noble buildings, and vineyards.[17]

MUHAMMAD V IBN YUSUF (1354–1359 AND 1362–1391)

It was during the reign of Muhammad V that Granada experienced its "golden age". Muslim Spain, from its very beginning in the eighth century, had been a multi-ethnic, multi-racial and multi-religious society – unique amongst all the countries of Western Europe. Now Andalusian society exhibited an even richer ethnic diversity. Catholics and Jews mixed with Muslims, both Spanish-born and those from North Africa and even from Egypt, Syria and Arabia. Granada in its golden age was a thriving oriental town with numerous markets divided according to craft, not unlike the old city of Fez in present-day Morocco. The silk merchants, for example, occupied a large section of the marketplace as silk was Granada's most important local commodity. A bustling caravanserai (travellers' inn) housed traders from distant towns and cities along with their pack animals and merchandise.

Muhammad V is most remembered for completing the Alhambra, the Nasrid royal palace built on the hilltop overlooking Granada. His long reign was interrupted by his nephew and brother-in-law who both seized the throne for brief periods.

DECLINE OF THE NASRIDS

By the fifteenth century, the Nasrids could not rely on fellow Muslim states to come to their assistance, if needed. The Merinids of Morocco were weakened and had their own internal conflicts. At the other end of the Mediterranean Sea, the Mamluk sultans of Egypt and the new Ottoman sultans in Turkey also offered no help to the Bani Nasr. In 1462, with the loss of Gibraltar to the Christians, the Kingdom of Granada was left stranded, cut off from any help, however small, that could have

[17] Ibn Battutah. *The Travels of Ibn Battutah*. trans. H.A.R. Gibb. New Delhi: Goodword Books, 2001:315.

possibly come from North Africa. In 1469, the marriage of the two most powerful Spanish monarchs, Ferdinand of Aragon and Isabella of Castile, led to a unified Spain that was determined to complete the *reconquesta* of the entire Iberian Peninsula.

ABU AL-HASAN 'ALI (1464–1482 AND 1483–1485)

The Nasrid dynasty in its final years was weakened by a series of pretenders to the throne. Sultan Abu al-Hasan 'Ali was the sole Nasrid ruler who was determined to turn the tide of history. He was ashamed of the behaviour of his predecessors; their willingness to join forces with the enemy to defeat other Muslims and their inability to defend Muslim territory. When the Spanish king, Ferdinand, sent an ambassador to the Nasrids demanding the annual tribute,[18] Abu al-Hasan 'Ali angrily replied:

> Tell your sovereign that the kings who paid tribute are no more. The mints of Granada no longer produce gold coins, but steel blades![19]

ABU 'ABDALLAH MUHAMMAD XII - BOABDIL (1482–1483 AND 1486–1492)

A final ten year-long war of survival began for the Nasrids of Granada. Unfortunately, Abu al-Hasan 'Ali's eldest son, Abu 'Abdallah – known as Boabdil in Spanish – proclaimed himself king in 1482 and instead of unity, there was discord amongst the Muslims of Granada as each king had his own supporters. In 1483, Abu 'Abdallah was captured by King Ferdinand and was only released under very severe conditions. First, he had to agree to permit the Christian army to pass through Nasrid territory in order for them to pursue his father, Abu al-Hasan 'Ali. Abu 'Abdallah also had to pay a large annual tribute of 12,000 gold *dinars* and had to hand over his own son as a hostage. Abu 'Abdallah had saved his throne, but at a great cost!

In 1485, Abu al-Hasan 'Ali fell ill and transferred all his power to his brother, al-Zaghal (Muhammad XIII). After a valiant defence of his country, al-Zaghal could not live as a slave of the Catholic Monarchs, Ferdinand and Isabella. Therefore, in 1486, he left his beloved homeland and settled permanently in a town in Algeria. Abu 'Abdallah was now the sole Nasrid ruler left to defend Granada against the encroaching Spanish army.

THE FALL OF GRANADA (JANUARY 2, 1492)

The Catholic Monarchs had launched a crusade against the last Muslim stronghold in Spain. Christians from all parts of Europe joined the Spaniards in this last attack on the Nasrid kingdom. The Muslims did fight one last time, making a very brave attempt to inflict a final blow on the enemy. In November 1491, the besieged city of Granada was starving so Abu 'Abdallah decided to negotiate a surrender. According to a treaty offered to them, Muslims were to be guaranteed almost all their rights under Christian rule. Only one Nasrid official, Musa ibn Ghassan, rejected the treaty outright and warned Abu 'Abdallah and all his advisers that the Christians could never and should never be trusted.

---

[18] Since the rule of Muhammad ibn al-Ahmar, the Nasrid sultans had been paying *parias* or tribute to the Christian kings of northern Spain.

[19] Rahman, Syed Azizur. *The Story of Islamic Spain*. New Delhi: Goodword Books, 2001: 288.

The treaty of surrender, however, was signed on November 25, 1491 and on the morning of January 2, 1492, Abu 'Abdallah handed over the keys to the magnificent Alhambra palace. Queen Isabella then released to Abu 'Abdallah his son who had been held hostage. Legend tells us that when Abu 'Abdallah and his entourage were leaving Granada, the former king looked over his shoulder and wept at seeing his beloved Alhambra for the last time. His mother chided her son, saying, "Stop weeping like a child for what you failed to defend like a man!" Abu 'Abdallah lived for one year in the mountains of Alpujarras to the south of Granada before finally settling in Fez, Morocco. He died in 1533, never forgetting the kingdom he had lost.

PERSECUTION OF MUSLIMS

Within a few years of the surrender of the last Muslim kingdom to the Christians, the Catholic Monarchs began their intentional, systematic persecution of Muslims. Approximately 170,000 Jews had already been expelled from Spain in 1492. Sadly, the terms initially agreed to in the Capitulation Treaty (regarding the protection of Muslim religious rights) were quickly forgotten. By 1499, Ferdinand and Isabella had reneged on many of their promises to Spanish Muslims.

Muslims were first given the choice of becoming Christian or leaving Spain for good. Thousands of Muslims converted to Christianity in order to stay in the land of their birth, the land that had rung with the call of the *adhan* for eight hundred years. For the next hundred years, the Spanish Christians tried unsuccessfully to Christianise the Muslim population of Spain. Outwardly, many appeared to have adopted their new faith, but inside they still professed belief in *La-ilaha illa Allah, Muhammad Rasul Allah*. These "converted" Muslims were called *moriscos* in Spanish and were always suspected of still adhering to the faith of their forefathers.

Eventually, the authorities forbade the speaking, reading or writing of Arabic. Their total intolerance of anything Islamic led to the destruction of whole libraries containing thousands upon thousands of valuable Arabic manuscripts, the accumulated knowledge of centuries.

Finally, between the years 1609 and 1614, the surviving remnants of the Muslims of Spain were rounded up and forcibly deported to cities in North Africa where their descendants live to this day still preserving their Andalusian heritage (see illustration 13-1). By 1614, almost 300,000 Muslims had been removed from their homeland. The Catholic Monarchs had apparently achieved their goal: a Spain ethnically cleansed of all Muslims and Jews. The precise reason for this final dehumanising expulsion has never been fully explained. It is thought that perhaps the Spanish monarchs might have feared an Ottoman invasion in support of the *moriscos*.

Although it was hoped that by the early seventeenth century, all (outwardly and inwardly) practising Muslims had been removed from Spain for good, extremely detailed Spanish Inquisition records indicate that for another hundred years or more, individuals accused of "Islamic behaviour" were still being brought before the Grand Inquisitor. Undoubtedly, some Spanish Muslims refused to emigrate and chose to outwardly accept Christianity. Just how successful they were at doing this and for just how long is still a matter of debate.

13-1   A WELL-TRAVELLED QUR'AN: After 1492, the *reconquesta* (the take over of all of Muslim Spain by the Catholic Monarchs) was complete. Despite promises made by the Spanish king and queen to permit the Muslims of Spain freedom to practice their religion, Muslims were soon forced to convert to Christianity. Those who refused, had to leave Spain for good. Thousands of Muslims could not bear the thought of seeing their children forced to eat pork meat, drink wine and repeat the Catholic prayers, so chose to leave their country of birth. Many of these Andalusian Muslims sought shelter in neighbouring Morocco, Algeria and Tunisia.

This is a page from a copy of the Holy Qur'an, handwritten in Spain almost six hundred years ago. It was taken from Granada to the city of Fez, in Morocco, by a family of refugee Spanish Muslims. This beautiful Qur'an is still read by the descendants of that family who now live in the "Andalusian" quarter of Fez. The interesting style of writing is called *khat al-andalus*, a unique way of writing Arabic that was once used throughout all of Muslim Spain. The incomplete ayahs on this page are from *Surah al-Qasas* (28:3-4): *Musa wa Fir'awna bilhaqqi liqawmin yu'minoon. 'Inna Fir'awna 'ala fil-'ardi wa ja'ala 'ahlaha shiya'an yastad'ifu ta'ifatam-minhum.*

LEGACY OF MUSLIM SPAIN

Few physical traces have remained of the eight-hundred year long Muslim presence in Spain. Gone forever are the hundreds of country villas skirting the banks of the *Wadi al-Kabir* (Guadalquivir River) in Cordoba; the royal palaces in all the provincial towns and the thousands of mosques, big and small, around which the lives of townspeople and villagers turned. Some mosques were converted into churches with their tall square bell towers still reminding us of the minarets they once were. The elimination of any vestiges of Islamic presence in the Iberian Peninsula has been so complete that of the tens of millions of Muslims who once thrived there, only a handful of inscribed gravestones are to be seen on display in the odd museum. But one outstanding architectural treasure has survived from the days of Muslim Spain – the famous Alhambra Palace, the home of the Nasrid monarchs in the royal city of Granada.

The Alhambra (from the Arabic *Al-Qal'ah al-Hamra'* meaning the red castle) was so-called probably because the rusted, iron rich earth, used to build the outer walls of the castle, changed the whitewashed walls to shades of red. In the late thirteenth century, Granada was built as a Muslim city with a *madinah* or city centre, and the sultan's fortress-palace built on a hill overlooking the city. The plain outer walls of the Alhambra give no indication of the exquisite beauty contained within (see illustration 13-2).

Visitors to the palace today – both Muslims and non-Muslims – are truly amazed at the artistry of the Nasrids: the amazing harmony between gardens, water channels, fountains and buildings. The Nasrids were never as wealthy as the caliphs of Cordoba so they could not afford to import expensive marble from Italy and Tunisia, or gold mosaic tiles from Constantinople. Nasrid craftsmen used more perishable materials like plaster, wood and ceramic tile to create a monument to the genius of Islamic art (see illustration 13-3). The Nasrid motto: *Wa la Ghalib 'ila Allah* (There is no Victor but Allah) can be seen painted on capitals and ceramic tiles, carved on wooden lintels and even into the plaster walls of the palace. The same motto was also very frequently placed on Nasrid gold and silver coins (see illustration 13-4).

The Muslim presence in Spain also left a lasting legacy, albeit minor, on the Spanish language. Spanish is a Latin-based language which was in its developmental stages when Arabic reached the shores of the Iberian Peninsula. Despite the eight centuries of Islamic presence in Al-Andalus, Arabic never really influenced Spanish in the way it did Turkish, Persian and Urdu. However, even today, some very common everyday Spanish words are unmistakably Arabic in their origin.

Above all, however, Al-Andalus will always be remembered as a glorious oasis in the hearts and minds of Muslims. Muslims there created a unique multi-religious culture of tolerance which was the envy of the world. This, then, is the most enduring legacy of the eight hundred year-long history of Al-Andalus – a legacy which still can, and should, inspire Muslims, even today.

13-2   A NASRID MASTERPIECE: The Bani Nasr, of the Nasrid dynasty of Muslim rulers, chose as their capital, Granada, a city whose fertile fields were fed by the clean, melted snow of the Sierra Nevada Mountains. The site was picturesque and idyllic, but the history of the Nasrids was anything but peaceful. There was the constant threat from the Spanish kingdoms that wanted to re-conquer all of Spain. Despite the dangers, the Nasrids did enjoy a short "golden age". During the last half of the fourteenth century, Granada was a multi-ethnic and multi-religious society which tolerated differences and flourished as an oriental town with numerous markets. After 1492, however, the Catholic Monarchs did their best to erase any trace of Muslim culture in Spain. However, one magnificent work of Islamic art was so dazzling in its beauty, even the Christians could not think of destroying it. The Alhambra Palace of the Nasrid kings of Granada remains the one surviving example in the region of the creative genius of Spanish Muslim architects. The illustration shows some of the palace buildings within the red walls of the Alhambra. It is impossible to imagine the beauty of their interiors by simply looking at the plain exteriors. Today, the Alhambra attracts many visitors who marvel at this gem of Islamic art which has survived intact from the golden age of the Nasrids, the last Muslim rulers of Spain.

13-3 BEAUTY IN DANCING TILES: The Nasrids of Granada were great patrons of Islamic art. Court poets wrote complex and imaginative verses of Arabic poetry, the best of which were often carved into the stucco walls of the Palace of the Alhambra. Unlike the much wealthier caliphs of Cordoba centuries before, the Nasrids made use of simpler building materials. While the Umayyad caliphs of Cordoba used imported marbles and gold mosaics to decorate their palaces, the Nasrids chose stucco and ceramic tile to astonishing effect. The example here shows a design unique to the Alhambra. The cut tiles of varying colours and the whirling shapes present a contrast. Such inventiveness can be seen throughout the palace. Many years after the last Muslim ruler of Granada, Abu 'Abdallah, had vacated the Alhambra, the Spanish king, Charles V, the grandson of Ferdinand and Isabella, visited the Alhambra for the first time. Upon seeing the exquisitely beautiful palace, he is reported to have sighed, "Ill-fated was the man who lost all this!"

13-4 SIMPLE SILVER COIN: For two and a half centuries, the motto of the Nasrid dynasty had been *wa la Ghalib 'ila Allah*, (there is no victor but Allah). This Arabic phrase was carved thousands of times on the stucco walls, wooden lintels, and stone columns of the Alhambra Palace in Granada. This historically important coin dates from the last days of the Nasrid dynasty. It is a silver quarter *dirham*. The Nasrid motto can be read on the left coin and the *kalimah* on the right. Although made of impure silver, and crude in design, this simple coin represents one of the last public statements made by Muslims in the land of Spain. *Masha'Allah*, it is a sincere statement of their *shahadah* – their belief in *Din al-Haq al-Islam*, the religion and way of life they had so courageously attempted to preserve.

CHAPTER FOURTEEN

THE MAMLUKS OF EGYPT (1250–1517)

It was the 'Abbasid caliphs who first made use of *mamluks*[20] (military slaves or slave soldiers) for their troops. These slaves, mainly of non-Muslim Mongol or Turkish origin, were later converted to Islam and given special training in military and administrative matters. The Fatimids of Egypt also employed *mamluks* as did Salah ad-Din and the Ayyubid dynasty. Many *mamluks* rose to positions of great power, such as army commanders; for example, the Mamluk commander of the Muslim forces in India, Qutb ad-Din Aybak, subsequently went on to found the Slave Dynasty of the Delhi Sultanate. It was in a similar manner that the Mamluk dynasty of Egypt was founded. There were two branches within this dynasty: the Bahriyyah Mamluks (1250–1382) and the Burjiyyah Mamluks (1382–1517).

MAMLUK ORIGINS

Both the 'Abbasids and the Ayyubids received their *mamluks* from the region to the north of the Black Sea, which is present-day southern Russia and the Ukraine. This area was inhabited by a nomadic Turkic people, the Qipchaqs. Over the years, many thousands of children or young adolescents were transported from their Qipchaq homeland to military barracks in Cairo. It is believed that dire poverty was the main reason these pagan (shamanic) Turks were so willing to sell their children to the *tajir al-mamalik* (slave dealer for the sultan). Another important source of *mamluks* was the region near the Caucasus Mountains, where the non-Turkic Circassians and Georgians lived.

Young *mamluk* recruits were regularly brought by sea to the ports of northern Egypt. They were then taken up the Nile River, or overland to Cairo, where they were assigned to specially prepared barracks in the citadel overlooking the old city. The *mamluks'* education began here. Firstly, the boys were introduced to the fundamentals of the Islamic faith. Only after having received a very thorough instruction in the principles of their new religion were the *mamluks* given any military training. The emphasis here was on horsemanship and archery. The *Al-Mamalik al-Sultaniyyah* (royal slaves) were all manumitted, or freed, upon graduation from the military school. Each *mamluk* graduate was awarded an *'itaqa* or diploma certifying his completion of all the necessary training and his manumission. The *mamluk*, was in fact no longer a "slave", but had now become a full-fledged soldier and thus a member of the fraternity of Mamluks.

Loyalty to one's former master or patron was very strong. Former *mamluks* still respected and honoured their masters as they would a father. And indeed, former masters treated their freedmen as their own sons. Freedmen, in turn, were all considered brothers-in-arms. These close "family" ties formed the basis for the smooth and successful running of the Mamluk system of administration.

---

[20] In this book the term *mamluk* denotes any rank and file "military slave" employed during specific periods in the history of Umayyad Spain, 'Abbasid Iraq, the Delhi Sultanate, or Egypt etc. The term Mamluk, however, refers to a particular dynasty employing such military slaves.

The *Al-Mamalik al-Sultaniyyah* were an elite guard. All its members had been purchased, trained and manumitted by the sultan himself. It was from this exclusive group that the ruling sultan (himself a former *mamluk*) would often choose his successor.

BAHRI MAMLUKS (1250–1382)

A group of mainly Qipchaq *mamluks*, based in a garrison on the island of Al-Manial in the Nile River, formed the bodyguards for Al-Salih Ayyub, one of the last Ayyubid rulers of Egypt. Upon Sultan Ayyub's death in 1249, his son, Turan Shah, succeeded him. However, in 1250, this Bahriyyah group of Mamluks killed the new sultan and power passed to Sultan Ayyub's widow, Shajar al-Durr. Under pressure, she married the *mamluk* commander, Aybak al-Turkumani, whose rule ended in his murder in 1257. Aybak's second-in-command, Qutuz, seized power for himself.

In 1259, the Mongols had begun their invasion of Syria. Qutuz, along with his powerful commander, Baybars, met the Mongol forces at 'Ain Jalut (Spring of Goliath), a village in Palestine.

BATTLE OF 'AIN JALUT (SEPTEMBER 3, 1260)

Hulagu Khan's unbeatable Mongol army was led by Kitbuga Noyon. The overwhelming strength of the specially-trained Mamluk forces quickly annihilated the Mongol's smaller army of horsemen. Hulagu was angered by the defeat on the battlefield and by the capture and subsequent killing of Kitbuga, but could not take revenge because of serious internal strife afflicting the Mongol Empire in the Far East. For the first time in history, the Mongol army had been defeated. The Egyptian Mamluks had employed their own military tactics and had won.

Although Sultan Qutuz had spearheaded the expedition from Cairo to meet the Mongols in Palestine, Baybars had clearly been the victor at 'Ain Jalut. Before the Mamluk sultan and his army could return to Cairo, Baybars murdered Qutuz on October 24, 1260 and immediately proclaimed himself the new Mamluk sultan of Egypt promising to aid his "brothers", the Bahriyyah Mamluks.

AL-ZAHIR BAYBARS I (1260–1277)

Despite his bloody rise to power as the true founder of the Egyptian Mamluk dynasty, Baybars was able to establish lasting institutions that strengthened it. He immediately bolstered his defences by repairing the Syrian castles destroyed by the Mongols. He also increased the number of Mamluk naval vessels in addition to expanding the size of his army. Baybars spent more than half of his reign away from his capital, Cairo, so he developed a very effective postal system, perhaps copying that of the earlier 'Abbasid one that had been modelled on the pre-Islamic Sasanian system. Horsemen relayed messages regularly from Cairo to all parts of the empire: Egypt, Syria and Palestine. It was said that a message sent from Cairo could reach Damascus (a distance of approximately seven hundred kilometres) in four days. An even speedier service using pigeons was also later developed.

Baybars consolidated his control over former Ayyubid territory by removing the Ayyubid princes there. He also used the formidable Mamluk army to lead major campaigns (a total of thirty-eight in Syria alone) against the crusaders who still held land principally along the Syrian/Palestinian coast. He destroyed their castles in order to prevent any future re-establishment of army crusader bases.

Baybars dealt with the local Isma'ili threat in the region by occupying their fortresses. At the end of his long reign, in 1277, he invaded the Ilkhanid territory in eastern Turkey and defeated a combined Seljuq/Mongol army there. He had personally led his forces in a total of fifteen battles.

Baybars had proved his worth as a warrior and had been successful against many odds. Enemies – Ayyubid princes, crusaders, Mongols and Isma'ilis – had surrounded him, but he had subdued them all. Before he died, Baybars wanted to establish a dynasty legitimising the succession of his son as sultan. We recall that several 'Abbasid princes had fled Baghdad after its destruction in 1258. In 1262, Baybars installed one, Al-Hakim I, as caliph and received from him the title of "Universal Sultan of Islam". Before his death in Damascus in 1277, possibly from a poisoned drink, Baybars had ensured that his son, Baraka Khan, would succeed him.

Even to this day, in Egypt and Syria, Baybars remains a national hero. His legacy is clear. He modelled himself as a second Salah ad-Din, successfully ridding the region of crusaders as well as uniting Egypt and Syria.

QALAWUN (1279–1290) AND AL-ASHRAF KHALIL IBN QALAWUN (1290–1293)

Despite Baybars' attempts to have his son succeed him, the Baybars dynasty was short-lived. Baraka Khan reigned for two years; his seven year-old brother, Salamish, for only a few weeks. Baraka Khan's father-in-law, Qalawun, suggested that Salamish was too young to rule and subsequently deposed him in August 1279. Baybars' three sons were then all exiled to a former crusader castle in Syria.

Qalawun, not unlike Baybars, spent much of his career negotiating alliances and capturing and destroying the last fortifications of the crusader states along the coasts of Syria and Palestine. Qalawun was the first Mamluk sultan to begin recruiting *mamluks* from the Caucasus region. These Circassian *mamluks* were to form the Burjiyyah dynasty, which over time would pose a threat to the Bahriyyah *mamluks,* mainly Qipchaq Turks.

Qalawun also wanted to establish a dynasty and in 1290 his son, Al-Ashraf Khalil, succeeded him. The following year Khalil was successful in capturing the last crusader outpost at Acre. Al-Ashraf Khalil continued recruiting Circassian *mamluks*, thus strengthening the Burjiyyah garrisons. Turkish Qipchaq *mamluks*, feeling threatened, eventually assassinated Khalil in 1293.

AL-NASIR MUHAMMAD (1293–1340)

Mamluk sultans, on average, had very short reigns. One exception was Sultan Al-Nasir Muhammad who ruled for three different periods between the years 1293 and 1340. He first succeeded to the throne at the age of ten and was deposed twice during the early years. By 1310, however, an older and much wiser Al-Nasir Muhammad returned to Cairo and with his rule, there would once again be stability in the Mamluk Empire.

The court of Al-Nasir Muhammad received ambassadors representing the kings of France, the Delhi Sultanate of India and Ethiopia. Al-Nasir Muhammad was so powerful that the Golden Horde of Mongols in southern Russia even sent him a Mongol princess to marry – the great, great granddaughter of Jenghiz Khan. His reign was a time of peace and prosperity and the golden age of the Mamluk dynasty. He completed several important construction projects such as the canal linking the city of Alexandria with the Nile River. Great mosques, *madrasahs*, palaces and public buildings were also constructed during this period (see illustration 14-1). Sultan Al-Nasir's mosque and *madrasah* complex is one of the most beautiful examples of Mamluk architecture and can still be seen in old Cairo today.

14-1 MAMLUK MONUMENTS: In two hundred and fifty years, the Mamluks of Egypt had constructed about seven hundred superb monuments in the Cairo area alone. Today, in old Cairo, a visitor can still view about two hundred of these architectural masterpieces, many with helmet-shaped domes, which dominate the skyline. Here we can see a forest of domes and minarets with the Pyramids of Giza in the background. The building frenzy during Mamluk times, in particular, forced some architects to begin using the Pyramids as a source of building material. Therefore, some of the monumental public works such as mosque complexes, *madrasahs*, hospitals, caravanserais, private villas and palaces built by the Mamluks, may contain stones pillaged from the four thousand year-old Pyramids.

One of Al-Nasir's sons, Sultan Hasan (1347–1351 and 1354–1361), also built an exceptional mosque, understood to be the most expensive Mamluk monument ever constructed (see illustration 14-2). In the large courtyard, each of the four schools of Islamic Law (Hanafi, Hanbali, Shafi'i, and Maliki) was given a special corner. Students of all four schools would study with their respective teachers in a separate wing of the open courtyard. Cairo had now replaced Baghdad as both the religious and economic capital of *Dar al-Islam*. In 1383, Ibn Khaldun, the great Arab social historian, visited Cairo for the first time and was very impressed with the city that was truly "the centre of the world".

> I beheld the metropolis of the World, orchard of the Universe, hive of nations ... human anthill, portal of Islam, throne of royalty bursting with palaces and portals within, shining on the horizon with convents and schools, illuminated by the moon and stars of its learned doctors, which appeared on the bank of the Nile, River of Paradise, flowing with waters of the sky.[21]

14-2 "LIGHT UPON LIGHT": During the daytime, open *iwans* (vaulted or flat-roofed halls) and windows permitted sunlight to stream into Mamluk mosques. At night, however, glass lamps (called *misbahs* in Arabic) were employed to lighten the mosque for the sunset and late evening prayers. Many beautiful examples of Mamluk glass have been preserved in museums around the world. Here is an exquisite mosque lamp made from enamelled glass. Qur'anic inscriptions were commonly placed on such lamps. When lit by a candle inside the lamp, the glorious verses of the Holy Qur'an, as well as the names and titles of the reigning sultan would be visible to all in the mosque.

---

[21] Raymond, Andre. *Cairo City of History*. Cambridge, Mass.: Harvard University Press, 2000: 145.

Hereditary succession had always been a problem for Mamluk sultans. Frequently, the son of one sultan would be deposed by another and would sometimes return to power at a later date. There was, consequently, always uncertainty when a sultan died. On the death of Sultan Al-Nasir in 1340, eight of his sons fought over the right of succession and all reigned for very brief periods as did four grandsons and great-grandsons.

BLACK DEATH (1348–1349)

The bubonic plague, the extremely contagious disease that had devastated large parts of Europe, finally struck Egypt in 1348, during the reign of Al-Nasir Hasan, one of Al-Nasir Muhammad's sons. It is thought the disease, transmitted by fleas infected by the black rat, originated on the steppes of Central Asia and had reached Egypt via the Black Sea trading ports.

The Black Death, as the plague was often called, resulted in the depopulation of entire regions of Egypt. Many *mamluk* recruits perished and it is said the number of Royal Mamluks was reduced by half. The army garrisons were also decimated and never fully recovered. The great Moroccan traveller, Ibn Battutah, was visiting Cairo during this period and commented on the vast numbers of dead he saw piled up in the streets. It is possible that as much as one-third of the city's population died in the pandemic. The Black Death ultimately affected the economy of the Mamluk state. With whole villages depopulated, once fertile farmlands reverted to barren wasteland. Egyptian industry also suffered from the loss of many skilled craftsmen such as important textile workers.

BARQUQ (1382–1389 AND 1390–1399) AND THE BURJIYYAH MAMLUKS

In 1377, a revolt in Syria spread to Egypt where Circassian *mamluks* (originally from the Caucasus region) seized power, thus deposing the ruling Bahriyyah dynasty in 1382.

Al-Zahir Barquq was the first in the line of Burjiyyah Mamluk sultans. The Burjiyyah (from the Arabic *burj* meaning tower) Mamluks had their barracks in the citadel in Old Cairo. Unlike the Bahriyyah Mamluks of Qipchaq Turkish origin, the Burjiyyah consisted of Circassian regiments. While the Bahriyyah Mamluks from the time of Baybars had to contend with the threat of a Mongol invasion, the Burjiyyah, a century and a half later, had to confront Timur-i Lang.

Sultan Barquq died in 1399 without having faced Timur on the battlefield. But Timur did arrive and seized parts of Syria including Aleppo in 1400. While Timur did not invade Egypt, Sultan Al-Nasir al-Faraj (1399–1405), the son of Barquq, had to flee Damascus and return to Cairo with his Mamluk army.

Sultan Barquq, not unlike most of the Mamluks, constructed some very imposing monuments in Cairo. His *madrasah* and *Khanqah* (dervish lodge) complex dates from 1386 and is considered one of the most important monuments in the heart of Old Fatimid Cairo. These buildings can still be visited today.

AL-ASHRAF QA'IT BEY (1468–1496)

Up until the fifteenth century, the principal enemy of the Mamluks had been the Mongols. However, during the reign of Al-Ashraf Qa'it Bey, the eighteenth Burji Mamluk sultan, Mamluk-Ottoman relations took a turn for the worse. The Ottoman sultan Bayezid II seized Mamluk-held territories such as Adana, in southern Turkey, after Qa'it Bey had given asylum to Bayezid's brother, Jem, who was a rival to the Ottoman throne. Finally, a major land war was fought between the years 1485 and 1491.

It was clear to the Mamluks that their obsolete army of sword-wielding horsemen was no match for the more modern Ottoman forces who employed firearms and cannon. The Ottomans had their own form of "slave soldiers", the Janissaries, who had proved to be an obviously superior fighting force.

Al-Ashraf Qa'it Bey is most remembered for the magnificent monuments (many of which are still extant) he constructed all over Cairo and in the cities of Damascus, Jerusalem, Madinah and Makkah.

QANSAWH AL-GHAWRI (1501–1516)

The world was changing and the Mamluks of Egypt were clearly behind the times and unable to catch up with the technological advances that had transformed warfare forever. Three large military powers loomed on the horizon: the Ottoman Turks to the north, the Safavid Persians to the east, and to the south, the maritime might of the Portuguese who wanted to exclude Muslims from using the Indian Ocean trading routes.

Qansawh al-Ghawri was almost sixty years old when he came to power. He understood the external threat to his Egyptian dynasty and did make an effort to strengthen the Mamluk army by issuing the troops handguns and by commissioning the first Mamluk cannon. Many *mamluks*, however, were reluctant to change and still believed in the efficacy of traditional weaponry.

The Ottoman sultan, Selim I, successfully defeated his archenemies, the Safavids, at the Battle of Chaldiran in August 1514. Exactly two years later, on August 24, 1516, Qansawh al-Ghawri – now well into his seventies – confronted Sultan Selim I at the decisive Battle of Marj Dabiq, north of Aleppo. There might have been some collusion between a Mamluk commander and the Ottomans which resulted in a disastrous defeat for the Egyptians. Qansawh died in battle and his body was never found.

The Mamluk dynasty did not end, however, until the Ottomans inflicted one last defeat at the Battle of Al-Raydaniyyah on January 23, 1517. The victorious Ottomans then entered Cairo and proceeded to hang Al-Ashraf Tuman Bay, the last Mamluk sultan who had been appointed viceroy by Qansawh before leaving Cairo for the Battle of Marj Dabiq the previous year.

AL-MUTAWAKKIL III (1509–1516 AND 1517)

It is frequently reported that when the Ottoman sultan, Selim I, occupied Egypt in 1517, he took over the title of caliph from the last 'Abbasid shadow caliph, Al-Mutawakkil III. In fact, Sultan Selim I had already referred to himself as "Caliph of Allah throughout the length and breadth of the Earth" three years before his conquest of Egypt. The formal transfer of caliphal power was made by Al-Mutawakkil III who was taken to Constantinople where he gave Sultan Selim I the sacred relics (the personal belongings of the Prophet Muhammad ﷺ) that had been held in trust by the 'Abbasids for eight hundred years. These relics are still preserved in the old Ottoman Topkapi Palace, in Istanbul. The Islamic world accepted the Ottoman sultans as caliphs even though they were not descended from the Quraysh, the tribe of the Prophet Muhammad ﷺ. Al-Mutawakkil III died in obscurity in 1543.

THE LAST MAMLUKS

After the Ottoman takeover of Egypt, thousands of Egyptian Mamluk nobles remained a wealthy land-holding class right up until the early nineteenth century. Mamluk governors in Ottoman times were called *beys* and were the most powerful class in Egyptian society.

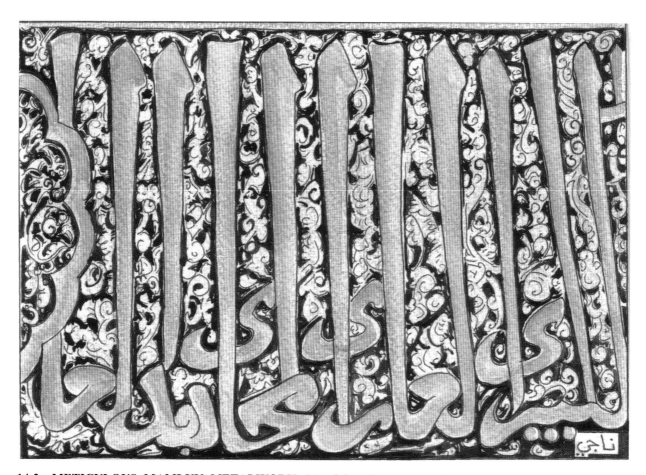

14-3 METICULOUS MAMLUK METALWORK: Mamluk sultans were all great builders. Today, hundreds of Mamluk monuments can still be seen in Old Cairo. The particular Arabic script that was used for many of their monumental inscriptions was *thuluth*. Besides building magnificent public and private works of art, the Mamluks of Egypt also considered metalwork an important art form. This is a beautiful example of Mamluk decoration on a brass candlestick with silver inlay. It is from the palace of sultan Qalawun (1279–1290). The Arabic inscription in *thuluth* reads: "the royal prince, the conqueror, the campaigner in holy wars . . .".

The French leader, Napoleon Bonaparte (1769–1821) invaded Egypt in 1798 and fought with Mamluk troops. When Napoleon left Egypt in 1801, he had some Mamluk soldiers in his Imperial Guard, or bodyguard regiment. He continued his campaigns in Europe and even used some Mamluk soldiers during the Battle of Austerlitz in 1805, between the combined forces of the Austrian and Russian empires. In 1806, the Albanian-born Muhammad 'Ali Pasha was chosen to be the new Ottoman governor of Egypt.

The history of the Mamluks of Egypt came to a sudden and violent end several years later. In 1812, Muhammad 'Ali Pasha invited the most important Mamluk leaders to his palace on the citadel in old Cairo. There, the Mamluk nobility were all ambushed and massacred to the last man. The Mamluk era was finally over when thousands of less important Mamluks from all over the country were rounded up and slaughtered.

LEGACY OF THE MAMLUKS

Almost fifty Mamluk sultans had ruled during a period of two and a half centuries. At the height of their power, the Mamluks had controlled territory from Libya to the borders of Iraq and from

Syria to the Hijaz in Arabia. At this time, they controlled the three Holy Cities: Makkah, Madinah and *Al-Quds* (Jerusalem). Not only did the Mamluks beautify their capital of Cairo with more than seven hundred magnificent monuments, they also built exceptional mosques and *madrasahs* in the three Holy Cities. Unlike so many important cities in the Islamic East which were destroyed by the invading Mongols and sometimes never rebuilt, the Mamluk monuments in Cairo and many parts of Syria and Palestine survived such a fate. They remain as some of the finest examples of Islamic art ever created (see illustration 14-3).

CHAPTER FIFTEEN

THE ILKHANIDS OF IRAN (1256–1353)

The Mongols were a nomadic people who, in the thirteenth century, became the rulers of the most extensive empire in history, stretching from Eastern China to the borders of Eastern Europe. What made the Mongols leave their ancestral home on the windswept grasslands of Mongolia? Historians claim that in 1217, a group of Mongol merchants was murdered while passing through the Khwarizm lands of Central Asia. To seek revenge, Jenghiz Khan and his Mongol army moved westwards and thus began the century long Mongol supremacy in the lands of Islam.

JENGHIZ KHAN (1206–1227)

The Mongols were pagans, believing in a form of nature worship called Shamanism. The god of Jenghiz Khan, for example, was *tengri*, the spirit (god) of the upper air or of the "Eternal Blue Sky". Jenghiz Khan believed that he had been sent to Earth to govern all peoples by the power of the Eternal Blue Sky. As they moved westward, some Mongols became Buddhist, while others converted to Nestorian Christianity. Their ability and willingness to change their religion ultimately shaped their future.

The Mongols were ruthless in their conquests. Besides the total destruction and depopulation of scores of cities and towns, farmland was also devastated. Orchards were cut down and salt was spread on once fertile land. For centuries, the inhabitants of the rural areas of Central Asia and Iran had dug and used a complex system of underground water canals called *qanats* to irrigate their fields. When this vast and complex system of canals was destroyed by the Mongols, much farmland was reduced to desert waste. It is reported that Jenghiz Khan despised cities and farmland because they denied him grazing lands for his vast army of mounted soldiers.

HULAGU KHAN (1256–1265)

In 1253, Hulagu Khan and Mongke Khan, grandsons of Jenghiz Khan, decided to pursue two separate military campaigns. While Mongke would move south from the Mongol capital in Karakorum (Mongolia) into Sung China, Hulagu would proceed westwards to eliminate the Isma'ili threat once and for all. Isma'ili terrorists had been a continual threat to many regimes in the Middle East. Any official not accepting the Isma'ili doctrine was open to assassination. The Isma'ilis had even plotted to assassinate the Great Khan Mongke in far-off Karakorum. This was one valid reason for Mongol expansion in the west; a second reason was to obtain the submission of the 'Abbasid caliph in Baghdad.

'ALA' AD-DIN 'ATA MALIK JUWAYNI (1226–1283)

The Persian historian 'Ata Malik Juwayni accompanied Hulagu Khan on his attack and destruction of the Isma'ili fortress of Alamut and followed him throughout his campaign in Persia and as far as

Baghdad. It is said that Juwayni drew up the terms of surrender for the last Isma'ili leader of Alamut and also prevented the destruction of the Isma'ili library there. He witnessed the dismantlement of all Isma'ili fortresses and thus the elimination of the Isma'ili threat. His first hand account of the Mongol invasions is recounted in his Persian-language chronicle, the *Tarikh-i Jahan Gusha* (History of the World Conqueror). He began writing it whilst living in Mongolia in 1252. As the only Persian historian ever to have visited Inner Asia and the homeland of the Mongols, his book offers a unique insider's view of Mongol culture.

After the capture of Baghdad and the end of the 'Abbasid caliphate in 1258, Juwayni was offered the post of governor of all former 'Abbasid territories. He amassed great wealth and several times was arrested on charges of embezzling state funds and even of collusion with the Mamluk enemy.

FATE OF BAGHDAD IN 1258

With Isma'ili terror now a thing of the past, Hulagu proceeded to Baghdad to seek the surrender of the 'Abbasid caliph. A proud and uncompromising Al-Musta'sim either thought Hulagu Khan was bluffing in his ultimatum to surrender, or he somehow believed that *Dar al-Islam* would come to his rescue and he would be saved from a Mongol attack. According to the Mongol rules of warfare (clearly practised by Jenghiz Khan on all his campaigns), a town or city which submitted unconditionally to Mongol suzerainty would be spared the sword. Any hesitation or non-compliance would result in its total annihilation. The Mongols would show no mercy on anyone resisting their invasions. It is reported that they "left no eye open to weep for the dead".

The caliph Al-Musta'sim chose to fight, but eventually had to surrender to Hulagu and was killed. On February 10, 1258, the Mongols entered Baghdad – for centuries the richest city in the world. There they proceeded unhindered to torch palaces and libraries and wantonly pillage and rape. After a one-week rampage, hundreds of thousands of inhabitants lay dead in the streets. Many Nestorian Christians, however, were spared the same fate because Hulagu's mother and favourite wife, Dokuz, were both Christian.

Hulagu Khan had accomplished his two goals in the region: the elimination of both the Isma'ilis and the 'Abbasids. Within a few years, Hulagu began to look covetously at lands, such as Egypt, further to the southwest. However, the Mongol war machine came to a sudden halt when it confronted the extremely well-trained forces of the Mamluk Egyptians. On September 3, 1260, the Mongol advance towards Egypt was curtailed at the Battle of 'Ain Jalut in Palestine. For the first time in its history, the Mongol Empire had been defeated by a Muslim army. But the Mongols did not leave the area. Hulagu's sons established a capital city in Iran from where they ruled as the Ilkhanid dynasty.

MONGOL RELIGIOUS FREEDOM

According to the Great *Yasa* (legal code) of Jenghiz Khan, there was to be freedom of religion throughout the Mongol Empire. Normally, no single religion prevailed in Mongol-held territories. The Mongol leaders themselves appeared to be quite open to the idea of switching faiths and were never fervently religious in any. Although neither Jenghiz Khan nor his brothers ever converted from their shamanist beliefs, Hulagu's sons seemed at first to favour Buddhism. While the vast majority of the Mongols who settled in Iran were Shamanists, the Buddhist Ilkhan leaders imported lamas (priests) from Tibet and even built some temples. There were many Nestorian Christians in Iran as well as pockets of Jews and even some Zoroastrians, who continued to practise the ancient faith of their Sasanian ancestors. The future Ilkhan ruler, Uljaytu Khan (1304–1316), as a child, had been baptised and given the name Nicholas. For a time, it appeared that the Mongols of Iran might all become Christian and, therefore, become aligned with Europe against the Muslims. This was not to happen.

In the year 1295, when Ghazan Khan, the great grandson of Hulagu Khan, formally accepted Islam, the Buddhists either converted to Islam or left Iran. From this moment on, the Ilkhanid dynasty became more and more committed to Islam and eventually all the Mongols adopted the faith of their new homeland.

FIRST ILKHANID RULERS

The Mongols were a new and totally foreign ethnic group to the Middle East. They spoke no Islamic language and believed in a totally different set of values. At Hulagu Khan's funeral in 1265, for example, a human sacrifice was offered to the pagan gods. But the Mongols, despite their terrible history of death and destruction, were able to adapt to change. The control of Mongol-held territories in Iran and Iraq now reverted to Hulagu Khan's son, Abaqa (1265–1282) who made Tabriz, in present-day northwest Iran, the capital of the new Ilkhanid dynasty.

The term *Ilkhan* derives from the Mongolian word meaning "subordinate" khan, i.e. subordinate to the Great Khan in China. Hulagu's descendants retained this title, but their dynasty was no longer dependent on any Mongol leader in the Far East.

A period of several short-lived governments followed the death of Abaqa until the appearance of Hulagu Khan's great grandson, Mahmud Ghazan Khan, in 1295.

MAHMUD GHAZAN KHAN (1295–1304)

Mahmud Ghazan Khan, son of the Ilkhan Arghun (1284–1291), was clearly the most important of all the Ilkhanid rulers and it was during his reign that the Ilkhanid state reached its zenith. Ghazan Khan was known to be ruthless and merciless to anyone who posed a threat to him. He was a polyglot of sorts, having a knowledge of some eight languages: Mongolian, Chinese, Tibetan, Kashmiri, Hindi, one European language (French or Latin), Arabic and Persian.

Ghazan Khan was the first Muslim Ilkhan ruler. In 1295, the year he ascended the throne, he embraced Islam along with most of the ruling Mongol nobles. Ghazan Khan's conversion was likely the single most important factor that led to the assimilation of the Mongols into Persian society. He immediately made Islam the state religion and ordered that a mosque be built in every village of his empire. The wearing of the turban also became common for all court officials. All existing Buddhist temples (many of which, as a Buddhist, he had earlier built) were converted into mosques. Buddhist lamas either converted or were sent back to India, Tibet or China. Jenghiz Khan's book of Mongol law, The Great *Yasa*, was adapted to make it conform to *Shari'ah*, or Islamic Law.

Many of Ghazan Khan's reforms helped to streamline the administration of the Ilkhanid state. Agricultural and tax reforms really protected the hard-working peasants from being oppressed. Ghazan's agricultural reforms included the *iqta'* system of parcelling out farmland to each Mongol soldier who received in lieu of a salary the net results of any harvest. Gaykhatu Khan (1291–1295), Ghazan Khan's predecessor and uncle, had attempted to introduce Chinese-style paper money, called *chao*, that bore both Chinese and Arabic inscriptions. Unfortunately, this proved unsuccessful as the populace were too attached to the old gold and silver coinage and the concept of paper currency was simply too alien to them. After the re-introduction of metal coinage, Ghazan Khan began his currency reforms. Ilkhanid coins would no longer bear inscriptions in Mongolian, Tibetan and Arabic. On his new coins, the Ilkanid ruler was identified, in Arabic only, as ruling "by the Grace of Allah". He was no longer a representative of the Great Khan in China.

Ghazan Khan is also noted for the many public works built during his reign and for several abortive attacks against the Mamluks. Many caravanserais and bridges were built throughout the territories. His capital city, Tabriz, was beautified with many public buildings of exceptional craftsmanship and became a major trading centre along the Silk Road between China and the West. The vehement anti-Mamluk sentiments of all Ilkhanid rulers automatically led to the possibility of closer diplomatic relations with Christian Europe, especially the Vatican in Rome, France and some crusader states in Syria/Palestine. Ghazan, himself, led two campaigns against the Mamluks in Syria. Both were disastrous for the Ilkhanids and no attempt was ever made again to conquer that land.

Our knowledge of the details of Ilkhanid history is due principally to the writings of one man, Rashid ad-Din al-Tabib, the great Persian historian and chronicler of the Ilkhanid dynasty. It was during the reigns of Ghazan Khan and his successor, Uljaytu Khan, that Rashid ad-Din became so influential.

RASHID AD-DIN AL-TABIB (1247–1318)

Rashid ad-Din, like his contemporary 'Ata Malik Juwayni, also wrote from first-hand Mongol sources. While Juwayni travelled with Hulagu Khan on his conquests and visited Mongolia, Rashid ad-Din had access to the inner courts of both Ghazan Khan and Uljaytu Khan. It is the authenticity of his writings that makes them so valuable.

Rashid ad-Din, originally a Jew, was born in the western Iranian city of Hamdan and converted to Islam at the age of thirty. He first worked as a physician in the court of the Ilkhan Abaqa and, for later Ilkhans, as an architect of many important public works. For the last twenty years of his life, he was a *wazir* to the Ilkhans.

Ghazan Khan, perhaps fearing that his people, now Muslim, would forget their history and origins after permanently settling in Iran, asked Rashid ad-Din to write a history of the Mongol people. Ghazan Khan, himself, was a direct source of information, but he also permitted Rashid ad-Din to study the *Altan Debter*, a very secret Mongolian chronicle. Rashid ad-Din met with a representative of the Great Khan who provided him with additional first hand knowledge of the Mongols, their history and traditions. The finished book, the *Tarikh-i Ghazani*, was presented to Ghazan Khan's brother and new sultan, Uljaytu Khan. The new sultan asked Rashid ad-Din to expand his book by including the history of all the peoples of the Mongol Empire. The fame of this author lies in this final work: the *Kitab Jami' al-Tawarikh* (The Universal History) which unquestionably is the best source available for the history of the Mongols.

ULJAYTU KHAN (1304–1316)

Ilkhanid sultans quickly became patrons of Islamic culture. Uljaytu Khan, Ghazan Khan's brother and great grandson of Hulagu Khan, was another very important Ilkhanid ruler. Born a Shamanist, he was later baptised and given the name Nicholas. He converted to Buddhism and later to Sunni Islam after his brother's conversion. Finally, towards the end of his life, as a Shi'ite Muslim, he repressed Sunni Muslims. However, during his life as a Muslim, Uljaytu Khan showed his devotion to Islam by commissioning some outstanding works of Islamic art (see illustration 15-1). He had several copies of the Holy Qur'an copied in the *rayhani* script. These beautiful Qur'ans, whose pages measure 72cm x 50cm, are some of the largest ever written.

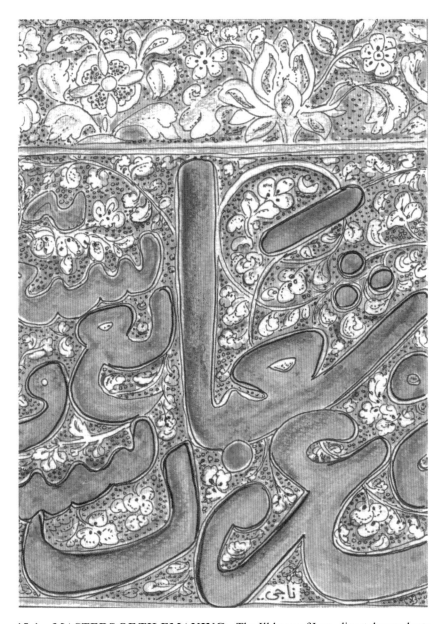

15-1   MASTERS OF TILEMAKING: The Ilkhans of Iran, direct descendants of the Mongols Jenghiz Khan and Hulagu Khan, became Muslims and patrons of Islamic art. Some of the most beautiful tile work ever produced came from Ilkhanid workshops. This superb example of Islamic art is a "lustre tile". Such tiles were produced in large numbers in the central Iranian town of Kashan. First, extremely intricate floral patterns were painted on the flat surface of the tile. The Arabic calligraphy was moulded in high relief and was painted a deep cobalt blue. Glazes were then applied, giving the tiles their characteristic metallic lustre. On this tile which dates from 1310, one can clearly read the Arabic month *sha'ban*, the month in which this work of art was made.

15-2   THE ILKHAN TAJ MAHAL: All that survives of the second Ilkhan capital at Sultaniyah is Uljaytu's famous mausoleum. In this remote region of northwestern Iran, the pink-coloured brick monument rises fifty metres above the single-storied mud houses of the village surrounding it. The egg-shaped dome was once covered with turquoise-blue tiles and eight tall minarets once proudly encircled it. Uljaytu's tomb, originally designed as a pilgrimage centre, was clearly made to impress. From a distance, on the flat wind-swept plains, this building must have reminded some of the Dome of the Rock in Jerusalem (see illustration 1-2), and others of a semi-circular nomadic Mongol tent.

In 1313, Uljaytu Khan transferred the Ilkhanid capital from Tabriz to the new city of Sultaniyah, further south. Uljaytu began constructing a large mausoleum that he intended for himself. When he converted from Sunni Islam to Shi'ite Islam, he decided to make the building a shrine for the mortal remains of Imam 'Ali ؏ and Imam Hussain ؏. Their bodies were to be transported from Iraq to Sultaniyah, thus making it an important Shi'ite place of pilgrimage. But this plan was not adopted and the gigantic building was used to house the tomb of Uljaytu when he died in 1316. The concept of placing the dead in tombs or mausoleums was not a *sunnah* of the Prophet ﷺ, but became a common practice in many Muslim societies. Today, the mausoleum of Uljaytu stands alone on a flat landscape as the last surviving Ilkhanid monument in Sultaniyah (see illustration 15-2). It is sometimes called the "Ilkhanid Taj Mahal" because of its imposing egg-shaped dome which was once covered in turquoise-blue glazed tiles. It is certainly a masterpiece of earth architecture and an early attempt by the Ilkhanid Mongols to identify with their new Islamic culture. The Mausoleum of Uljaytu Khan, even in ruins, is one of the most beautiful buildings in all of Asia.

ABU SA'ID (1316–1335)

The golden age of Ilkhanid rule had now passed. Abu Sa'id, the son of Uljaytu Khan, became sultan on the death of his father in 1316. He was the first Mongol ruler to be given a Muslim name at birth (see illustration 15-3). He restored Sunni Islam as the state religion and also made peace with the Mamluks of Egypt who had been the Ilkhanid archenemy for decades.

Abu Sa'id left no sons, so upon his death in 1335, the Ilkhanid state disintegrated. Regional governors established their own short-lived dynasties such as the Jalayrids of western Iran and Iraq and the Muzaffirids of Shiraz in southern Iran. An anarchy of sorts prevailed until the arrival of Timur-i Lang.

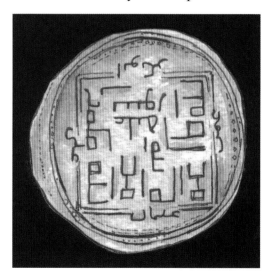

15-3 ABU SA'ID SILVER: Although not as famous as his son Uljaytu Khan, the Ilkhan ruler Abu Sa'id did restore *sunni* Islam as the state religion. This beautiful example of Islamic art in miniature dates from the time of Abu Sa'id (1316–1335). It is a silver *dirham* and bears the *kalimah* inside the square. Encircling it are the names of the four *Khulafa' ar-Rashidun* (the Rightly-Guided Caliphs).

LEGACY OF THE ILKHANIDS

The Black Death (the deadly bubonic plague) that killed millions of victims in Europe and many parts of Asia in the fourteenth century, did not spare the Middle East. The civilian population of Ilkhanid cities suffered as well as soldiers in the Ilkhanid army. It may be said that the real reason Mongol rule ended was because the ethnic Mongol population of Western Asia had simply become too small to govern so vast an area.

The Mongols arrived in Iran as oriental nomadic warriors having a culture alien to that of the Islamic states that were being conquered. Within a century, however, they had become totally assimilated into Islamic society. Mongols for the first time in their history gave up their nomadic lifestyle replacing it with farming, an occupation once considered beneath their dignity. They learned Arabic, Persian and Turkish which, in time, replaced their native Mongol tongue. Finally, by embracing the religion of the society they had conquered and by marrying indigenous women, the assimilation was complete.

Perhaps the most enduring legacy of the Mongols is the fact that the borders of the Ilkhanid state seven hundred years ago closely resemble those of present-day Iran.

CHAPTER SIXTEEN
THE TIMURIDS (1370–1506)

Perhaps the most important event after the great destruction caused by the first Mongol invasion of Muslim lands was the conversion of the Mongols from Shamanism, Buddhism and Christianity to Islam. The hordes of Jenghiz Khan first appeared in Western Asia in the early thirteenth century and by the end of the century, his great grandsons had all become Muslim. Because of this, Islamic culture and civilisation were further enriched by those who had once intended to destroy it forever. After the death of the last important Ilkhanid sultan, Abu Sa'id in 1335, a series of weak governments could not bring unity to the empire. The power vacuum created was soon filled by yet another world conqueror from the East: Timur-i Lang. But unlike Jenghiz Khan and Hulagu Khan before him, this new Turkicised Mongol invader claimed to be a Muslim.

TIMUR-I LANG (1370–1405)

The name Timur derives from a Chaghatai Turkish word meaning "iron"; indeed, the modern Turkish word for iron is *demir*. Timur was born in a small town, Shahr-i Sabz (Green City), about fifty kilometres south of the Uzbek city of Samarqand in the year 1336. He was the son of the leader of a Turkic tribe, the Barlas, who had joined forces with Jenghiz Khan a century before. This tribe had, over the years, lost its Mongol identity and become more Turkish.

Timur was a Turkish nomad who grew up on the plains of Central Asia. In his early years he led the life of a bandit. While still in his twenties, he was wounded by an arrow in his right leg, which left him with a permanent limp. He was thus known by his Persian name, *Timur-i Lang* (Timur the Lame or Tamerlane in English).

Because of his defence of Transoxania against the nomadic raids from Mughulistan (areas co-extensive with the present-day Xinjiang province of western China and Kirghiztan), Timur's fame increased. Finally, in 1370, he gained control of Balkh in northern Afghanistan, became its ruler and returned to Samarqand proclaiming himself *amir* of the Chaghatai Khanate and restorer of the Mongol Empire. Over the next ten years, Timur fought all his neighbours until he had expanded his empire into western China and most of Central Asia. He was to spend the remaining twenty years of his life attempting to re-conquer lands once held by Jenghiz, the Great Khan. Most of his adult life was thus spent waging a series of endless campaigns of conquest which sadly resulted in the wanton destruction of countless cities and towns of Western Asia, such as Isfahan, Baghdad and Damascus, whose beautiful centres of Islamic culture were plundered and their populations slaughtered.

Timur was not a Mongol and was in many ways very different from the founder of the empire he wished to restore. He fabricated a genealogy linking him to the Great Khan. In fact, Timur's life resembled neither that of his hero, nor that of a God-fearing Muslim. He actually believed he had been sent by Allah as a punishment to Muslims. Despite the amazing architectural wonders Timur had built for himself in Samarqand and the flowering of Islamic culture that eventually emanated from the Timurid dynasty, his senseless slaughter and almost sadistic pleasure in torturing his victims clearly mark him as a human failure.

TIMUR'S CONQUESTS

Timur might have been a gifted military leader, but, unlike Jenghiz Khan, lacked the political acumen to be able to retain the lands he conquered. After his capture of the lands between the Black and the Caspian Seas and some Russian territories, Timur began his successful conquest of Persia. Between 1383 and 1394, all the previous Ilkhanid territories were now added to Timur's expanding empire. The local descendants of the Ilkhanid dynasty could not oppose the might of Timur's organised army. First, Herat and all of Khorasan and eastern Iran fell, followed by southern Iran, Iraq and the Caucasus Mountains region (including Azerbaijan, Armenia and Georgia). During all of these campaigns, Timur showed his penchant for ruthless slaughter. In 1387, for example, the inhabitants of Isfahan rejected the Timurid occupation of their beautiful Persian city and ended up massacring a garrison of some 3,000 Mongol soldiers. Upon hearing this, Timur returned to Isfahan and punished the city by beheading 70,000 of its citizens! The heads were made into two huge pyramids and placed at the entrance to the city. This reign of terror was brought to all the lands he conquered.

INVASION OF INDIA (1398)

Timur was more than sixty years old when he set his eyes on Delhi, the wealthy capital of the *mamluk* sultanate of northern India. Historians maintain he invaded India in the belief that the Muslim sultans of Delhi had shown too much tolerance to their Hindu subjects. On September 24, 1398, Timur crossed over the mighty Indus River and then began his bloody march towards Delhi. On December 17 of the same year, Timur and his army met the forces of Sultan Mahmud Tughluq on the banks of the Yamuna River, between Panipat and Delhi.

Mahmud Tughluq and his army were totally defeated in battle. Timur then proceeded to Delhi where he crowned himself "Emperor of Hindustan". The city was left in ruins and the population decimated. An enormous amount of booty was taken from the pillaged capital and transported to Samarqand. A caravan of ninety elephants loaded with the spoils of war along with captured artisans, architects and engineers proceeded north to Timur's capital, which ironically, he had transformed into a flourishing cultural oasis of immense artistic beauty.

OCCUPATION OF DAMASCUS (1401)

Within a year, Timur once again made his way westwards to confront the Mamluks of Egypt who always seemed to be in conflict with the Mongols. In 1401, Timur entered Damascus prompting the young Mamluk sultan, al-Faraj, son of Sultan Barquq, to lead a military campaign against the Timurids. Travelling along with al-Faraj and his Mamluk army was the great Arab social historian, Ibn Khaldun.

Ibn Khaldun (1332–1406) is credited as being the "father of sociology". A Tunisian by birth, he had spent years working at the courts of both Spanish and Moroccan rulers. However, he spent the last years of his life in Cairo working as a Maliki *qadi* for various Mamluk sultans.

We are told that Ibn Khaldun rather reluctantly left Cairo along with the Mamluk army and the new inexperienced Sultan al-Faraj. On reaching the walls of Damascus, al-Faraj was told of an uprising in Cairo. He deserted his army, leaving them without leadership, and fled back to Cairo. Ibn Khaldun remained in Damascus for seven weeks during which time he conducted several historic meetings with Timur who was fascinated by Ibn Khaldun's erudition. Apparently Ibn Khaldun, tied with ropes, was lowered down the walls of Damascus in order to conduct these meetings. Timur questioned Ibn Khaldun extensively about the geography, peoples and customs of North Africa while Ibn Khaldun used the opportunity to increase his knowledge of Mongol history. Unfortunately, Ibn Khaldun was unsuccessful in dissuading Timur from pillaging Damascus. For three days, Timur's soldiers ran amok in the city's streets, totally destroying the "pearl of Syria". Only skilled artisans and Islamic scholars were spared the sword and they were immediately transported to Samarqand to begin work on another one of Timur's grandiose building projects or to teach in one of the many large *madrasahs* there. But Timur's notoriety preceded him wherever he went and, until his death, no one really felt safe in his vast realm.

BATTLE OF ANKARA (JULY 28, 1402)

Timur, as the restorer of the empire of Jenghiz Khan, thought it only natural for him to be the inheritor of all Anatolian territories which had been formerly held by the Seljuqs of Rum and the Ilkhanids. Bayezid I, the sultan of the fledgling Ottoman state, came directly into contact with Timur when the Ottomans occupied the town of Sivas in eastern Anatolia in the summer of 1398. Two years later, Sivas was taken by Timurid forces, thus initiating the conflict that almost ended Ottoman rule for good.

On July 28, 1402 on the open plain of Chubuk (on the outskirts of present-day Ankara, Turkey), the two armies met and fought a battle whose humiliating defeat and subsequent civil war and succession struggles between surviving Ottoman princes were never to be forgotten by the Turkish people. The Battle of Ankara lasted one full day. The Ottoman army was approximately half the size of Timur's. The Ottoman troops had been marching from the west over the parched waterless Anatolian plateau and when they arrived at Chubuk, they were exhausted and thirsty. Timur had cleverly diverted the flow of the Chubuk Creek, the only source of water in the area. Bayezid's tired and thirsty troops fought poorly and many deserted to Timur's ranks or simply refused to fight. The battle, not surprisingly, was an utter defeat for the Ottomans. Sultan Bayezid I was captured along with his son, Musa. Only his eldest son, Sulaiman, and two younger sons, Isa and Mehmed, escaped the battlefield with the remnants of the Ottoman forces.

The story of Bayezid being transported like a caged animal to be exhibited in the grand public square in Samarqand is pure fiction. He simply died of natural causes in 1403. He left a newly founded empire in tatters - an empire that would suffer a long and bitter dynastic crisis before it could be restored twelve years later, with Mehmed I finally being proclaimed Ottoman sultan.

With total dissension in the Ottoman ranks and brother vying against brother for control of the throne, the ancient Greek Byzantine Empire centred in Constantinople was given another half century to live. It was only in 1453 that a new Ottoman sultan, the young Mehmed II, was finally able to bring that city and the surrounding lands into the Ottoman realm and the fold of Islam.

TIMUR'S DEATH

Qubilai Khan (Hulagu Khan's brother) and his descendants had successfully ruled China for a century, but by 1368, the Mongol Yuan dynasty had been replaced by the Chinese Ming dynasty. After the campaigns in western Anatolia, Timur, now an old man in his late sixties, returned to Samarqand where he planned a military attack on the Ming emperor of China with the aim of restoring Mongol rule there.

In December 1404, Timur set out on what would be his last campaign. He died of a fever at his campsite at Otrar (north of Samarqand in present-day Kazakhstan) on February 18, 1405. His body was placed in a black coffin and buried in a magnificent mausoleum in Samarqand – the *Gur-i Amir* (see illustration 16-1).

Thus ended the life of the iron-willed Timur-i Lang, a world conqueror whose violent life was one full of contradictions. To this day, in the Arab and Persian worlds, Timur is known as "Timur the World Conqueror", or *Jihan Gusha*, in Persian.

His vast, but fragile empire, would soon disintegrate as governors in the remoter areas asserted their independence. But led by his sons and descendants, the Timurid Empire, despite its reduced size – now comprising only *ma wara' an-nahr* (Transoxiana) and Afghanistan – survived for another century.

SAMARQAND

Timur conquered many ancient cities in Western Asia, but at a cost. So many beautiful historical cities of culture were left in utter ruins. It is not surprising, therefore, that Samarqand became Timur's favourite city and his capital. Throughout his life, Timur would always return to Samarqand with new ideas of beautifying it.

Samarqand, in present-day Uzbekistan, was situated in Transoxiana. This region became part of *Dar al-Islam* very early in the eighth century when the army of Qutayba ibn Muslim captured the major cities of Transoxiana, including Samarqand.

The city soon became an important centre of Islamic scholarship, especially after the Arabs learned the art of papermaking. Chinese captives had been brought to Samarqand after the Battle of Talas in 751 and the secret of papermaking was then revealed to the Arabs. Many subsequent Persian and Turkish dynasties continued to beautify the city.

But, unquestionably, it was during the reign of Timur that Samarqand became one of the greatest cities of the world. Timur, as we have seen, would pillage and destroy cities of wealth and beauty but made sure that the most gifted craftsmen and scientists were carried off to work on his on-going construction projects in Samarqand. Not surprisingly, therefore, the master stonemasons from Delhi and Isfahan, the ceramic tile experts from Shiraz and countless other experienced woodcarvers, weavers, glass-blowers and ironmongers from all over Western Asia, produced works of art that had few rivals. Even today, Timur's public buildings (mosques, *madrasahs* and mausoleum complexes), covered in the most exquisite multi-coloured tile mosaics, continue to amaze and remind all who see them of the time when Samarqand was known as the "centre of the world".

SHAH RUKH (1409–1447)

There were definite similarities – both in life and in death – between Timur and his great predecessor, Jenghiz Khan. When Timur died in 1405, the vast Timurid Empire was divided amongst his two sons, Miranshah and Shah Rukh. Miranshah had been given the western territories of Iraq, Azerbaijan and Georgia to govern while Shah Rukh had received Khorasan. Within two years of Miranshah's death in 1407, Shah Rukh was able to reunite most of his father's empire except for areas of Anatolia and parts of Iran and Iraq which were lost to Turkish tribes.

Samarqand was located on the fabled Silk Road linking China with the Mediterranean seaports and was a constant source of revenue for the Timurid dynasty. During the reign of Shah Rukh, economic prosperity gave birth to a thriving new Timurid cultural centre in the capital of Herat in northwestern

16-1   TIMUR'S TOMB: In life, Timur-i Lang waged war against the civilised Muslim world. He claimed to be a pious Muslim, but would leave city after city in ruins with their inhabitants dead and sometimes decapitated. The only ones saved from the slaughter of innocents were skilled craftsmen. Timur would transport such artisans to Samarqand, to beautify his capital. Like the Ilkhans of Iran, for Timur and his descendants, architecture was very important. Timur's conquest and reign of terror ended with his death in 1405. He lies buried in his tomb, the *Gur-i Amir* (tomb of the prince, in Persian), in Samarqand. In this building, we see for the first time, a ribbed dome placed on a high drum base. Glazed bricks below the ribbed dome spell out in Kufi script, *al-Baqa' li-llah*, or "Eternity is for Allah". The melon-shaped dome is covered with priceless turquoise and blue tiles. After six centuries, this building continues to impress all who see it. In fact, many architects consider the *Gur-i Amir* to be one of the most perfect buildings ever constructed.

Afghanistan where artists and writers found a welcoming patron. Shah Rukh was extremely curious about foreign lands and welcomed foreign delegations to Herat. Some of them have left written accounts of their visits to the Timurid court.

Herat, during Timurid rule, became a lively centre of Persian culture where the multi-ethnic origins of the Timurid rulers also influenced artistic production (see illustration 16-2). Besides Arabic, Chaghatai Turkish was used by court poets and writers who generated a considerable amount of fine poetry in this language. Finally, Gawhar (Jawhar) Shad, Shah Rukh's wife, outshone her husband by commissioning the construction of two superbly beautiful Timurid mosque and *madrasah* complexes: one in Herat, the other in Mashhad (see title page illustration).

Finally, mention must be made of Prince Baysunqur (lived 1399–1433), the second son of Shah Rukh who served a *wazir* in his father's court at Herat. He never became sultan as court astrologers had predicted a short life for him. Baysunqur was, however, a gifted artist and a patron of the arts. He was an accomplished calligrapher and in his lifetime produced some true works of art. Initially, he copied the Qur'an in miniature, but was rebuked by his elders for thus diminishing *Kitab Allah*.

16-2 TIMURID TILE WORK: Despite being an infamous "world conqueror", Timur-i Lang is known equally for his incredible patronage of Islamic art. The Timurid capital of Samarqand was a city of great wealth and visitors to it wrote of beautiful tiled palaces set in flowering gardens. Timurid architects made use of tile in all the buildings they erected. Here is an example of the famous "star tile" made of stone paste. Hundreds of such colourful tiles would be placed in brick walls to create a truly dazzling effect.

Baysunqur later transcribed the Qur'an onto pages seventy inches in length. Sadly, only several pages of this astonishingly beautiful Qur'an survive; they are housed today in the Museum of the Imam Reza Mausoleum in Mashhad, Iran.

ULUGH BEG (1447–1449)

Perhaps the greatest of all Timur's successors was his grandson, Ulugh Beg, the eldest son of Shah Rukh. On the death of his father in 1447, Ulugh Beg became the new sultan. He was born in Sultaniyah, the Ilkhanid capital, in 1394 and travelled with his grandfather, Timur, on many of his conquests. Even though he ruled for only two years, Ulugh Beg made Samarqand an important centre of Islamic culture.

When Shah Rukh transferred his capital to Herat in 1409, he named his sixteen-year-old son, Ulugh Beg, governor of Samarqand. As governor, he transformed the city – which already had been bestowed with amazing monuments by his grandfather – into the intellectual capital of the Timurid Empire. Ulugh Beg was clearly unlike his grandfather, whose main interest had been territorial conquest. By nature, he was a scholar and it is thus befitting that the two buildings he spent time erecting were both educational institutions: his *madrasah* and his observatory.

Between the years 1417 and 1421, Ulugh Beg constructed his immense *madrasah* whose façade was covered in intricate, multi-coloured, glazed tile mosaics. It was here to the magnificent *madrasah* in one corner of Samarqand's famous Registan Square that Ulugh Beg invited renowned astronomers and mathematicians.

But it is for his observatory and important astronomical writings that Ulugh Beg is most remembered. In fact, many scientists today claim he was the most important observational astronomer of the fifteenth century. In 1428, he built his three-storey circular observatory, the *gurkhaneh-i zij*. For the first time in history, astronomical instruments were permanently fixed inside an observatory. As the telescope was yet to be invented, Ulugh Beg made use of complex, over-sized sextants in his observations. The so-called Fakhri sextant that he used was a sixty-degree stone arc having a radius of almost forty metres! Sadly, all that remains of this unique observatory is the large semi-circular cut in the earth in which the sextant was mounted. It is not an exaggeration to claim that Ulugh Beg's observatory was the most important one of its kind ever constructed in the pre-modern Islamic world.

Ulugh Beg's greatest contribution to science was his *Zij-i Sultani* (Catalogue of the Stars) in which he identified the precise position of almost one thousand stars. Such accurate calculations could only have been made by using the most advanced astronomical instruments available at the time. Using mathematical data obtained from his observatory, he calculated the length of the year to be 365 days, 5 hours, 49 minutes and 15 seconds. These amazing contributions to the world of knowledge were recognised even by the non-Muslim world; to honour Ulugh Beg, a crater on the Moon was named after him in the nineteenth century.

Ulugh Beg, as a Muslim scientist, had made Samarqand the astronomical capital of the world. His research and interest in astronomy was the culmination of centuries of Islamic scholarship. Complex astronomical tables had first been produced in Baghdad during the time of the caliph Ma'mun in the ninth century. Ibn Yunus, another great Muslim astronomer, worked in his own Cairo observatory during the Fatimid caliphate of Al-Hakim in the early eleventh century. Even the Ilkhanid sultans had built an observatory which Nasir ad-Din Tusi (1201–1274) used to produce the Ilkhanid tables (*Zij-i Ilkhani*). These extremely accurate "star catalogues" were painstakingly collected over many years and are an important contribution to scientific knowledge.

DECLINE OF THE TIMURIDS

Ulugh Beg's eldest son, 'Abd al-Latif, was unhappy about his father's many secular interests and hired an assassin to kill him. However, the following year, in 1450, 'Abd al-Latif himself also died.

In 1452, Abu Sa'id, grandson of Miranshah, brought the remnants of the empire under his control. His successor, Sultan Husayn Bayqara (1470[?]–1506), a grandson of yet another of Timur-i Lang's sons, Umar Shaykh, ruled for almost forty years. During his reign, he ushered in a short-lived, but truly remarkable, Islamic Renaissance. Herat flourished as a centre of learning and the creative arts. Three luminaries exemplify this period: the Chaghatai Turkish poet 'Ali Sir Nava'i, the founder of Turkish literature; Bihzad, the painter of exquisite miniatures; and Jami', the last of the great classical Persian poets.

The period after Timur's death had surprisingly become the golden age of the Timurid dynasty, a time when his sons, lacking their father's desire for bloodthirsty conquest, had all become patrons of the arts and sciences. However, shortly after the death of Sultan Husayn Bayqara in 1506, the Uzbek army of Muhammad Shaibani put an end to Timurid rule in the region.

The last Timurid ruler of Ferghana, Zahir ad-Din Babur, a fifth generation descendant of Timur, was finally deposed in 1511. He fled south to Afghanistan for protection. Several years later, Babur founded his own dynasty: the Mughals of India.

CHAPTER SEVENTEEN
THE OTTOMANS (1281–1922)

Many of the Islamic dynasties discussed so far in this book lasted for no more than a century or two. The longest surviving Islamic dynasty and also the greatest in many ways was that of the Ottoman Turks. The Ottoman Empire at its zenith extended from western Algeria across North Africa to the Arabian coast of the Persian Gulf and from the dense forests of Central Europe to the craggy mountains of Yemen. For more than six hundred years, their unique culture dominated Southeastern Europe and much of the Middle East. A total of thirty-eight rulers – all direct descendants of the dynasty's founding father – governed Ottoman territories beginning in the late thirteenth century and ending in the early twentieth century.

SELJUQ CONNECTIONS

The ancestral homeland of the Turkish people was the grassland of Mongolia in East Asia. The first Turks to arrive in present-day Turkey were the nomadic Seljuq tribes led by Alp Arslan in 1071, the year in which the Byzantine emperor was defeated at the Battle of Malazgirt. Much of eastern Turkey was subsequently inhabited by these Turkish-speaking nomads who had all embraced Islam a century before. The Seljuq Turks were *ghazis*, always extending the borders of *Dar al-Islam*.

The Seljuqs who remained in Anatolia established their own dynasty, the Seljuqs of Rum whose capital was Konya. By the end of the thirteenth century, the Seljuq state had weakened after the Mongol invasions of Hulagu Khan and was divided into many small principalities each headed by a tribal chief or *bey*. Many of these nomadic Turkish tribes had entered Seljuq territory years before. One such group of nomads was the Sőğűt who settled near the Sakarya River in Western Turkey. When its chief, Ertoğrul, died in 1280 or 1281, his son, Osman, became leader.

OSMAN I (1281–1326)

Osman Bey conducted many raids against the Byzantine (Eastern Greek) Christians whose capital was Constantinople. Many Byzantine towns and villages in western Turkey fell to the Muslim *ghazis* led by Osman. Just before he died, Bursa, the largest Byzantine city in Anatolia was captured in 1324. Osman's son, Orhan (1326–1359), continued his father's practice of conquest and after 1357, brought Macedonia, Serbia and Bulgaria under Turkish control. The third ruler of this growing empire, Murad I, seized power in 1359 on the death of his father, Orhan. By 1372, the majority of Byzantine territory had been captured by Turkish forces. Murad I led his troops even deeper into Europe. In 1383, he proclaimed himself sultan and the dynasty founded by his grandfather, Osman, was officially given the name *Osmanli* (supporters of Osman) or Ottoman.

BATTLE OF KOSOVO (JUNE 28, 1389)

Murad I led a large army of Turkish soldiers and volunteers from neighbouring countries and met the Serbian king, Lazar, on the Plain of Kosovo (in the southwestern part of the former Yugoslavia) in the summer of 1389. This was a concerted effort on behalf of the Serbs to expel the Turks from the Balkans. In the ensuing battle, both sides suffered catastrophic losses. Murad I died of a stab wound from a poisoned dagger while Lazar and most of the Serbian nobility (an estimated 150 knights) all perished on the battlefield.

Murad's son, Bayezid, had been in his father's tent when the latter was assassinated. As the new Ottoman sultan, Bayezid I (1389–1402), he successfully routed the Serbian forces ensuring victory for the Ottoman Turks. Bayezid I then clinched an alliance with the Serbs by marrying the daughter of King Lazar. In time, the Serbs allied themselves with their former enemies. A few years later, in 1402, the Serbs even fought alongside Bayezid I at the Battle of Ankara.

It was at this battle that Timur-i Lang entered Ottoman territory and defeated Bayezid I on the plains just outside of Ankara – the present-day capital of Turkey. The great Sultan Bayezid I, known as *yıldırım* or "the Thunderbolt" because of his speedy and successful military campaigns, had extended the frontiers of the Ottoman Empire to include northern Greece. Now, in facing Timur-i Lang, he was battling a different foe and lost. Bayezid was captured in battle and died shortly thereafter. His death led directly to a chaotic struggle for power among his four sons. Historians agree that this interregnum enabled the tiny Byzantine Empire to survive for another half century. No strong united Ottoman force was able to confront the waning Byzantine state until the middle of the fifteenth century.

Janissaries

The result of the Ottoman defeat at the Battle of Ankara and the death of Bayezid I, led to an internal struggle for power between the remaining sons. Eventually, Mehmed I succeeded to the Ottoman throne. He moved the capital from Bursa (in Asian Turkey) to Edirne (north of Istanbul, in European Turkey). Leading the Ottoman army into Europe in the spring became an annual event for each Ottoman sultan. By now, the Ottoman Empire needed a large army to defend its expanding borders. The great victories over Byzantine and Serbian troops had been due to the extremely well-trained and efficient Ottoman infantry units. These troops were called the Janissaries (or *yeni cheri*, Turkish for new troops). They became the bodyguard of the sultan and their loyalty to him and the Ottoman state was unquestioned.

The Janissary troops, the real "fighting machine" of the Ottomans, have an interesting history. Early Ottoman leaders discovered that soldiers from their own Turkish tribes could not always be trusted; their loyalty could be bought or sold. In the fourteenth century, during the time of Murad I, a system of recruiting "slave soldiers" (very similar to the *mamluks* in Egypt) from non-Muslim lands was introduced. A quota of young Christian boys (between the ages of seven and fourteen) was regularly taken from Ottoman territories – mostly Albania, Bosnia and Bulgaria – and educated in very special training schools in the capital.

Although *devshirmeh*, the practice of recruiting young boys for government service, was detested by some parents who hated to lose their sons, others saw it as a means to ensure a better social status for their children. Most of the boys became Muslim and considered the sultan as their father. For almost five hundred years, the Janissaries protected the Ottoman sultans and, as individuals, some rose to positions of great power. All the major military campaigns in Ottoman history involved Janissary troops. They formed the backbone of the Ottoman Empire until they were considered an undesired anachronistic detriment to attempts at modernising the Ottoman army. The Janissary corps were finally disbanded by the reform-minded Sultan Mahmud II in 1826.

MEHMED II (1444–1446 AND 1451–1481)

Mehmed II, grandson of Mehmed I, was one of the greatest of all Ottoman rulers. He first became sultan in August 1444, at the age of twelve, after his father, Murad II, had made peace with the Karaman princedom in central Anatolia. After two years, Mehmed persuaded his father to reclaim the throne. But when his father died in 1451, Mehmed II became sultan for a second time. He had received a good education and is reported to have been fluent in seven languages, including Turkish, Byzantine Greek, Arabic, Persian, Hebrew and Latin. He was also a great patron of Muslim scientists and artists.

By the middle of the fifteenth century, the Ottoman state had expanded from Asia into many parts of Southeastern Europe. The once great Byzantine Empire had been reduced to the area around its capital, Constantinople. The conquest of this city had always been a goal of Muslims since the earliest days of Islam. The following well-known and oft-quoted *hadith* of the Prophet ﷺ is found in the *Musnad* of Ahmad ibn Hanbal, among other collections of *ahadith*.

> Verily you shall conquer Constantinople [Istanbul]. What a wonderful leader will her leader be, and what a wonderful army will that army be!

Many later historians thus believed Muhammad ﷺ had prophesised Mehmed II's conquest of the city.

In 1452, Mehmed II, decided to conquer the great Byzantine city and make it his "capital of the world". By way of preparation, he built a large stone fortress (see illustration 17-1) on the shores of the Bosphorus Straits just outside of Constantinople. He named the castle *Rumeli Hisari* (European fortress). By the following year, the twenty-one year old Mehmed II was ready to attack and was able to finally capture the Byzantine capital on May 29. The one thousand year-old Church of Haghia Sophia was quickly converted into a mosque as were other churches. Christians and Jews were not evicted from the city. Indeed, the Ottoman Empire became a refuge for Jews fleeing persecution in Christian Europe. The Jewish community found in Istanbul today are descendants of Jews who fled from Spain five centuries ago.

CONSTANTINOPLE, THE OTTOMAN CAPITAL

After the conquest of Constantinople, Sultan Mehmed II became known as Mehmed *al-Fath*, the Conqueror. He immediately began to make the city a world capital. It was first repopulated as people from all over the empire were invited to live in the rapidly growing city. Building projects greatly changed the character of Constantinople, but without destroying the older parts. Mosque and *madrasah* complexes (some still active today), caravanserais, covered markets, public baths and palaces all made the new Ottoman capital a wondrous city to behold. The great age of the Ottomans had begun!

With the capture of Constantinople, Mehmed II was able to consolidate his control over Anatolia. He now believed he was the new "Roman Caesar" and, therefore, attempted an invasion of Rome in 1480 with the aim of reviving the Roman Empire as an Islamic Empire. However, military links were sabotaged by an Albanian rebel named Skander-beg, which resulted in a defeat by the overwhelming strength of the army lead by Pope Sixtus IV in 1481. However, Mehmed II did come amazingly close to conquering Italy.

17-1 MEHMED II'S FORTRESS: Before his conquest of Constantinople in 1453, the young Ottoman sultan, Mehmed II, built a stone fortress just outside the city, on the shores of the Bosphorus. The walls are seven metres thick in some places. This is an eighteenth century miniature painting of the *Rumeli Hisari* (European castle/fortress). This restored fortress is still standing along the Bosphorus and is an important tourist attraction.

OTTOMAN TURKISH LANGUAGE

Constantinople soon became a multi-ethnic society. Traders, students and scholars from all over the Empire resided in the city. Arabic, Persian, Albanian, Armenian, Bosnian, Georgian, Greek, Kurdish, and many other languages could be heard on its streets. The educated Ottoman nobility spoke a very refined form of Turkish called *osmanlija*, which also used many Persian and Arabic words and grammatical structures.

A speaker of *osmanlija* was accepted as an *osmanli* or true "Ottoman" while the uneducated villager who spoke a Turkish dialect was referred to as a "Turk".

SELIM I (1512–1520)

Sultan Selim I was another very important Ottoman ruler. His father, Bayezid II, had succeeded Mehmed II as sultan in 1481. Bayezid II is remembered for sending the fledgling Ottoman navy to Spain in order to rescue Jews who were fleeing the Spanish Inquisition in 1492.

Selim I dethroned his father and immediately had his own brothers and nephews killed to eliminate any potential rivals, a policy initiated by Mehmed II to prevent any succession turmoil resembling that which took place after the capture of Bayezid I in 1402 at the Battle of Ankara. But it is because of his habit of frequently having his grand viziers executed that he is known as "Selim the Grim".

In the early part of the sixteenth century, a new rival empire appeared on the eastern borders of the Ottoman state. A young Shah Isma'il had forcibly converted his people from Sunni to Shi'ite Islam and had established the Safavid dynasty of Persian kings. For two hundred years, the Safavids and Ottomans would be at war. In order to prevent Shah Isma'il from expanding his empire further west into Syria and Palestine, Selim I confronted the Egyptian Mamluks whose territories included Syria, Palestine and the two Holy Cities of Makkah and Madinah in Arabia.

Selim I defeated the Mamluks at the Battle of Marj Dabiq in northern Syria in 1516. The following year, the victorious Ottoman sultan entered Cairo, the Mamluk capital. The Ottoman Janissary troops had played a major role in the military defeat of this once powerful dynasty.

The "shadow caliph", Al-Mutawakkil III (1509–1517) – the last of the 'Abbasid caliphs who had ruled from Cairo alongside Mamluk sultans ever since the fall of Baghdad in 1257 – was taken to Constantinople. He relinquished all rights to the caliphate and surrendered the sword and cloak of the Prophet ﷺ to Selim I. The title and power of the 'Abbasid caliph was thus passed on to the Ottoman sultans who held it until the beginning of the twentieth century. During the reign of Sulaiman I (Selim's son), Al-Mutawakkil III was permitted to return to Cairo from his exile in the Ottoman capital.

During his relatively short reign, Selim I had more than doubled the size of the empire through his many successful campaigns. Selim was a gifted poet and his poems in Ottoman Turkish and Persian are still read today.

SULAIMAN I (1520–1566)

The Ottomans experienced a golden age during the long reign of Sulaiman I. During this period, the Ottoman Empire reached its zenith and became the most powerful state in the world.

Upon the death of his father, Selim I in 1520, Sulaiman I became the new Ottoman sultan at the age of twenty-six. Like his predecessors, he possessed military acumen and personally led his army into battle as a true *ghazi*. The borders of the Ottoman Empire were extended to include parts of the present-day countries of Russia, Iran and Saudi Arabia as well as Turkey, Greece, Albania, Bulgaria, Bosnia, Croatia, Macedonia, Yugoslavia, Romania, Hungary, Algeria, Tunisia, Libya, Egypt, Palestine, Lebanon, Syria, Jordan, Iraq and Kuwait. Even parts of Sudan, Eritrea, and Yemen were at one time all Ottoman domains. Sulaiman I ruled for forty-seven years, thirty of which were spent campaigning.

Sulaiman I was known in Turkish as *kanuni*, or the "law giver", but in Europe, he was admiringly referred to as "Sulaiman the Magnificent". During his reign, both Qur'anic and new temporal laws were codified as never before. He truly believed that Allah had given him the entire world as a gift. As the supporter and protector of any Muslim country in danger, he accepted the title of Caliph of Islam very seriously. He even invaded Islamic lands – for example, the Holy Cities in Arabia – when he believed they were being ruled by weak Muslims.

When Sulaiman I saw the dilapidated condition of Islam's third holiest city, Jerusalem, he immediately ordered the construction of massive city walls that still encircle the Old City today. The religious tolerance guaranteed by the Sulaimanic Laws was most evident in Jerusalem where mosques, churches and synagogues could be found on the same street.

But it was for Sulaiman's desire to make Constantinople the cultural capital of the Islamic world that he is most remembered. He beautified Constantinople with some of the most impressive architectural monuments the world had ever seen and he was fortunate to have had the architect Sinan to help build them for him.

Mimar Sinan (1489–1588), "Sinan the Architect", was born into a Christian family in a village near Kayseri in eastern Anatolia. At a young age, he was taken to Constantinople where he was educated in one of the Palace schools. He became a Muslim and very quickly showed promise as a skilled architectural engineer. He first worked as a member of the engineering corps that travelled with Selim I on his military campaigns. He became the Ottomans' chief architect after Selim I's capture of Cairo in 1517. During his extraordinary long life, Mimar Sinan was chief architect for four consecutive sultans: Selim I, Sulaiman I, Selim II and Murad III. He was an exceptional master craftsman and many hundreds of bridges, mosques, *madrasahs* and public buildings designed by him can still be admired in many parts of the former Ottoman territories – from Hungary, Bosnia, Greece and Bulgaria in the Balkans to Syria, Palestine, Iraq and the Holy Cities of the Hijaz.

The Sulaimaniye complex of buildings in Istanbul is remarkable. In a period of seven short years, Mimar Sinan built a monument to Sultan Sulaiman I, commemorating both the great sultan and the golden age which had been his reign. The complex was constructed on a specially prepared part of the city with a magnificent view of the Golden Horn. Besides the great Sulaimaniye Mosque (see illustrations 17-2, 17-3, 17-4, 17-5) which still dominates the city skyline of Istanbul, the complex includes a *madrasah*, a dormitory, soup kitchen, hospital and the sultan's tomb.

Mimar Sinan died in Constantinople after a long life devoted to building extraordinary monuments. Today, his tomb can be seen just outside the walls of the Sulaimaniye Mosque.

Sulaiman I was not only a brilliant military tactician, but not unlike many other sultans who learned a trade, he also became a skilled goldsmith and poet. Of all the Ottoman sultans, Sulaiman I is considered

17-2   OTTOMAN EXCELLENCE: The Ottomans continued the interest in ceramic tile making first developed by the Seljuq Turks. During the golden age of the Ottomans, there was a huge demand for high quality tiles to decorate the magnificent monuments being constructed all over the empire. The most beautiful examples of Ottoman tiles come from the workshops of İznik, a town in western Turkey. The example here comes from an İznik factory and dates from the late sixteenth century. The Ottoman Turks perfected the art of tile making in the Islamic world and introduced stylised tulips, carnations, and roses – like the ones here – as new designs.

to have been the most gifted poet. Many of his verses have become proverbs and are often quoted by educated Turks even today. Perhaps his most famous verse is the following:

> In all creation, there is nothing more esteemed than the powerful governance of a stong state. But, in truth, there is no wealth in this world equal to one healthy breath![22]

Sulaiman I died in 1566 on the eve of a great Ottoman military victory at Szigetvar, in Hungary. During his long reign, he had truly made Constantinople – the largest city of its time – the centre of the Islamic world. When asked who he was, he replied, "I am Sultan Sulaiman Khan, son of Sultan

---

[22] Author's translation.

17-3   SINAN'S SULAIMANIYE: After the conquest of the Byzantine city of Constantinople in 1453, the new capital quickly became Muslim in character. Mehmed II, the Conqueror, set a precedent by building an enormous mosque complex in his name. All subsequent sultans seemed compelled to build larger and grander mosques. Within a century, Constantinople had become a city bursting with imperial mosques. The most famous architect of the Islamic world must surely be Mimar Sinan. In his long life (1489–1588), he produced more than one hundred buildings of exceptional quality. For sultan Sulaiman the Magnificent, the protector of *sunni* Islam and the caliphate, he erected one of the most outstanding architectural achievements: the Sulaimaniye complex (1550–1557). Besides the enormous mosque, shown here, the site included seven colleges, a hospital, public bath, a hostel, a *madrasah*, and a public soup kitchen. Fountains, shops, and tombs completed the complex which covered 60,000 square metres!

17-4 CALLIGRAPHIC EXCELLENCE: By the mid-sixteenth century, Constantinople had become the "capital of the world". Building projects converted the city's skyline into its familiar one of domes and minarets. In the many *madrasahs*, master calligraphers (professional scribes) taught their pupils the techniques of writing the various styles of Arabic. Ottoman calligraphers were universally acclaimed to be the best in the world. It was often said that the Qur'an was best written by the Turks, but best recited by the Egyptians! Here is a superb example of Ottoman calligraphic excellence. On this panel of twenty-four hand painted İznik tiles, the *ustaz* (master calligrapher) has written the second half of the *shahadah: wa ashhadu anna Muhammadan 'abdu-hu wa rasuluhu*. The first half of the *shahadah* was placed on the mosque wall to the right of the *mihrab* (prayer niche); the second half was placed to the left. The fine art of handwriting is still taught today by Turkish masters who have spent many years perfecting their remarkable skills.

Selim Khan, son of Bayezid Khan. I am Sulaiman. To the East, I am the Lawgiver, to the West, I am the Magnificent."

BATTLE OF LEPANTO (OCTOBER 7, 1571)

After the death of Sulaiman I in 1566, a series of weak and incompetent sultans ascended the Ottoman throne. Until this time in their history, the Ottomans had been masters of the Mediterranean Sea.

One of the most decisive naval battles in history took place on October 7, 1571 in the Ionian Sea off the west coast of Greece. A massive flotilla of more than two hundred galleys was met by the naval might of the Holy League, a weak coalition of the Christian states of Habsburg Spain, Venice, Genoa, Naples and Malta all led by the Pope in Rome. This was the last great naval battle in world history which was mounted using rowing vessels only.

The outcome of the Battle of Lepanto did not signal the decline of the Ottoman Empire as is so often reported. For the Turks, the defeat was a shocking blow, but they soon rebuilt their navy and

17-5   A TILED GARDEN: We have seen how important ceramic tiles were for the Ilkhans of Iran (see illustration 15-1) and the Timurids (see illustration 16-2). For both these dynasties, it became common to cover entire walls and domes with tile work. The Ottomans also used tiles extensively in their building projects, but in a different way. Because Ottoman buildings were constructed largely from stone, and not brick, outside surfaces were never covered in tiles. Ottoman tile work was used to beautify particular areas inside the mosque, such as the *mihrab*, or prayer niche. As the Islamic city of Constantinople grew, the demand for high quality tiles remained high. The tile workshops of İznik (one hundred kilometres to the southwest of the capital) provided most of the Ottoman tiles until the seventeenth century. Tiles, like the ones shown here, are typical of the period when the Ottomans ruled the world. The Ottomans perfected the fine art of tile making and even today the interiors of the mosques in old Istanbul resemble beautiful "tiled gardens".

regained suzerainty of at least the eastern Mediterranean. What had changed, however, was the era of vast territorial conquest. By the end of the sixteenth century, the Ottoman Empire had indeed reached its zenith.

DECLINE BEGINS

The Ottomans had fallen behind in keeping up with the technological developments being made in Europe and so the seventeenth century saw them attempting to adapt to the rapid changes occurring elsewhere in the world. Various sultans tried to introduce reforms in order to halt the slow decline of the Empire. But after the failure of the last serious attempt to capture Vienna in 1683, the Ottomans rapidly began to lose territories in Europe, Africa and Asia. As a result of the Treaty of Karlowitz in 1699, concluding the fifteen year-long war between the Austrians and the Turks, the Ottomans ceded almost all of Hungary and parts of present-day Romania, losing at one stroke of the pen, almost half of their European territories to Austria. This signalled the loss of Ottoman control in the region and the ascendancy of the Habsburgs as the dominant power in Southeastern Europe.

THE TULIP ERA (1718–1730)

A unique period in Ottoman history was inaugurated during the reign of Sultan Ahmed III (1703–1730). The era became known as the *lale devri*, the "Tulip Era", because of the sultan's love of the tulip flower. During this brief interlude, the Empire was at peace and Ahmed III thoroughly indulged himself in pompous pleasures. He erected extravagant public fountains and pavilions throughout Constantinople. One such opulent fountain (*sebil*) can still be seen today in front of the entrance to the Topkapi Palace. He patronised the arts (see illustration 17-6) and authorised the installation of the first printing press in the Ottoman capital. Some important reforms also took place during the reign of Ahmed III. The Conte de Bonneval, a French convert to Islam, helped to reform the Ottoman army by establishing military colleges in which medicine and mathematics were taught.

Unfortunately, because of his excesses, Ahmed III was forced by a Janissary insurrection to abdicate in favour of his nephew Mahmud I (1730–1754). Ahmed III died six years later in the palace apartments earlier vacated by Mahmud.

SELIM III (1789–1807)

Selim III, Ahmed III's grandson, thoroughly understood the need to reform the Ottoman state. He began with plans to increase educational opportunities. French military officers were employed to train a small select group of new troops in several military academies. However, religious conservatives and an increasingly jealous and rowdy Janissary corps openly revolted. Selim III was dethroned and eventually stabbed to death in his own palace in 1807.

Attempts at reform continued during the reign of Mahmud II (1808–1839). In 1826, he was able to successfully abolish the Janissary corps. This long-standing Ottoman institution had served the empire well, but by the beginning of the nineteenth century had become no more than a group of irreligious bandits. Mahmud II now wished to develop a more modern, disciplined and technology-savvy Ottoman army.

17-6 "PLENTY OF ISLAM": In this book, we have seen many examples of how Islamic coins can help us better understand our history. Here is yet another example. This coin is a gold *sultani* from the time of the Ottoman sultan Ahmed III dated 1703. This sultan was a great patron of Islamic art and during his reign, beautiful public fountains were constructed, some of which can still be seen in Istanbul today. On this coin, we see the standard Arabic formula for identifying the mint (the place of production) and date. The coin reads in Arabic *dhuriba fi islambol* ("was struck [minted] in Islambol"). On most Ottoman coinage – right up to the twentieth century – the Arabic/Ottoman Turkish word *Qustentiniyah* (Constantinople) was used to indicate the mint. On this unique coin, however, sultan Ahmed III placed the name *Islambol* as the place of production. The colloquial name for the city was "Istanbul". In Turkish, *bol* means "plenty of". So, on this coin, sultan Ahmed III is telling us that, in his capital city, there is *Islambol*, or "plenty of Islam"!

TANZIMAT REFORMS (1839–1876)

The period of real westernisation in Ottoman history began in the mid-nineteenth century starting with the *tanzimat* (re-organisation) reforms. European educated bureaucrats like Midhat Pasha worked along with reform-minded sultans. Reforms begun during the reign of 'Abdul Majid I (1839–1861) were designed to ensure security for all subjects (see illustration 17-7). Tax collection was regulated and military conscription modernised. Public education was to be modelled after the French system. Even the marble palaces built in Constantinople looked like luxurious European villas. From 1839 onwards only religious clerics, the *'ulema,* were permitted to wear turbans and robes in public. For the rest of the population, traditional Islamic clothing was replaced by the fez and European-style trousers. By such symbolic reforms, it was naively hoped that the psychology of

17-7 THE TURKISH TUGHRA: This five *kurush* silver coin was minted during the reign of the Ottoman sultan 'Abdul Majid (1839–1861). Great reforms in Ottoman society had been introduced by his predecessor, sultan Mahmud II. For centuries, coins had been "hammered", or hand struck. This coin, however, was machine made and is clearly more "modern"-looking. The decorative inscription here has a long and interesting history. The central symbol, called the *tughra*, in Turkish, was first used by the Seljuq Turks on their flags and standards. It was later employed by Ottoman sultans as their official signature or stamp. It, therefore, appeared on all formal documents such as imperial decrees, flags, coins, and postage stamps. The *tughra* became a complex monogram of the sultan's name and titles. Whenever a new Ottoman sultan was enthroned, a master calligrapher working at the court would have to devise a new *tughra* for the new sultan. On this coin, the name of the Ottoman sultan, 'Abdul Majid, is included in the complex *tughra*. The *tughra*, however, was never really meant to be read. Its unique shape became synonymous with the power of the Ottoman state: the sultan and the caliphate. The use of the *tughra* as a royal symbol was copied by rulers in the Sudan, Saudi Arabia and even by the Nizam of Hyderabad, in India.

an entire people might be altered. Ironically, less than a century later, Mustafa Kemal Atatürk, the founder of the modern Turkish Republic, inaugurated a similar set of "clothing" and "hat" reforms for precisely the same purpose.

The Tanzimat reforms were a last ditch attempt by the Ottoman state to halt the decline of the Empire. In many ways, it proved utterly futile. The European-style schools graduated a European-minded elite who very quickly opted in favour of a constitutional monarchy (and later a republic) rather than the propping up of the old Ottoman state. Another far reaching result of these reforms was the growth of Zionism.[23] For example, Tanzimat reforms had enabled Russian Jews who had suffered anti-Semitic persecution in Europe to purchase land in Palestine, thus signalling the start of large-scale Jewish emigration to the region.

FINAL YEARS OF THE OTTOMAN EMPIRE

The final years of the Ottoman Empire were chaotic. The government could no longer pay its foreign loans and this created an economic crisis. In 1875, the Ottoman state declared bankruptcy. The situation was exacerbated by the fact that the last Ottoman sultans had chosen to lead an ostentatious lifestyle in their pseudo-European marble palaces which dotted the Bosphorus. In 1876, with the ascent of sultan 'Abdul Hamid II (1876–1909), a constitutional monarchy was proclaimed. This was short-lived, however, and was annulled two years later.

The Ottomans' one ally in Europe was Germany who sincerely wanted to help modernise the Ottoman state. This friendship, surviving until the dying days of the Empire, in fact helped contribute to its demise.

YOUNG TURKS

By the end of the nineteenth century, the Ottoman Empire rapidly shrank in size. In 1881, the Ottomans lost Tunisia to the French and in 1882, the British annexed Egypt in order to protect their interests in the Suez Canal.

Within the Ottoman Empire itself, a group of radical Turkish nationalists – mainly students called *Gench Turkler*, the "Young Turks" – wanted to see the dissolution of the Empire which had become known to the West as the "sick man of Europe". These activists created dissent that shaped the last decades of the Empire.

After Sultan 'Abdul Hamid II annulled the constitution in 1878, the Young Turk movement was forced underground where they fought for the establishment of a constitutional monarchy. Once this goal was achieved in 1908, promises made to the non-Muslim and non-Turkish minorities in the Empire were not honoured. The Ottomans continued to lose their last territories in the Balkans and in 1912 lost Libya to Italy.

Contrary to popular belief, the Young Turks were not liberal; they were an elitist group who never planned to accept parliamentary democracy. They were adamantly secular and were thus accused by the *'ulema* of trying to create a new religion. Their extreme nationalistic tendencies were based on a belief of racial superiority. The Young Turks, therefore, laid the foundation for the nationalistic, secular revolution of Mustafa Kemal Atatürk that subsequently led to the formation of the Turkish Republic of today.

FOREIGN OCCUPATION OF TURKEY

When World War I began in 1914, the Ottomans were neutral. Eventually, however, they joined Germany in the war and suffered the bitter consequences of defeat in 1918. The Ottoman government, not surprisingly, collapsed at the end of the war.

---

[23] A nineteenth century Jewish movement whose original aim was the re-establishment of a Jewish homeland in Palestine.

France and Great Britain, being the victors of World War I, immediately began to carve up the former Ottoman lands of the Middle East. Greece and Italy were given much of present-day Turkey, while France and Britain occupied Syria, Palestine, Iraq and North Africa. Of course, the Turkish people justifiably refused such foreign occupation and began a war of liberation. Some Young Turks and other resistance fighters were led by Mustafa Kemal Atatürk. Turkey was liberated and the Greek occupiers were forced to retreat across the Aegean Sea.

Mehmed VI (1918–1922)

The final Ottoman sultan, Mehmed VI Vahdettin, took office in 1918. As the thirty-sixth Ottoman sultan, he witnessed the demise of the once illustrious Ottoman Empire. The Treaty of Sevres, signed on August 10, 1920, imposed extremely severe demands on the Turks. Former Ottoman territories now became mandates of European powers. The Turkish state was reduced in size and the two Holy Cities of Islam became part of an independent Hijazi Arab state.

Turkish nationalists led by Kemal Atatürk established a new government in Ankara. The Grand National Assembly, the new Turkish parliament, enacted the separation of the sultanate and caliphate on November 1, 1922. On November 17, 1922, with the abolition of the sultanate, Mehmed VI left his marble palace, the Dolmabahçe Palace, which stretched half a kilometre along the banks of the Bosphorus. He was exiled to Malta and later to Italy, where he died alone in 1926; Mehmed VI was subsequently interred at the Mosque of Selim I, in Damascus. With the abolition of the sultanate, the Ottoman dynasty had come to an end.

The last caliph of the Ottoman dynasty, 'Abdul Majid II (Mehmed VI's first cousin), reigned from November 19, 1922 until March 3, 1924. He was installed as caliph by the Turkish National Assembly in Ankara but was soon expelled from Turkey along with his entire family when the title of caliph was officially abolished. For a brief period, Atatürk had permitted the continuation of the caliphate co-existing with his presidency. But he soon saw the need to sever the second head of the two-headed serpent that for him had been the degenerate Ottoman state. All Ottoman princes were sent into exile and it was only in 1974 – precisely fifty years after the abolition of the caliphate – that any male members of the Ottoman dynasty were ever able to return to Turkey. 'Abdul Majid II died in Paris in 1944 and was buried in Madinah. He had been the one hundred and first caliph in line from Abu Bakr ﷺ and the last of the Ottoman caliphs.

The Ottoman Empire had been founded by a *ghazi* who had battled the Byzantine Greeks and again, rather ironically, the Ottoman dynasty came to an end with another *ghazi*, Mustafa Kemal Atatürk, who also fought the Greeks on Turkish soil. He proclaimed the new state, the Republic of Turkey, on October 29, 1923.

Of all the Islamic dynasties, that of the Ottomans lasted the longest. For thirteen centuries, *Dar al-Islam* had never been without a caliph to lead the Muslims. For four hundred years the caliphate had resided in Constantinople, but after its abolishment in 1924, there was little protest from the *ummah*. The fall of the Ottoman Empire resembles to some degree the fall of the Roman one. In the end, the Ottoman state was simply unable to control the unrest amongst the Empire's many diverse ethnic populations. The Tanzimat reforms of the nineteenth century had come too late to provide succour to the ailing empire.

The *raison d'etre* of the Ottoman state had always been the extension and preservation of *Dar al-Islam* and to ensure its security. The history of this dynasty clearly shows evidence of having done just that. Today, any visitor to the modern Turkish city of Istanbul can marvel at the well-preserved mosques (see illustration 17-8), palaces, covered markets, and public fountains that remain from the days when it truly was the centre of the world.

17-8 POPULAR MIHRAB AYAH: The Ottoman Turks understood the importance of writing Arabic well. In their *madrasahs* (traditional religious schools), all school children were taught the proper way to write and pronounce the Holy Qur'an. Special *khat*, or calligraphy (the art of "good penmanship") classes were offered and students would even learn how to cut the ends of their reed pens to ensure the proper width and shape of the letters they were learning to write. Some of the best handwritten copies of the Holy Qur'an were produced by Ottoman calligraphers. These masters of Arabic handwriting were also hired by tile workshops in İznik and Kütahya, the two great tile making centres in Ottoman Turkey. They would produce large works of calligraphic art that were then transferred onto blank ceramic tiles. It became the custom in Ottoman times to place a specific *ayah* above the *mihrab* of all Ottoman mosques, whether they were in Algeria, Bosnia, Yemen, or Iraq. The middle section of the carefully chosen *ayah* 37 of *Surah Aal 'Imran* was either carved into marble, or placed on tiles, as we see here. This section of the beautiful *ayah* reads: "Whenever Zakariyah visited her [Maryam *'alayha as-salaam*] in the sanctuary, he found her provided with food." This is a panel of hand painted ceramic tiles that has been produced in modern times. Such tiles are purchased whenever a new mosque is being built in Turkey and are placed on the *mihrab* wall. In the same *ayah*, Maryam *'alayha as-salaam* answers that Allah alone grants *rizq*, or sustenance to whom He wills.

CHAPTER EIGHTEEN
THE SAFAVIDS (1501–1722)

One of the two great superpowers of the pre-Islamic Middle East had been the Persian Sasanian Empire, which included most of present-day Iran. For centuries, the Sasanians had governed a unified state with an official written language, Pahlavi, and a state religion, Zoroastrianism. After the Sasanian Empire collapsed with the Arab takeover of its winter capital at Ctesiphon (outside of Baghdad) in 637 (see illustration 3-1), it would take hundreds of years before Iran once again had a powerful central government able to regain the geographical borders of the Sasanian state. Persia – or Iran – as a political entity simply did not exist. Many people in the region spoke Persian (*farsi*, from the ancient southern Iranian province of Fars), but others spoke Arabic, Kurdish or Baluchi. The various provinces of today's Iran once belonged to different ruling states in the region: the 'Abbasids, Samanids, Ghaznavids, Seljuqs and others. It was not until the early sixteenth century that Iran was reunited under the Safavid shahs.

ORIGINS OF THE DYNASTY

The Safavid rulers were descended from a militant religious group of *Sufis* (Muslim mystics), the *Safaviyah*, led by Safi ad-Din (1252–1334). His Sufi religious order or *tariqah*, had its centre in Ardabil, a city in Azerbaijan, a Turkish-speaking area west of the Caspian Sea in northern Iran. The *Safaviyah* were Sunni Muslims, but by the early fifteenth century had become ardent Shi'ites who vowed to spread Shi'ism by any means, even military. It was precisely because of this ardour that Shi'ite Islam became the state religion of Iran and has remained so to this day.

In 1501, Shaikh Haydar, a Safavid teacher, was killed. His thirteen year-old son, Isma'il, set out to avenge his father's death. By the following year, Isma'il and his forces of Qizilbash Turkoman tribesmen had defeated the ruler of Azerbaijan in the Caucasus Mountains and had secured the city of Tabriz, in northwestern Iran. Successful conquests continued in Khorasan and Armenia and finally in 1502, Isma'il, now fifteen years old, was proclaimed the first Safavid *shah* (king) of Iran in Tabriz, their capital.

SHAH ISMA'IL (1502–1524)

The Safavids wanted to reclaim all territories that had once comprised the Sasanian Empire. Shah Isma'il, therefore, claimed Baghdad, northern Iraq and parts of western Afghanistan. At the same time, he enforced Shi'ite Islam as the state religion, but this was a difficult task because Shi'ites were still in the minority in Iran. He was successful, however, and Iran today is still overwhelmingly Shi'ite. Shah Isma'il claimed to be a descendant of the Prophet Muhammad ﷺ through 'Ali and Fatima ؉ and also to represent the Twelfth or "Hidden Imam". Besides this, he boasted of having royal Sasanian blood. Shah Isma'il was a prolific poet and much of his mystical Sufi poetry written in Azerbaijani Turkish and Persian is still read today.

SAFAVID-OTTOMAN CONFLICT

In neighbouring Turkey, the Ottoman sultans became the protectors of Sunni Islam in the Muslim world. Through a series of letters, the Ottoman sultan Bayezid II had warned Shah Isma'il to stop destroying Sunni mosques and graveyards in Safavid territory. A bitter two hundred year-long conflict with the Ottoman Empire had begun.

BATTLE OF CHALDIRAN (AUGUST 23, 1514)

An important battle was fought on the plains to the west of Tabriz on August 23, 1514. Shah Isma'il had some 80,000 troops while the Ottoman sultan Selim I had more than double that number. The Safavid army with their swords, spears and bows were simply no match for the far superior Ottoman one bearing state-of-the-art weaponry: muskets and artillery. The defeated Shah Isma'il I, while wounded in battle, was able to flee eastwards with the remnants of his army. In retreat, he employed a "scorched earth" policy ensuring that pursuing Ottoman troops could not easily occupy Safavid lands. Selim I entered Tabriz but soon withdrew before the onset of winter.

As a direct result of this battle, the borders between the Ottoman and Safavid states were established and after five hundred years, remain virtually the same today.

In defeat, Shah Isma'il and his men were left utterly confused. Shah Isma'il had become a semi-divine leader who truly believed that Allah would guarantee victory for him in all battles. The Ottomans now seized the opportunity to reclaim lands lost to the Safavids who concentrated on expanding their empire north of Khorasan province into Central Asia. During this period, the *Qizilbash*[24] tribal chiefs represented the Safavid shah in all provinces of the Empire.

Shah Isma'il's wife had been taken hostage by the Ottomans during the Battle of Chaldiran. Not willing or able to accept the exorbitant demands for her release, Shah Isma'il died ten years later – it is said – of a broken heart.

SHAH TAHMASP I (1524–1576)

Shah Isma'il's eldest son, Tahmasp, became ruler at the age of ten on the death of his father in 1524. At this young age he was not able to be a strong and effective ruler, and consequently lost considerable territory to the new Ottoman sultan, Sulaiman I.

Shah Tahmasp I is most remembered for having introduced *mamluks* into his court and army. These "slave soldiers", loyal to the shah, were taken as prisoners from various regions of the Caucasus Mountains such as Georgia and Armenia.

Like the Janissary troops of the Ottomans, some of these slave soldiers reached positions of high office. Because of the continual warfare between the Ottoman and Safavid states, in 1514, Shah Tahmasp I transferred his capital from Tabriz in the northwest to Qazvin, a city further east.

Shah Tahmasp I is also remembered for his generosity in allowing the exiled Mughal emperor Humayun to be a guest at his court for ten years. It was during this period away from India that the Mughal dynasty became so infatuated with all things Persian. This influence can be detected in

---

[24] The Turkoman tribesmen were called "redheads" in Turkish (*qizil*, red and *bash* head) because of their distinctive colourful caps.

Mughal architecture, miniature painting, poetic writing styles, the design of royal gardens and even in Mughal cuisine.

SHAH 'ABBAS I (1587–1629)

The *Qizilbash* Turkoman tribes whose chiefs had been representing the Safavid shah in outlying provinces began to demand more autonomy. But when Shah 'Abbas I was enthroned, he had all the rebellious *Qizilbash* chiefs replaced. Now all the regions of the empire were to be administered from a central government.

Thus began the reign of the greatest of all Safavid kings and one of the most remarkable in all of Iranian history. In Persian, Shah 'Abbas I is still referred to as *'Abbas-i Buzorg*, 'Abbas the Great, because of his success in reforming and reuniting his country.

Early in his rule, he was able to rout the Uzbek Turks from their hold on the northeastern province of Khorasan. At the historic battle near Herat in 1598, 'Abbas defeated the Uzbeks and recaptured the two important towns of Khorasan: Herat and Mashhad. A long series of military campaigns followed. Parts of Georgia in the Caucasus were secured and Baghdad was reoccupied for a brief period in 1623. In 1602, he forced the Portuguese navy to relinquish control of Bahrain and in 1622, he removed the English navy from the strategically important island of Hormuz in the Persian Gulf.

'Abbas I's many military successes could be attributed to his effective new army. In 1598, two English travellers and adventurers, Robert and Anthony Sherley, arrived in Persia. On the advice of these two brothers, the Persian army was completely reorganised along European models. The new divisions included crown and artillery corps recruited from the Caucasus territories (Armenia, Georgia and Circassia), and musketeers recruited mostly from the local peasantry. Officers in all divisions of the army were to receive a salary. These costly reforms needed financing, so all the provinces became crown lands that were to be taxed.

During his military campaigns, Shah 'Abbas I transported thousands of business-oriented Georgians and Armenians to various cities within Persia. This varied ethnic mix is evident even today in Iranian society. Today, in the area of New Julfa in Isfahan, a large group of Armenian Christians are directly descended from people transported there from Julfa in Azerbaijan some four hundred years ago.

From the new Safavid capital of Isfahan, 'Abbas sent his diplomatic envoys west to Europe, north to Muscovy in Russia, and the Tatar region of Crimea, and east to Mughal India. Despite his many efforts to establish friendly ties with European powers, he was never able to persuade them to join him in an alliance against Ottoman Turkey.

ISFAHAN - "HALF THE WORLD"

In 1598, Shah 'Abbas I transferred the Safavid capital from Qazvin to Isfahan, a beautiful city in central Iran. Under his wise rule, he began an extensive building programme there that resulted in the construction of some of the most magnificent buildings in the entire Islamic world. Shah 'Abbas was a great patron of the arts and encouraged the production of fine silk, luxurious hand-woven carpets, ceramic tiles, metalware and miniature painting. The art of weaving was no longer just a nomadic art form. Extremely large and intricate palace carpets were woven in state-of-the-art work-shops and exported to eager markets in Europe.

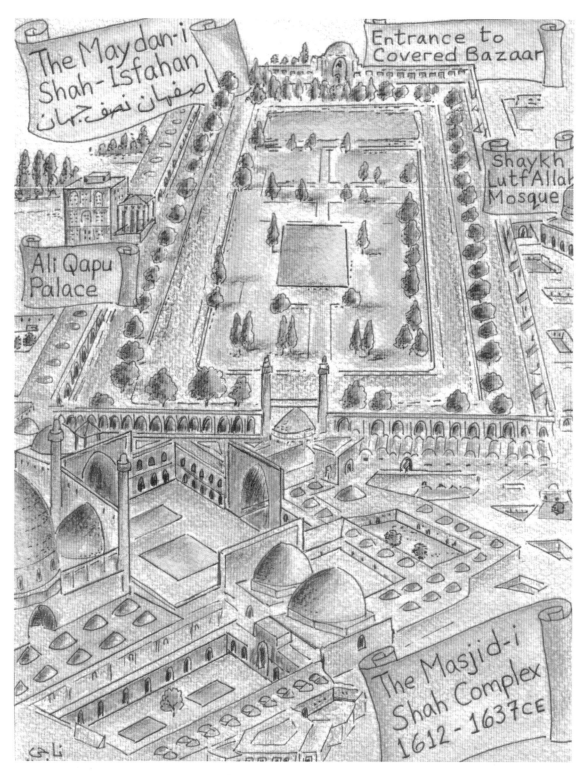

18-1 A SPECTACULAR PUBLIC SQUARE: The greatest of all Safavid monarchs was clearly 'Abbas I (1587–1629). Single-handedly, he converted the backward provincial town of Isfahan into one of the great cities of his age. Unlike Contantinople, whose magnificent Ottoman mosques were of dull grey stone, the Isfahan of Shah 'Abbas I, had buildings whose exteriors were covered in dazzling blue ceramic tiles. The huge (500m by 150m) open rectangle of the *Maydan-i Shah* (Persian for royal square) became the heart of the new Safavid capital.

18-2 SAFAVID CALLIGRAPHY: The *Masjid-i Shah*, or "royal mosque", built for Shah 'Abbas I between 1612 and 1637, is one of the most beautiful mosques ever built. It is estimated that eighteen million honey-coloured bricks and 500,000 ceramic tiles were used in its construction. Its large dome is covered with multi-coloured painted tiles. Beneath the dome, on the drum surrounding it, are spectacular mosaic tile inscriptions. A three-level inscription in praise of the Safavid dynasty encircles the dome. The large band of calligraphy in rigid Kufic style contains the final words of the Arabic prayer: *Allahumma salli 'ala Muhammad wa-aal Muhammad wa-sallim* (O, Allah, bless Muhammad and his family and grant them peace). This magnificent mosque, at one end of the *Maydan-i Shah* in Isfahan, can accommodate thousands of worshippers and is today a major attraction for all who visit Isfahan, the beautiful city, once known as "half the world".

Royal architects created perhaps the most exquisite public square (*maydan* in Persian) found anywhere in the world. The long rectangular public square – the length of several football fields – beautified the centre of Shah 'Abbas's new capital (see illustration 18-1). At one of the shorter ends of the *maydan* was the entrance to a superb covered *bazaar* (Persian for marketplace), and at the other, the great blue-domed *Masjid-i Shah* (Royal Mosque) or *Masjid-i Imam*, Imam's Mosque as it is now called (see illustration 18-2). On the two longer sides of the square, Shah 'Abbas built a palace whose extravagant gateway was called the *'Ali Qapu*, the "Sublime Porte" or "High Gate" in Persian (see illustration 18-3) and the beautiful Shaykh Lutfallah Mosque. Skirting the square were

18-3   A PALACE WITH A VIEW: The golden age of the Safavids was experienced during the reign of Shah 'Abbas I in the early seventeenth century. Isfahan, the new capital, became a city filled with garden pavilions, palaces, mosques, *madrasahs*, and fine public buildings, such as covered bazaars, *khans* (caravanserais), bridges and bath houses. All these were constructed using the best materials available. The Safavid palace was not a secluded residence. Shah 'Abbas I lived in the centre of his capital, along one side of the *Maydan-i Shah*. Here is the gateway to his palace, called in Persian, the *'Ali Qapu*, or "Sublime [High] Gate". The upper levels of the six-storey building offered wonderful views of the skyline of Isfahan. The balcony gave the shah, his family and invited foreign ambassadors, a grandstand view of all the ceremonies that took place in the square below. Typical of Safavid architecture are the delicate, slender wooden columns supporting a decorated wooden ceiling. This interesting building, along with all the others skirting "the royal square", are today open to the public. Standing on the high balcony of this palace, one can easily imagine what it must have been like during the golden age of Shah 'Abbas I.

scores of one-room shops selling all kinds of goods. In other parts of the city, wonderful *madrasahs*, bridges, palaces, and public and private gardens were built. Shah 'Abbas also had well-equipped hospitals constructed.

International trade was encouraged and foreign merchants were welcomed to his city. Safe highways were built to help in the transport of goods over long distances. It was at this time that enormous numbers of intricate hand-woven Persian carpets were exported to many cities in Western Europe. The keen interest in Oriental Persian carpets dates from this period.

All foreign visitors to Isfahan were dazzled by its astonishing beauty and many wrote flattering accounts of their stay in the city. For the Safavids, the city of one million inhabitants was truly unique and worthy of every praise. A popular Persian saying at the time described the city as:

Isfahan nisf-i jihan
Isfahan is half the world!
[i.e. the one who has seen Isfahan has surely seen 'half the world'!]

Remarkably, many of the architectural treasures from the time of Shah 'Abbas have been perfectly preserved and can be appreciated if one visits Isfahan today.

DECLINE OF THE SAFAVIDS

The Safavid Empire had reached its zenith under the reign of Shah 'Abbas I. Safavid domains had once included Iran, Iraq, the Caucasus regions of Armenia, Georgia, Azerbaijan and also parts of Turkmenistan, Uzbekistan, Afghanistan and Pakistan.

Historians agree that after his death in 1629, no ruler was capable or disciplined enough to confront the Ottoman threat in the west and the Uzbek Turks to the north. The Safavid dynasty did survive for another century, however. Two main reasons are suggested for its decline and final fall. First, for all the apparent good he did for his people, Shah 'Abbas I grew to fear his own sons. Instead of permitting them to rule as provincial governors, Shah 'Abbas began to imprison his sons in enclosed palace gardens where they lived in total ignorance of the real world. The result was a string of weak, poorly educated and feeble-minded shahs who were simply incapable of ruling properly.

The second reason for the decline of the Safavids was the forcible conversion of all Sunni Muslims to Shi'ite Islam. During the reign of Shah Sultan Husayn (1694–1722), the last important Safavid monarch, all forms of Sunni Islamic practice were forbidden and non-Muslim minorities in Iran (i.e. the Zoroastrians, Jews, Christians) were persecuted. But pilgrimages to the tombs of Shi'ite saints were encouraged. The total incompetence of Shah Sultan Husayn hastened the demise of the Safavid dynasty (see illustration 18-4).

A militarily weak Safavid state enabled the Afghan leader Mahmud to invade Iran and take over the Safavid capital of Isfahan in 1722. Shah Sultan Husayn had to abdicate, passing authority to Mahmud. The Afghan invasion led directly to the death of Shah Sultan Husayn and the partitioning of northwestern Iran between the Ottomans and the Russians. Historians agree that 1722 clearly marks the end of the Safavid dynasty.

From 1722 until 1732, Tahmasp II, the son of Shah Sultan Husayn, claimed his father's throne and led a resistance movement. He gained support in several parts of Iran, most notably from the

18-4   SAFAVID SILVER: Many non-Arab dynasties have shown a profound interest in Arabic calligraphy. We recall Uljaytu Khan, the Ilkhan ruler of Iran, commissioning the writing of oversized Qur'ans in the beautiful *rayhani* script. Some Ilkhanid coins also depict extremely complex Arabic inscriptions. The Safavids produced some outstanding works of art besides the turquoise domed mosques and tiled garden pavilions of Isfahan. Here is another example of Islamic fine art – in miniature. This is a Safavid silver abbasi from the reign of Shah Sultan Husayn (1694–1722). The beauty of this coin lies in the exquisite composition of the Arabic letters and their shape. The Safavids, being the first Shi'ite dynasty to rule all of Iran, have placed the Shi'ite version of the *shahadah* on this coin: *la ilaha illallah, Muhammad ar-rasulullah wa 'Ali wali Allah.*

Turkoman tribe of Afshar nomads in the northeastern province of Khorasan. By 1729, Tahmasp II had consolidated his power throughout most of Iran.

Several years later, in 1732, a very competent Afshar general, Nadir Shah, seized power but permitted 'Abbas III, the infant son of Tahmasp II, to continue as nominal ruler of Iran. Nadir Shah Afshar successfully expelled the Afghans and reunified the country. By the year 1736, Nadir Afshar deposed the still very young Safavid Shah 'Abbas III. Nadir Afshar crowned himself shah, thus ending the line of Safavid dynastic monarchs. Unfortunately, both Tahmasp II and his son, 'Abbas III, were murdered in 1740 to prevent any possible restoration of the Safavid dynasty.

A short-lived regional Afsharid dynasty replaced the Safavid one, but it too ended with the death of Nadir Shah in 1747. In that same year, the Qadjar shahs of Iran established their dynasty which survived into the twentieth century.

SAFAVID LEGACY

The most obvious legacy of the Safavids must surely be the glorious city of Isfahan and its well-preserved gardens, gateways, bridges, mosques and *madrasahs*. Shah 'Abbas I and his skilled architects and artisans set an exceptionally high standard of craftsmanship that was never again equalled by succeeding generations of Persian monarchs.

The long period of Ottoman-Safavid rivalry in the region eventually resulted in peace treaties that demarcated the present-day borders between Iran and her western and northern neighbours. The permanent unification of Iran under Shah 'Abbas the Great also helped foster the strong national identity that exists in Iran today.

CHAPTER NINETEEN
THE MUGHALS OF INDIA (1526–1858)

In India the term *mughal* – the Persian equivalent of the word "Mongol" – came to mean anyone coming from Central Asia. Not surprisingly, the word *mughal* eventually was applied to the last dynasty of Indian rulers who originated from Central Asia. For more than three hundred years, the Muslim Mughal emperors governed a predominantly Hindu India and surrounding areas from opulent marble palace-cities whose splendour was rivalled only by Isfahan under the Safavids and Constantinople under the Ottomans. The Mughals were the longest-lasting of all the Muslim dynasties of India and historically, the most interesting. Even today, the mere mention of the Mughals conjures up both fabulous wealth and, at the same time, ruthless brutality.

BABUR SHAH (1526–1530)

Babur Shah founded the Mughal dynasty of Indian emperors. He was the last of the Timurid rulers of Central Asia being a fifth generation descendant of Timur-i Lang. Babur's mother, however, was a descendant of the Mongol Jenghiz Khan. He was born in 1483 in the town of Andijan in modern Uzbekistan. His mother tongue was Chaghatai Turkish, but he was also fluent in Persian, the preferred language of Central Asian nobility.

By the time Babur began to rule as the last of the Timurids, his kingdom had been reduced to a very small one based in Turkistan. The vast empire that had once belonged to his Turko-Mongol ancestors was but a memory. Modern technology, however, helped Babur regain some of the greatness of his illustrious ancestors. After the Battle of Chaldiran in 1514, during which the Safavid Shah Isma'il was defeated by the Ottoman army, both Babur and Shah Isma'il were eager to acquire the latest in warfare technology: the musket and siege weaponry such as cannons. By using firearms for the first time in waging wars in the region, Babur was immediately successful in his later campaigns.

With a small army, Babur quickly conquered Afghanistan in 1504 and made Kabul his capital – the city he came to love the most and the one in which he was finally buried. He was not successful, however, in attempting to regain control of his homeland in Samarqand. Even with help from the Persian Shah Isma'il, he was only able to hold on to power in Samarqand for three years. In 1514, Babur was defeated by an invading army of Uzbek Turks. With no chance, therefore, of ever returning to the grand former Timurid capital of Samarqand, Babur retired to Kabul from where he began to look south towards India. Babur, on reflection, later believed his loss of Samarqand to be one of Allah's greatest blessings.

FIRST BATTLE OF PANIPAT (APRIL 21, 1526)

In 1526, an opportunity arose enabling Babur to enter India with his army. The last ruler of the Delhi Sultanate, Ibrahim Lodi (1517–1526), was of Afghan origin. He was detested by his Indian subjects, but even some of his Afghan countrymen despised him. They eventually called on Babur for military help.

Babur with his relatively small army of 12,000 soldiers (or possibly up to 25,000, as reports vary), confronted Ibrahim Lodi and his much larger army of some 100,000 troops on April 21, 1526. The ensuing First Battle of Panipat took place at a site about eighty-six kilometres to the north of Delhi.

Babur, although greatly outnumbered, skilfully employed his musketeers and artillery – the new technology he first introduced into India. Ibrahim Lodi and his outdated army and clumsy elephants were simply no match for Babur and his modern army. The five-hour-long battle ended with the death of Ibrahim Lodi – the only ruler of Delhi ever to be slain while fighting.

Babur quickly seized the cities of Agra, the Lodi capital, and Delhi. Before his death in Agra four years later in 1530, Babur had had little time to secure his military victories. But he had established the Mughal dynasty which came to be known as the "first gunpowder empire".

Babur was a man of varied interests. When settled in India, he immediately began landscaping exquisite Persian gardens in all parts of his empire. He was also an accomplished poet and calligrapher and wrote some musical compositions. But it is for his diary, the *Babur Nameh*, that he is most remembered today. These amazing memoirs comprise what is truly the first autobiography in Islamic history. It is written in Chaghatai Turkish and has been translated into several European languages. Babur reveals his keen interest in the history, geography, flora and fauna of all regions of his world. Today, selections from the *Babur Nameh* are compulsory reading in many schools in Central and South Asia.

The following one-paragraph excerpt from the *Babur Nameh* – a lucid description of the fabled city of Samarqand – illustrates the effective, succinct style of writing Babur employed throughout his personal memoir.

> Few cities in the civilized world are as pleasant as Samarqand. …Samarqand is the seat of the province, which is Transoxiana. Because it has not been stormed and seized by enemies, Samarqand is called *balda-i mahfuza* [well-protected town]. Samarqand became Muslim during the time of the caliph 'Uthman. One of the Companions, Qutham son of 'Abbas ﷺ, went there, and his tomb outside the Iron Gate is now called Mazar-i Shah. Samarqand is supposed to have been built by Alexander the Great. The Mughals and Turks call it "Semizkand" (fat city). Timur-i Lang was the first to make it his capital.[25]

An interesting legend surrounds the death of Babur. His son and successor, Humayun, a young man of about twenty-one years of age, lay severely ill in bed. A Sufi mystic told Babur to walk three times around his son's bed and then to offer himself to Allah in place of his sick son. Humayun quickly recovered while Babur died shortly thereafter.

About nine years after Babur died, his remains were taken to their final resting place: Babur's beloved garden in the cooler climes of Kabul. His tomb is still there and bears a Persian inscription which reads: "If there be an Earthly paradise, surely it is here, it is here!"

HUMAYUN (1530–1540 AND 1555–1556)

Humayun, the second Mughal emperor and son of Babur, succeeded his father in 1530. Of all the Mughal emperors, his life was perhaps the most tragic. In the first ten years of his reign, he lost one of the largest empires in the world at that time. Babur had given control of the northern regions

---

[25] *The Baburnama*. (ed. trans. by Wheeler M. Thackston). New York: The Modern Library, 2002: 55.

of the empire (the area around Kabul and Lahore) to Humayun's half-brother, Kamran Mirza. Humayun was to govern the rest of the empire. While Kamran Mirza became a rival for power, Humayun's main threat came from Afghans who still laid claim to the old sultanate of Delhi. Even some of his own people disputed Humayun's right to become emperor.

By 1540, rebellions forced Humayun to flee India. He first escaped north into Afghanistan with a small entourage which included his wife and infant son, Akbar. The group suffered great hardships in the Afghan mountains in winter. When they arrived in Khorasan, however, they were warmly greeted by the Persian Safavid governor. As Humayun continued travelling west, he could not help but be impressed by the amazing architectural treasures of the region. For example, in Mashhad, he saw the magnificent *Masjid-i Gawhar Shad*, the imposing Friday Mosque commissioned by Gawhar Shad (d.1438), the wife of Shah Rukh. Humayun was proud that such works of art had been commissioned by some of his Timurid ancestors.

Eventually, Humayun and his followers reached the Safavid capital of Qazvin in central Iran. At the court of the young Shah Tahmasp I, Humayun was entertained lavishly by his host. Tahmasp I even offered to help Humayun in his attempt to regain the Mughal throne. Humayun's half-brother, Kamran Mirza, had sent word to Tahmasp I asking him to hand over Humayun, dead or alive. As a bribe, Kamran offered to give the Safavid monarch control of the city of Kandahar. Tahmasp I rejected Kamran's offer outright. But all this expensive entertaining and offers of assistance to Humayun came at a cost: Tahmasp I expected Humayun to convert to Shi'ite Islam. Outwardly, Humayun professed to be Shi'a and therefore received all the help he had requested from the Persians. After a year in exile, Humayun prepared for his return to India.

Persian troops aided in the capture of both Kandahar and Kabul from Kamran. The people of Afghanistan were only too happy to welcome Humayun and see the tyrannical Kamran defeated. Humayun was of course happy to once again be reunited with his wife and three-year-old son, Akbar. Athough Kamran Mirza had made several attempts to have Humayun assassinated, Humayun showed mercy on his half-brother by reluctantly having him blinded. Kamran died near Makkah while performing the Hajj.

Humayun encountered little resistance from the remnants of the Sher Shah Sur dynasty in his push into India. In July 1555, after a fifteen year absence, Humayun entered Delhi and reclaimed the capital of the Mughals.

Unfortunately, Humayun was to be given very little time to savour victory. Six months later, in January 1556, Humayun died of injuries sustained from a fall down a flight of stairs in his own private library in Delhi. Many historians consider the life of the second Mughal emperor a tragic failure. As the prolific nineteenth century British writer Stanley Lane-Poole once remarked, "Humayun stumbled out of life as he had stumbled through it."

HUMAYUN'S LEGACY

Humayun's important legacy is the love of Persian culture that he bequeathed to his son Akbar. As Mughal culture developed, Persian influences became very strong. These are most pronounced in the magnificent tomb of Humayun, built after his death by his wife (see illustration 19-1).

When the Mughals arrived in India, Sanskrit, the classical language of Hinduism, was the language spoken by the educated Hindu priests. The uneducated spoke regional Indian dialects. Babur spoke Chaghatai Turkish as did the soldiers in his invading army. Persian had been the language

19-1 HUMAYUN'S TOMB: The Mughals were of Central Asian origin and came to India in the early sixteenth century speaking Persian and Turkish. Persian influence in Mughal culture became stronger after Humayun returned from his exile in Iran. When he died, his wife assembled Indian and Iranian architects and craftsmen to build the first great monumental structure erected by the Mughals. The Tomb of Humayun (1565), situated to the south of Delhi, is considered one of the finest tomb complexes in the world. Humayun's wife intended it to be used first as a tomb for her husband, and later to be used as a mausoleum for all Mughal descendants. While Persian tombs displayed glazed ceramic tiles on the outside, Humayun's tomb used carefully cut pink and yellow sandstone with white marble inlay. The building proved popular and became a model for later Mughal tombs including the Taj Mahal, which Shah Jahan built for his wife.

of the Timurid court and had become the preferred language of educated Muslims in Central Asia. Over time, the "national language" of the Mughal Empire became Urdu, an Indian language with Sanskrit roots, but with many Turkish, Persian, and later, Arabic influences.

AKBAR (1556–1605)

At the time of Humayun's death, much territory still needed to be recaptured from the Afghans who had attempted to end the fledgling Mughal dynasty of rulers. This task of imperial conquest was left to Akbar, the thirteen-year-old son of Humayun.

Akbar, considered the greatest of all Mughal rulers, is often called *Akbar-i Azam* or "Akbar the Great". For five years, a Shi'a Turkoman named Bayram Khan acted as regent and led the military conquests in Akbar's name. A low-class Hindu upstart, Hemu, posed the first serious threat to Akbar's dynasty. But in November 1556, Hemu and his superior forces were defeated by Akbar's army at the Second Battle of Panipat. Within a year, Akbar's control over India was secure.

In 1561, a more mature Akbar took full control of his government which he ran like an army, with himself being the commander-in-chief. Akbar worked hard at enforcing his many policies that helped shape the ever-expanding Mughal state which now extended from Kabul in Afghanistan to Bengal in east India and from Kashmir in the north to the Deccan Plateau of India in the south. Akbar's greatness clearly lay in his administrative skills.

Akbar is often cited as being the only illiterate Mughal ruler. The extremely chaotic early years of his life, when as an infant he fled with his father Humayun to remote Afghanistan, must have had an influence on his development. Akbar himself was proud to remind his subjects that prophets were illiterate and even suggested that Muslim families keep one of their sons illiterate.

While later Mughal emperors received an extensive education in palace schools, Akbar spent his youth in the rugged Afghan mountains learning to fend for himself. Unlike his bookish father, Akbar became adept at hunting, playing sports and excelling in the martial arts. His interests were varied and ranged from philosophy to politics. Akbar's library contained religious books in several Indian languages as well as in English, Greek, Arabic and Persian. Books from his vast library were regularly read to him aloud. Today, revisionist historians argue that Akbar was indeed literate, but simply not to the extent of his predecessors or successors.

AKBAR'S *DIN-I ILAHI*

Akbar is remembered for his policies of assimilation. He accepted the fact that the land he ruled was multi-ethnic, multi-religious and multi-linguistic. By abolishing the *jizya* (the required poll tax levied on the non-Muslim population), Akbar might have endeared himself more to the Hindu masses; but no ruler has the right to abolish a Qur'anic command. By so doing, Akbar exhibited a flagrant disrespect for *Kitab Allah*. To show his sincerity to the non-Muslims in his realm, in later years, he became a vegetarian and is reported to have said he did not believe it right for a man to make his stomach the grave of animals! Akbar even stopped hunting, which had been a very popular Mughal pastime.

Akbar adopted an official policy of assimilation which even encouraged interfaith marriages between Mughals and Hindu nobility. The Rajputs were a notorious clan of Hindu warriors and in order to pacify relations with them, Akbar married a Rajput Hindu princess who became the mother of Salim Muhammad, a future Mughal emperor.

Akbar did not impose Islam on his subjects. All religions in the land – Hinduism, Jainism, Buddhism, Zoroastrianism and Christianity – were tolerated. To this end, Akbar encouraged religious debates in specially constructed *ibadet khanahs* or houses of worship. Akbar himself was seen celebrating *Diwali*, the Hindu "festival of lights". He leaned towards Sufism, but in the end invented a personality cult that in essence rejected all formalised religions.

Akbar's new religious path, *din-i ilahi* or divine faith, was never intended to be a religion as such. He initiated this new exclusive brotherhood in 1582. It was never meant for the masses even though Akbar demanded veneration from them. As a "divine monarch", he believed he offered his subjects just and honest governance.

Akbar's *din-i ilahi* was offered to a small group of courtiers only. According to some accounts, only eighteen people were ever initiated into the secret brotherhood. Akbar, of course, led the initiation ceremony. Initiates greeted each other with *Allah-u Akbar* and responded with *Jalla Jalaluhu*. When they met with Akbar, disciples of *din-i ilahi* would prostrate themselves in *sajdah* before him!

Akbar likely intended his personality cult to be open to only those select few who would show utter loyalty and fealty to him. *Din-i ilahi* died a natural death when its leading practitioners all predeceased Akbar, the object of their veneration.

The concept of tolerating one another's differences was not totally new to Indian society. Not everyone, however, could accept Akbar and his deviant cultic order. For most orthodox Muslims, Akbar was an apostate who had clearly left the fold of Islam.

There are many contradictions in Akbar's life; he was most certainly a very complex individual who some say was possibly epileptic. One day he would establish a new city and call it Allahabad (the City of Allah); the next day, he would order the wearing of silk and golden garments during the daily prayers.[26]

Despite Akbar's personal unorthodox religious practices, many Indians today still revere him as a ruler who genuinely attempted to be the protector of all his subjects, irrespective of their religion.

FATEHPUR SIKRI (1571–1585)

We recall that the 'Abbasid capital was shifted from Baghdad to Samarra' for a brief period in the early ninth century. After Samarra' was abandoned in 892 and the seat of government restored to Baghdad, it reverted to a simple market town.

Akbar similarly chose to relocate his capital from Agra to the newly built palace city of Fatehpur Sikri, situated forty kilometres to the west of Agra. Apparently Agra had been unlucky for Akbar as all his children born there had died in their infancy. However, his son Salim (whose mother had been a Rajput princess), was born in Sikri in 1569 and had survived. It was, therefore, on a whim that Akbar then decided to build his new palatial capital covering five square kilometres at Sikri. It remains Akbar's greatest architectural legacy and even today is one of the most impressive sights in all of India. As craftsmen were commissioned from all over the empire, the architecture is a unique fusion of styles with Islamic and indigenous Jain and Hindu influences.

Building began in 1571 and by 1573 Fatehpur Sikri (City of Victory) had become the new Mughal capital. Initially, the new city was to encompass the shrine of the Sufi saint Sheikh Salim of the Chisti *tariqah*. But Akbar's successful conquest of Gujarat in 1573, enabled him to celebrate his victory by constructing a series of grand and extremely impressive gateways, mosques, conference centres (the *ibadet khanahs*), and of course the extensive multi-storied palace complex. In 1575, Akbar inaugurated the famous "conference of religions" in the newly constructed *ibadet khanah*. Representatives from all the major religions in India attended; these included Muslims, Hindus, Jains, Zoroastrians, and even Catholic Christians from the Portuguese port of Goa on the Indian Ocean.

Surprisingly, after only fifteen years, Fatehpur Sikri was suddenly abandoned in 1585. Most historians cite a chronic water shortage as the main reason for the permanent evacuation of the city. The impressive red sandstone city, which still attracts visitors today, was as original as its founder.

---

[26] It is not permissible for Muslim men to wear silk or gold.

Akbar's Final Years

Portuguese Jesuits unsuccessfully tried to convert Akbar to Christianity; Greek Christians attempted to do the same. The flame of a Zoroastrian altar burned for a time in Akbar's palace. He supposedly even recited at noon the 1,001 Sanskrit names for the sun. After meeting with Jain savants, Akbar restricted animal slaughter and the caging of birds. But Akbar was simply curious about other faiths and it is not believed that he ever really denounced Islam for any other religion. Still, Akbar remains one of the most intriguing, if not tormented, personalities in Islamic history.

Towards the end of his long reign, Akbar had to contend with tempering his rebellious sons. Murad died young of excesses as did Daniyal soon after. Salim, Akbar's sole surviving son, was over thirty and very impatient; he wondered when he would become enthroned as emperor. Akbar tried hard to save Salim from self-destruction.

In 1604, Akbar's beloved mother – Humayun's wife – passed away. Within a year, Akbar himself lay on his deathbed. He forgave Salim for his faults and invested him as the new Mughal emperor.

Akbar died in 1605 and was interred in a specially built mausoleum. But in 1691, a band of brigands desecrated the tomb and threw Akbar's bones into a fire. Ironically, the Mughal emperor who had often ridiculed his own Islamic faith, in the end, received a Hindu funeral of sorts.

Jahangir (1605–1627)

Akbar the Great died in 1605 and was succeeded by his son, Salim, who chose the regal name Jahangir (World Conqueror) when he succeeded to the Mughal throne. Jahangir was the first Mughal ruler whose mother was neither Turkish nor Persian, but of pure Indian Rajput blood.

Jahangir, unlike his father, received the best education possible at the time. The best tutors instructed him in Turkish, Persian, Arabic and all the sciences. Just as the rebellious Salim had once tried to wrestle the throne from his father, he, now as emperor, soon had to deal with the aspirations of his equally rebellious son, Khusraw, who attempted to capture Lahore and unseat his father. The example set by Humayun in punishing his half-brother Kamran Mirza by blinding, now became the norm for successive Mughal emperors. Khusraw was subsequently blinded. Jahangir, as sovereign, no longer believed parental or fraternal relationships were of much importance.

During Akbar's reign, the Portuguese had established small colonies such as Goa along the coast of the Indian Ocean. Now more Europeans, including the British East India Company, arrived and were able to establish trading posts in various parts of India. This formal permission granted by Jahangir to the British merchants is often cited as his greatest political blunder. Once the British gained a foothold in South Asia, they were very reluctant to leave and, in time, became rulers of the entire subcontinent.

The Mughal emperors, living amongst millions of Indians, never forgot their Mongol (Timurid) roots. Jahangir, for example, inquired about the conditions of his ancestor's tomb in Samarqand. He offered to pay for the maintenance of the *Gur-i Amir*, Timur-i Lang's mausoleum. This wonderful structure inspired the Mughals to also build great tombs (see illustration 16-1).

Jahangir wished to be known as a just ruler. To this end, he inaugurated a unique device called the "chain of justice". An elaborate system of long ropes and bells was employed in his palace whereby any subject of the realm could complain directly to the emperor regarding any injustice. Once the bell was rung, royal clerks would investigate the complaint.

Jahangir constructed some impressive buildings in Allahabad, Agra and Lahore. Indeed, this period of creative building is often referred to as the "Age of Mughal Splendour". Jahangir became a patron of all Mughal arts, especially miniature painting and was himself a connoisseur of fine art and an accomplished calligrapher. He was a scientist who adored nature and wrote some worthy zoological studies, still appreciated today.

But Jahangir was also an aesthete (someone having an excessive admiration for all things of beauty), who was always meticulously groomed, bejewelled and clothed. Moreover, he was helplessly addicted to the pleasures of this world and was quite content to while away the time in his magnificent palatial gardens in Kashmir. He had obviously inherited his love of Persian gardens from his great-grandfather, Babur.

Nur Jahan, Jahangir's last wife, being a Persian princess, wielded enormous influence at the Mughal court which attracted and welcomed many Persian artists and scholars. Thus, the strong Persian influences introduced by Humayun after his exile in Iran, became even more evident.

Jahangir had married Nur Jahan in 1611. Her intelligence and innate gifts made her an extremely competent administrator. While the pleasure-loving Jahangir was incapacitated, he permitted his wife along with her Persian father and brother, to become the *de facto* rulers of the Mughal Empire. Nur Jahan was also instrumental in arranging the marriage between her son, Prince Khurram, and the daughter of her brother. It was for this bride, Mumtaz Mahal, that the future Shah Jahan was to build the Taj Mahal.

Jahangir encouraged the mass conversion of non-Muslim Indians to Islam although he himself was quite irreligious during his life. The emperor Akbar, inquisitive as ever, had witnessed with great interest the birth of a new religion in India, Sikhism. Unfortunately, Jahangir was much less tolerant than his father regarding non-Muslims, and is blamed for the death of one of the Sikh holy men, Guru Arjan Singh in 1606. The Sikh guru had given Jahangir's rebellious son, Khusraw a sum of money and had, therefore, become guilty of aiding and abetting his treacherous son. Years later, tension between the Muslim Mughals and the fledgling Sikh faith only intensified when Jahangir's grandson, Aurangzeb, murdered the ninth Sikh Guru Tegh Bahadur.

In his final years, Jahangir had to contend with court intrigues and a rebellion by Nur Jahan and her son, Khurram. The emperor died en route from Kashmir to Lahore in 1627. He had lived a pampered life and had succumbed to its excesses. Prince Khurram was now ready to rule without his mother's interference.

SHAH JAHAN (1627–1658)

Jahangir's son, Prince Khurram, upon ascending the Mughal throne, assumed the title of Shah Jahan, Persian for "Lord of the World", a name he had received from his father in 1617 after a victorious military campaign.

Shah Jahan spent the early part of his reign heading mainly unsuccessful military campaigns to extend the Mughal control southwards into the Deccan Plateau and the northwest. Enormous sums from the state treasury were spent on these extensive campaigns. Taxation of the peasants financed the Mughal army which had become an enormous military machine. Unfortunately, many tax collectors were corrupt and would return to the imperial treasury only part of the revenue collected.

Mughal emperors were all great builders, but Shah Jahan surpassed them all in his many lavish constructions, some of the finest ever built. These extensive buildings, of course, were extremely expensive and once again almost drained the state treasury (see illustration 19-2).

An effective series of highways and waterways connected the many important towns and cities and ports throughout the empire. Cities like Lahore, Delhi and Agra became commercial and artistic centres (see illustration 19-3).

In 1638, the capital was moved from Agra to the newly-founded walled city of Shahjahanabad (City of Shah Jahan), whose site is now referred to as Old Delhi. The city was planned by the chief architect of the Taj Mahal and took ten years to construct. Shahjahanabad had wonderful avenues, waterways, gardens, mosques and mansions. Most importantly, it featured an immense fortified palace known as the *Lal Qila* (Red Fort). This palace became the principal royal residence and the centre of Mughal administration until the last days of the dynasty in the mid-nineteenth century. Besides the impressive Red Fort, other buildings such as the *Moti Masjid* and *Jama Masjid* – the largest mosque in all of India – can still be visited today.

19-2 MUGHAL MASTERPIECE: Although the Mughal emperors were wealthy beyond belief, the extensive building projects undertaken by them were costly and did, on occasion, drain their treasury. Master calligraphers skillfully designed monumental Arabic and Persian inscriptions for many large public buildings. Other calligraphers worked on a much smaller scale and produced miniature Mughal masterpieces such as this silver *rupee* from the reign of Shah Jahan (1627–1658). It was common practice for all Muslim rulers to place the *kalimah* on all their coins and the Mughals were no exception. Shah Jahan's grandfather, Akbar the Great, however, abolished the *kalimah* after creating his new religion. On his new *ilahi* coins, he placed a different motto: *Allahu akbar jalla jalalahu* (Allah is the Greatest; glorified be His Glory). On this beautiful silver *rupee* of superb craftsmanship, the *kalimah* is back again and fills the entire square on this side of the coin. Around the sides, the four *Khulafa' ar-Rashidun* (the Rightly-Guided Caliphs), are identified: *bi-sudq Abu Bakr,* (by the truth of Abu Bakr); *wa 'adl 'Umar,* (and the justice of 'Umar); *bi-azram 'Uthman,* (by the modesty of 'Uthman); and *wa 'ilm 'Ali,* (and the wisdom of 'Ali). It is not surprising that a work of such beauty as this coin was commissioned by Shah Jahan. Coins like these – miniature works of art – were used to finance much larger works of art, such as the Taj Mahal – the building many believe to be the most perfect ever constructed.

19-3 FROM A MUGHAL GARDEN: The Persian influence on Mughal culture was profound; the word *Mughal* itself is the Persian word for "Mongol". The Persian language and its lyrical poetry were avidly studied in Mughal times. Architecture was also influenced by Persian styles and tastes. Even Mughal tile work shows clear traces of Persian Safavid influence. The example here comes from the Mosque of Wazir Khan in Lahore, Pakistan and dates from 1634. Of all the hundreds of Mughal buildings, this mosque contains the richest variety of ceramic tile decoration. This is a wonderful example of a cut-tile mosaic showing stylised iris flowers. The brilliant, earthy colours of this piece of Islamic art are uniquely Mughal.

TAJ MAHAL (1631–1648)

The greatest architectural achievement of the Mughals was of course the magnificent Taj Mahal, the mausoleum for Shah Jahan's beloved wife, Mumtaz Mahal. This beautiful building symbolises the power and stability of the Mughal dynasty.

This quintessential Mughal building derived its inspiration from Timur-i Lang's *Gur-i Amir* tomb in Samarqand and Humayun's tomb outside Delhi. The fusion of Turkish, Persian and Indian influences is clearly evident in the Taj Mahal. But while many Mughal buildings were constructed of red sandstone, Shah Jahan's architects employed only dazzling white marble, inlaid with semi-precious stones. It is reported that these gems were taken from mines as far away as China, Badakhshan (northern Afghanistan), Sri Lanka, Tibet and Arabia.

Craftsmen were brought from all over the empire to work on the construction of the Taj Mahal. Ustadh 'Isa and 'Isa Muhammad Effendi were two imminent artisans who had both been trained by the great Ottoman master architect, Mimar Sinan.

In 1657, when Shah Jahan became ill, reports were circulated that he had died. This news led to a prolonged and bloody struggle for succession. Each of the emperor's four sons (of the same mother, Mumtaz Mahal) attempted to seize the throne. The infirmed Shah Jahan could only helplessly watch the tragic events unfold. The battle of succession eventually left three sons dead: Murad Bakhsh, Dara Shikoh and Shah Shuja.

Aurangzeb, the sole surviving son, claimed victory, always asserting that he had waged war on his brothers in the defence of Islam. He immediately arrested his father who was deposed in 1658. The following year, Aurangzeb was formally enthroned as the new emperor in a lavish ceremony in the Red Fort at Delhi. It proved to be the grandest enthronement ceremony in Mughal history.

An ungrateful Aurangzeb imprisoned his sick father in a suite in the Agra Fort where he lived for another eight years, cared for by his eldest daughter. He died there a broken and forgotten man. According to legend, Shah Jahan on his deathbed, took one last look at the Taj Mahal from his confined quarters. He was later interred alongside his wife in her mausoleum.

By the middle of the seventeenth century, India was still one of the greatest empires in the world. Mughal culture had reached its zenith. Exquisite gardens, like the Shalimar in Lahore, as well as the fine art of miniature painting and the reading and writing of Persian poetry were all enjoyed by the wealthy Mughal nobility. Shah Jahan had beautified his empire and had built a new capital city. However, the one thing he did not accomplish in his life was the creation of a unified Sunni state linking India with Central Asia.

AURANGZEB (1658–1707)

Aurangzeb is recognised as the sixth and last of the Great Mughals. He was succeeded by a series of weaker rulers known as the later or lesser Mughals. During his long reign of almost fifty years, the empire expanded to its furthest extent with only a small part of the southern tip of India not conquered. Aurangzeb lived longer than any other Mughal emperor and died at the age of eighty-nine. Despite his deep religiosity, most religious minorities today in South Asia consider Aurangzeb an intolerant despot. Indeed, one might identify the on-going Hindu-Muslim conflict in India today as stemming from the severe policies of Aurangzeb.

Aurangzeb's intolerance of the religious minorities of India was in stark contrast to many of his predecessors. He passionately wanted to Islamise all of India. But in a multi-ethnic, multi-religious empire, Aurangzeb's tough policies against non-Muslims only reaped hostility, especially from the Sikh and Hindu communities.

Aurangzeb, throughout his life, followed a very strict orthodox interpretation of Islam. He codified his edicts in a large thirty-three volume compilation called the *Fatawa-i Alamgiri*. In 1659, Aurangzeb displayed his ultra-orthodox character by prohibiting the usual engraving of the Arabic *kalimah* on his newly minted coins. He feared the defilement of the *kalimah* in the hands of non-Muslims. Interestingly, this view was in direct contradiction to most Muslim monarchs of the day who saw the inclusion of the *kalimah* on their coinage as a necessary statement of the presence of Islam in their realm. Such overtly Islamic coinage was also seen as a means of propagating the faith with each inscribed coin acting as a *da'i*, or Islamic missionary.

Also in direct contrast with his predecessors who made their palaces centres of Islamic art and culture with resident artists and musicians, Aurangzeb forbade music, representational art and singing. Thousands of architectural images were subsequently destroyed in the enforcement of his edicts.

Aurangzeb was a committed workaholic who spent most of his life extending the frontiers of the Mughal Empire. He was a very complex character who often exhibited great kindness to some, but extreme brutality to others. He dressed simply, forbade the wearing of silk in his court and cultivated the outward appearance of a saintly *fakir*, or dervish. In his earlier years, he had memorised the entire Qur'an. He led an almost ascetic life. He wove prayer caps and was an accomplished calligrapher writing copies of the Qur'an which showed meticulous penmanship. Aurangzeb sold both his prayer caps and Qur'ans, earmarking the proceeds for his funeral.

After hundreds of years of Muslim rule, Aurangzeb found it intolerable that Hindus should still be prosperous. He decreed that no new Hindu temples could be built or old ones repaired. The rebuilt Hindu temple of Somnath, once destroyed by Mahmud of Ghazna, was yet again demolished by Aurangzeb along with the systematic destruction of countless other idolatrous temples throughout India.

The *jizya* was re-introduced by Aurangzeb, having been previously abolished by Akbar. Not surprisingly, these policies and attempts to forcibly convert Hindus and others to Islam led to open rebellion and costly wars. The ensuing chaos directly weakened and eventually caused the collapse of the Mughal Empire later in the eighteenth and nineteenth centuries. As a direct result of Aurangzeb's discriminatory policies, Indians, for the first time, identified themselves according to their religion, not ethnic origin or geographic location.

An example of Aurangzeb's intolerance is the execution in 1675 of Guru Tegh Bahadur, the ninth Sikh Guru, for refusing to convert to Islam. Even today, Guru Tegh Bahadur's martyrdom is still mourned by the Sikh community. The death of this guru caused the Sikh religion to be transformed into a more militant brotherhood of "saint soldiers" aimed at destroying the Mughals.

In 1681, Aurangzeb's many years of attempting to rule devoutly all came to naught when his own son, Akbar, attempted to depose his father by proclaiming himself the new emperor. Akbar failed to win the necessary support for such a coup and therefore, lived the rest of his life as a fugitive in remote parts of India and Iran where he died in 1704, predeceasing his father by three years.

The last years of Aurangzeb's rule were pathetic ones. As was so often the case with Mughal rulers, Aurangzeb worried about his sons initiating a bitter war of succession after his death. Such a war, of course, was inevitable with not only several princes vying for power, but many grandsons and even great-grandsons also eager to claim the Mughal throne.

Earlier in his life, Aurangzeb had killed off his rival brothers and had imprisoned his old and infirm father. Despite these contradictions, he had attempted to live his life with piety at its centre. Now, at almost ninety years of age, Aurangzeb appeared a sad and almost tragic figure whose life as both father and ruler had been one big disappointment. His asceticism and peculiar interpretation of Islam had only resulted in him winning enemies.

In 1707, Aurangzeb, the last of the Great Mughals, died alone, having outlived many of his peers. He was unceremoniously buried in a simple open-air grave. Today, he is remembered and admired by some for his codified edicts, but is also criticised by Hindus and Sikhs for being a religious zealot.

THE LESSER MUGHALS - THE DECLINE OF THE DYNASTY (1707–1858)

On the death of Aurangzeb in 1707, a very unstable and rebellious empire – which had now reached its zenith encompassing nearly ninety percent of South Asia – was bequeathed a series of fourteen weak descendants known as the "Lesser Mughals". Aurangzeb had requested in his will that the Empire be divided amongst his four sons in order to avoid a war of succession, but the will was ignored.

Without a strong, central leadership, many regional governments proclaimed their independence. The once great Mughal Empire had dissolved into a series of "successor states", both Muslim and Hindu. In 1739, the true weakness of the Mughal Empire became all too clear when the Persian ruler, Nadir Shah, pillaged Delhi and took seven hundred elephants loaded with Mughal treasure back to Iran. The famous *taht-i tavous* (Peacock Throne), for example, was removed from the *diwan-i khas* (private audience hall) of the Red Fort in Delhi.

The Mughal dynasty survived Nadir Shah's invasion, but Shah 'Alam II and his Mughal army was defeated by the British in a decisive confrontation near Allahabad in 1763. From now on, the British and their East India Company became the new masters of India and Shah 'Alam II was forced to cede all state revenue to them.

The British pretended they were just administering the Mughal Empire on behalf of the emperor, but the destitute royal family was kept as virtual prisoners in the Red Fort after the British occupied Delhi in 1803. The once all-powerful Mughal emperor had been reduced to a mere "puppet king" of Delhi.

BAHADUR SHAH ZAFAR II - THE LAST MUGHAL (1837–1858)

Of the dozen or so "Lesser Mughals", the life of the last ruler of the dynasty, Bahadur Shah Zafar II, is perhaps the most fascinating.

By 1837, the year in which Bahadur Shah II was enthroned as emperor, the Mughal Empire had virtually ceased to exist. While the titular Mughal rulers essentially only commanded the city of Delhi, they still attempted to keep up courtly appearances. But the days when corpulent emperors were weighed on scales balanced by a virtual mountain of precious stones were long gone. The Mughals were now an impoverished family held hostage in the Red Fort and totally submissive to the British, the new rulers of India.

THE SEPOY REBELLION OF 1857

Bahadur Shah II was a man of letters who had little or no administrative ability. Poets do not make good military commanders, yet the feeble old man of eighty-two was coerced into supporting the Sepoy Rebellion (or Mutiny) of 1857, often called the First War of Indian Independence by today's Pakistanis and Indians. Indeed, for many resident historians of the subcontinent, the events of 1857 were tantamount to a "revolution" with "mutiny" and "rebellion" simply being too inadequate to describe an uprising of the people against a foreign occupier that had plundered the country and made India a pauper.

The mutiny of *sepoys* (native Indian soldiers of the Bengal army working for the British East India Company) began when they were issued with new rifles. A rumour soon spread that the cartridges to be used were greased with lard and tallow (beef fat). Both Muslims and Hindus were offended. The mutiny spread and Bahadur Shah II (probably unwillingly) signed a proclamation making him emperor of the whole of India. Within months, he had coins minted in his name and the *khutbah* mentioned him too. The fact remains that Bahadur Shah II had simply gotten caught up in the turmoil of the times. In all likelihood, he very reluctantly gave his blessings to the insurgents.

The Sepoy Rebellion had started in January 1857 and very soon spiralled into the most serious anti-colonial uprising of the nineteenth century. By late summer of the same year it was crushed once Delhi had been retaken by the British. Bahadur Shah II fled to Humayun's tomb where he was soon captured by British troops. The next day, two of his sons along with a grandson were shot and their heads presented to the grieving monarch. Within a short period of time he was also to witness the total destruction of his beloved garden city of Old Delhi, and in turn, his dynasty, the Mughals. After the rape and slaughter of its inhabitants, Delhi was pillaged and almost overnight, any remnants of the Mughal aristocracy that had survived the chaos were left penniless.

In January 1858, a year after the start of the uprising, Bahadur Shah II was tried for treason and complicity in the murder of Europeans. The show trial was held in the ruins of his old palace. He was subsequently exiled[27] along with his remaining family to Rangoon in Burma, where he died a prisoner four years later. He was very intentionally buried in an anonymous grave.

Bahadur Shah II, not unlike many Ottoman and Safavid monarchs, was a talented poet. Much of his Urdu poetry has been lost, but what remains is of outstanding quality and is still read and enjoyed today. Having been denied any real power by the British, Bahadur Shah II had still been able to initiate a minor cultural renaissance at his Delhi court. Being associated with the First War of Indian Independence, Bahadur Shah II today is often hailed as one of the first Indian nationalists to rise up against British occupation. Today, the only known descendants of Bahadur Shah II survive in lower class neighbourhoods in Delhi, Calcutta and Hyderabad.

As a result of the Sepoy Rebellion, India was now to be ruled directly from London. The ninety year-long period known as the *Raj* had begun. With the death of Bahadur Shah II in 1862, the Mughal dynasty finally came to an end. The British monarchs, beginning with Queen Victoria in 1877, became the new emperors of India, a title they held until 1948.

---

[27] Such was the loathing felt by the British towards the last Mughal emperor, that Bahadur Shah II was forced to vacate his beloved Delhi on a peasants' bullock cart.

It might be argued that had it not been for the "revolution" of 1857, there might never have been the birth of national movements that eventually forced the British to quit India, once the biggest jewel in the imperial crown.

LEGACY OF THE MUGHALS

Apart from the extensive architectural treasures – tomb complexes, forts, palaces, gardens and mosques – the most enduring legacy of the Mughals must certainly be the Urdu language. Rulers of the Delhi Sultanate as well as the Mughals were all originally Turkish speakers. But since the time of the Samanids (mid-tenth century), the newly invigorated Persian language had become popular at royal courts all over Central Asia. The Mughals, as we have seen, brought Persian culture to India. The Persian language with its beautiful lyrical poetry greatly influenced the language which the Muslims in India were speaking.

Over the centuries, a hybrid language emerged mixing Persian and Arabic with the Sanskrit-based Hindustani language spoken by the majority of the population of northern India. This new language became known as Urdu (the language of the Exalted Court), a word derived from the Old Turkic word for "military camp". Indeed, the modern Turkish word for "army" is *ordu*. Today, Urdu is the official language of Pakistan and is the mother tongue of millions of Muslims in India. The legacy of the once-great Mughal dynasty, therefore, must surely be this rich and vibrant spoken language.

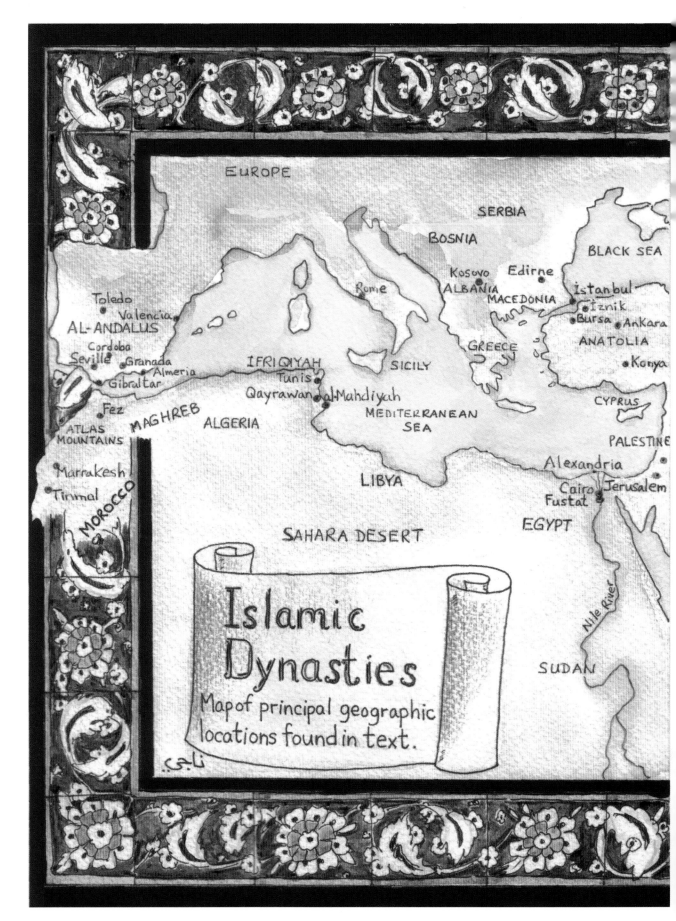

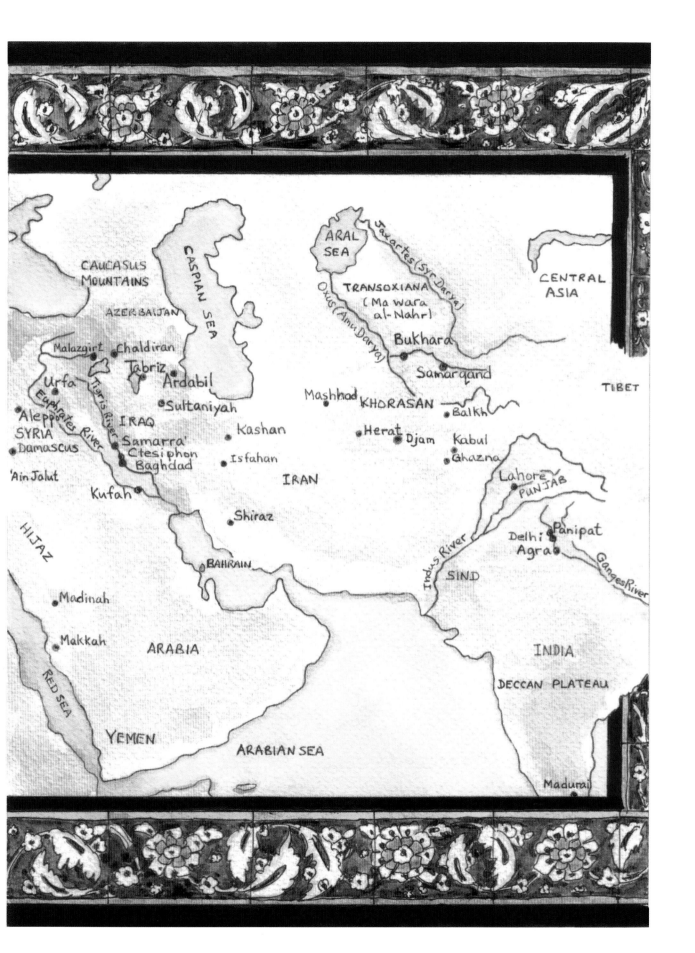

GLOSSARY

'Abbas I: great Safavid shah who made his capital, Isfahan, a city of magnificent Islamic architecture

Al-Abbas ibn 'Abd al-Muttalib: uncle of the Prophet ﷺ

'Abbasids: second great Islamic dynasty that replaced the Umayyads

'Abd al-Malik ibn Marwan: fifth Umayyad caliph; remembered for his reforms and building projects

'Abd al-Mu'min: second Almohad ruler; built the Kutubiyah Mosque in Marrakesh

'Abd ar-Rahman I: Syrian-born founder of the Umayyad dynasty of Spain

'Abd ar-Rahman II: ruler of Muslim Spain who made his capital, Cordoba, rival Baghdad in greatness

'Abd ar-Rahman III: greatest of all the Spanish Umayyad rulers; reigned during the golden age of caliphal Spain

Abu al-'Abbas as-Saffah: first 'Abbasid caliph; known as the "blood-shedder" for shedding Umayyad blood

Abu Bakr: Companion of the Prophet ﷺ and the first of the four "Rightly-Guided Caliphs"

Abu al-Hasan 'Ali: Nasrid king of Granada opposed to collaboration with Spanish Christians

Abu Sa'id: son of Uljaytu Khan and last of the great Ilkhanid rulers of Iran

Al-'Adid: last Fatimid caliph of Egypt; Salah ad-Din took control of Egypt on his death in 1171

Afsharids: short-lived Iranian dynasty founded by Nadir Khan of the Afshar Turkoman tribe

Aghlabids: famous dynasty of Arab rulers who once controlled parts of North Africa including Tunisia

Ahadith: Arabic for the collected "traditions", or reported deeds and sayings of the Prophet ﷺ

'Ain Jalut: site in Palestine of the battle between the Mamluks and Mongol forces of Hulagu Khan

Akbar: Mughal emperor who showed great tolerance towards the multi-ethnic make-up of his empire

'Ala ad-Din al-Khalji: ruler of the Delhi Sultanate who defeated the Mongols and brought Islam to central India

Alarcos: victorious battle for Almohads in Spain in 1195

Alhambra: famous palace of the Nasrid sultans of Granada in Spain

'Ali: son-in-law and Companion of the Prophet ﷺ; fourth and last of the "Rightly-Guided Caliphs"

Alp Arslan: Seljuq ruler who defeated the Byzantines at the Battle of Malazgirt in 1071

Amir: Arabic for emir or "prince"

Amir al-Mu'minin: Arabic for "Commander of the Faithful"; popular title used by many Muslim leaders

Amir al-'Umara': Arabic for "commander of the commanders"; title given to the head of 'Abbasid *mamluk* troops

Anatolia: Asia Minor, or present-day Turkey

Al-Andalus: Arabic for the Muslim territories in Spain and Portugal

Ankara: site of famous battle in central Turkey in 1402 between Timur and Ottoman sultan Bayezid II

Assassins: group of Isma'ili terrorists who conducted political assassinations throughout the Middle East

Atabeg: Turkish word meaning "guardian of a prince"; became powerful rulers after the death of Malik Shah

Atatürk: Turkish for "father of the Turks"; the new name for Mustafa Kemal, founder of the Turkish Republic

Aurangzeb: last of the great Mughal emperors; murdered his three brothers and imprisoned his father

Aybak: founder of the Mamluk dynasty of Egypt

Al-Azhar: the great Islamic university in Cairo; first established as a Fatimid Isma'ili training centre

Babur: descendant of Timur who became the founder of the Mughal dynasty of India

Bahadur Shah II: last Mughal emperor of India; exiled by the British to Burma in 1857

Bahri: Arabic for "sea-based"; the first group of Mamluk rulers of Egypt

Balkh: ancient city in northern Afghanistan destroyed by Mongols; birthplace of poet Jalal ad-Din Rumi

Bani Nasr: Arabic for "sons of Nasr"; the Nasrids of Granada, the last Muslim dynasty of Spain

Barlas: name of the Turkic tribe of Timur-i Lang

Barmakids: the Persian-speaking family who supplied many chief ministers to early 'Abbasid caliphs

Baybars: true founder of the Egyptian Mamluk dynasty who seized power from Qutuz in 1260

Bayezid I: Ottoman sultan defeated at Battle of Ankara in 1402

Bayqara: last important Timurid sultan; welcomed poets and artists to his court in Herat

Bayt al-Hikmah: Arabic for "house of wisdom"; the famous translation centre in 'Abbasid Baghdad

Bayt al-Mal: Arabic for "public treasury"

Berbers: original non-Arab inhabitants of North Africa; embraced Islam in the seventh century

Bey: Turkish word originally meaning "tribal chief"

Bihzad: great master of miniature painting who worked at the court of the Timurid Sultan Bayqara in Herat

Al-Biruni: great Muslim scholar associated with the Ghaznavid dynasty; wrote the superb *Kitab al-Hind*

Boabdil: Spanish for Abu 'Abdallah, the last Nasrid king of Granada, Spain

Bukhara: capital city of the Samanid dynasty; city in present-day Uzbekistan

Burji: Arabic for "of the citadel"; the second group of Egyptian Mamluk rulers

Bursa: large Byzantine city captured by the Ottomans; became an early Ottoman capital

Buyids: a dynasty of Persian Shi'ites who ruled for a century from Baghdad during 'Abbasid times

Byzantine: name given to the East Roman (Greek Orthodox) Empire whose capital was Constantinople; along with the Sasanian Empire was one of the two superpowers during the lifetime of the Prophet ﷺ

Catholic Monarchs: Spanish King Ferdinand and Queen Isabella; retook Spain from the Muslims in 1492

Chaghatai: the Central Asian Turkish language spoken by Babur Shah and his army

Chaldiran: site in eastern Turkey of a battle in 1514 between the Ottomans and Safavids

Charlemagne: Holy Roman Emperor; his army of Franks tried to reoccupy Muslim land in Spain

Constantinople: the old Greek name for Istanbul; the capital of the Byzantine Greeks for 1000 years

Cordoba: city in southern Spain; capital city of the Spanish Umayyads

Crusades: military expeditions originating in Christian Europe to retake Holy Land from Muslims

Ctesiphon: the pre-Islamic Sasanian capital city; ruins located outside of present-day Baghdad

Da'i: Arabic for "missionary"

Damascus: ancient city in Syria; capital of the Umayyad dynasty

Dandanqan: battle in 1040 in which the Ghaznavid sultan Mas'ud lost half his empire to the Seljuq Turks

Dar al-Islam: Arabic for "the abode of Islam"; the Islamic world

Defoe, Daniel: famous seventeenth century British writer; his book *Robinson Crusoe* was influenced by an Ibn Tufayl novel

Delhi Sultanate: series of five Islamic dynasties based in Delhi, India

Din al-Haq al-Islam: Arabic for "the religion of the Truth, al-Islam"

Din-i ilahi: Arabic for "divine religion (faith)"; name given to a new religious path created by the Mughal emperor Akbar

Dinar: the standard gold Islamic coin

Diogenes Romanus: Byzantine emperor defeated by the Seljuq Turks at the Battle of Malazgirt in 1071

Dirham: the standard silver Islamic coin

Diwali: famous Hindu "festival of lights"; celebrated by the Mughal emperor Akbar

Diwan-i khas: Persian for "private audience hall"; room in the Red Fort in Delhi

Drachm: the Sasanian Persian silver coinage

Druzes: small religious minority in Syria and Lebanon whose origin was the Fatimid caliph Al-Hakim

Edirne: second Ottoman capital; city to the north of Istanbul

Farsi: Persian word for the "Persian language"

Al-Fath: Arabic for "the conqueror"; name given to the Ottoman sultan Mehmed II after the 1454 conquest of Constantinople

Fatimids: North African dynasty which founded the city of Cairo; most powerful Shi'ite dynasty in history

Firdawsi: Persian poet who wrote the Persian national epic, the *Shahnameh*

'first gunpowder empire': term applied to the Mughal Empire in India

Fustat: the old district of Cairo originally founded by 'Amr ibn al-'As ﷺ

Gench Turkler: Turkish for "young Turks"; a group of radical Turkish nationalists opposed to the Ottomans

Al-Ghazali: great theologian who taught at the Nizamiyah College in Baghdad

Ghazi: Arabic for "frontier warrior of the faith"

Ghazna: capital city of the Ghaznavid Empire; the present-day city of Ghazni in Afghanistan

Ghaznavids: dynasty founded by a Turkish slave; remembered for sultan Mahmud's Indian invasions

Ghurids: the Afghan dynasty that replaced the Ghaznavids; builders of the Minaret of Djam

Granada: Arabic *Gharnata*; the beautiful capital city of the Nasrids in southern Spain

Great Yasa: Book of Mongol Law; adapted by the Ilkhans of Iran to conform to Islamic Law

Gur-i Amir: Timur's famous and beautifully decorated tomb complex in Samarqand

Hadith: Arabic for "tradition", or the reported deed and saying of the Prophet ﷺ

Haghia Sophia: Greek for "Holy Wisdom"; the ancient Byzantine church was made into a mosque in 1453

Al-Hakim: eccentric Fatimid caliph whose proclaimed divinity led to the founding of the Druze religion

Hayy ibn Yaqdhan: Arabic for "Alive, Son of Awake"; the famous allegorical book by Ibn Tufayl

Herat: ancient city in northwestern Afghanistan; capital of Shah Rukh's Timurid state

Hijrah: Arabic for "migration"; the Prophet's ﷺ flight from Makkah to Madinah in September 622

Hilm: Arabic for "civilised restraint"; the way in which Mu'awiyah, the first Umayyad monarch, ruled

Hittin: site of a battle in Palestine between the crusader king of Jerusalem and Salah ad-Din

Hulagu Khan: Mongol leader who sacked Baghdad in 1258 and ended 'Abbasid rule there

Humayun: second Mughal emperor; lost his empire to Afghans, regained it, but died shortly thereafter

Hussain: second son of 'Ali ؓ and grandson of the Prophet ﷺ; murdered at Karbala

Ibn al-Aghlab, Ibrahim: 'Abbasid governor of Tunisia who established his independent Aghlabid dynasty

Ibn al-Ahmar, Muhammad: founder of the Nasrid dynasty of Granada in southern Spain

Ibn Battutah: the "traveller of Islam"; the fourteenth century Moroccan-born Arab traveller and writer

Ibn Hanbal, Ahmad: Islamic scholar punished in Baghdad for his belief in the uncreated Qur'an

Ibn al-Haytham: greatest Arab physicist; wrote on optics at the court of the Fatimid caliph Al-Hakim

Ibn Hisham: early Islamic biographer of the Prophet ﷺ; his *sirah* is still read today

Ibn Jubayr: Andalusian traveller whose *rihlah* described the Middle East during the time of Salah ad-Din

Ibn Khaldun: famous Tunisian-born Arab historian; the "father of sociology"

Ibn Qasim, Muhammad: Arab leader who captured areas of western India during the Umayyad period

Ibn Sina: great Musl im scholar of the Middle Ages; his medical textbook was used in Europe for centuries

Ibn Tashfin: greatest of the Almoravid Berber rulers; founded the city of Marrakesh in southern Morocco

Ibn Tufayl: great Andalusian Arab philosopher; wrote his famous novel at the Almohad court in Marrakesh

Ibn Tughluq, Muhammad: ruler of Delhi Sultanate who brought Islam to remoter regions of southern India

Ibn Tumart: founder of the Almohad Berber dynasty of North Africa

Ibn Yunus: important Muslim astronomer who worked in Cairo during the reign of the Fatimid caliph Al-Hakim

Ibna' as-sabil: Arabic for "sons of the way"; people entitled to receive financial aid from the public treasury

Idris ibn 'Abdallah: relative of 'Ali ﷺ; founded the Idrisids, the first Arab dynasty in Morocco

Ilkhan: name of the first Mongol dynasty to rule parts of the Middle East; centred in Iran

Iltutmish: second "slave sultan" of the Delhi Sultanate; son-in-law of Qutb ad-Din Aybak

Al-'Iqab: Arabic for "the punishment"; Arab name for the Muslim defeat in 1212 at Las Navas de Tolosa

Isfahan: beautiful city in central Iran; Seljuq and Safavid capital

Isfahan nisf-i jihan: Persian for "Isfahan is half the world"; popular saying describing the city of Shah 'Abbas

Isma'il: first Safavid shah of Iran; at constant war with the Ottoman Turks

Isma'il Saman: Samanid ruler whose tomb in Bukhara is the greatest example of Samanid architecture

Isma'ilism: deviant religious doctrine that grew out of Shi'ite Islam; official religion of the Fatimid caliphs

Jabal Tariq: Arabic for "Tariq's mountain"; the site in southern Spain known today as "Gibraltar"

Jahangir: son of Akbar the Great; welcomed Persian scholars and artists to his court

Jain: follower of ancient Indian religion who believes in the transmigration of souls

Janissaries: *mamluk* slave soldiers who formed the backbone of the Ottoman Empire

Jenghiz Khan: first of the Mongol leaders to wantonly sweep across Asia and the Middle East

Jizya: Arabic for "poll tax"; paid by non-Muslims for protection by Muslims

Kai-Qubad I, 'Ala' ad-Din: greatest ruler of Seljuqs of Rum; beautified his capital, Konya, with splendid tiled buildings

Kanuni: Arabic for "lawgiver"; name given to the Ottoman sultan Sulaiman I

Karbala: site in southern Iraq of the massacre of Hussain ibn 'Ali ﷺ

Khalifah: Arabic for "caliph"; title first used by Abu Bakr ﷺ

Al-Khalifah as-Salih: Arabic for "pious caliph"; title given only to the Umayyad ruler 'Umar bin 'Abd al-'Aziz

Al-Khirqah al-Sharifah: Arabic for the cloak of the Prophet ﷺ; worn by ʻAbbasid caliphs for ʻ*eid* prayer

Khorasan: historically important province of northeast Iran

Al-Khulafa' ar-Rashidun: the four "rightly-guided caliphs" who succeeded the Prophet ﷺ as leaders

Al-Khusraw, Nasr: Iranian Isma'ili missionary who wrote an account of his travels to Fatimid Cairo

Khutbah: Arabic for "sermon"; usually delivered in a mosque on Friday

Kilij Arslan: Seljuq of Rum ruler who successfully fought the crusaders

Kitab al-Hind: Arabic for "The Book of India"; Al-Biruni's objective analysis of Hindu culture

Konya (*Qonya*): beautiful garden city in central Turkey; capital of the Seljuqs of Rum

Kufa: important Shi'ite pilgrimage centre in southern Iraq

Kurd: non-Arab ethnic minority inhabiting many parts of the Middle East; Salah ad-Din was a Kurd

Kutubiyah Mosque: beautiful Almohad mosque in Marrakesh, Morocco

Lahore: city in Pakistan that was the second and last Ghaznavid capital; known as "little Ghazna"

Laqab: Arabic for "title of honour"; very popular with ʻAbbasid caliphs and many other Muslim rulers

Las Navas de Tolosa: battle in 1212 in which the Almohad army was defeated in Spain by Christian armies

Lepanto: naval battle in 1571; the Ottoman navy defeated and lost control of the western Mediterranean Sea

Litham: Arabic for "veil"; worn by Tuareg Berber nomads (male) of the Sahara Desert

Lodi: last dynasty to rule the Delhi Sultanate; Ibrahim Lodi was defeated by Babur in 1526

Al-Madinah al-Munawwarah: Arabic for "the City of Light"; the city of the Prophet ﷺ in Saudi Arabia

Al-Madinat as-Salam: Arabic for "the City of Peace"; the round-walled city of ʻAbbasid caliph, Al-Mansur

Madrasah: Arabic for "school"; the traditional schools of Arabic learning

Mahdi: Arabic for the divinely-guided leader for the end of time

Al-Mahdiyah: first capital city of the Fatimids; coastal city in Tunisia

Mahmud Ghazan Khan: most important Ilkhanid ruler; first Mongol Ilkhan leader to embrace Islam

Mahmud ibn Sebuktigin: most famous Ghaznavid ruler; made annual raids into India

Mahmud II: Ottoman sultan who disbanded the Janissaries in 1826

Al-Maghreb al-Aqsa': Arabic for "the lands of the farthest west"; the countries of Northwest Africa

Malazgirt: site of famous battle in eastern Turkey in 1071 between the Byzantines and the Seljuqs

Malik Shah: son of the great Seljuq ruler Alp Arslan; killed by the Assassins

Mamluks: Turkish "slave soldiers" employed by various Islamic dynasties as a defence force

Al-Ma'mun: son of Harun al-Rashid; most important of all 'Abbasid rulers

Maristan: Persian word referring to the hospitals built in the Middle Ages in Old Cairo, Damascus etc.

Marrakesh: city in southern Morocco; capital of the Almoravid and Almohad Berber dynasties

Al-Masjid al-Aqsa': Arabic for the "Al-Aqsa' Mosque" in Holy Jerusalem, the third most sacred site in Islam

Masjid-i Shah: Persian for "Royal Mosque"; the great Safavid mosque built by Shah 'Abbas I in Isfahan

Masmuda: nomadic Berber tribe of the Atlas Mountains of Morocco

Mas'ud: son of Mahmud of Ghazna; lost the western half of his father's empire to the Seljuq Turks

Mathnawi: Arabic/Persian name of the most famous book of poetry by Jalal ad-Din Rumi

Mawali: Arabic for "clients"; the many non-Arabs who converted to Islam in the early period of Islamic history

Ma wara' an-Nahr: Arabic for "that which lies beyond the river"; the territories between the *Amu Darya* (Oxus) and *Syr Darya* Rivers; Transoxiana

Maydan: Arabic/Persian/Turkish word meaning "public square"

Mehmed II: Ottoman sultan who captured Constantinople from the Byzantines in 1453

Merinids: the Bani Merin, Moroccan Berber dynasty; succeeded the Almohads at time of Nasrids of Spain

Mihnah: Arabic for "testing" or "trial"; the Islamic "Inquisition" during time of caliph Al-Ma'mun in Baghdad

Mihrab: Arabic for "prayer niche"; that part of the mosque indicating the direction of Holy Makkah

Mimar: Turkish word for "architect"; name given to the great Ottoman architect Sinan

Minaret of Djam: immense victory tower/minaret built by the Ghurids in central Afghanistan

Minbar: Arabic for "pulpit"; placed to the right of the *mihrab* in a mosque

Mount Moriah: Jewish and Christian name for *Bayt al-Maqdas* in Jerusalem

Muadhdhin: Arabic for "caller to prayer"

Mu'awiyah: son of Abu Sufyan and nephew of 'Uthman ﷜; the first Umayyad caliph

Mughal: Persian word for "Mongol"

Mughals: longest-lasting of all the Muslim dynasties of India

Muhaddith: Arabic for "scholar of *hadith*", or the traditions of the Prophet ﷺ

Muhtasibs: Arabic for "inspectors" of the public markets

Muhammad 'Ali Pasha: Albanian-born Ottoman governor of Egypt

Muhammad V: sultan during the golden age of Nasrid Spain

Al-Mu'izz: Fatimid ruler who successfully conquered Egypt in 969

Muluk: Arabic for "kings"; often used to refer to the Umayyad caliphs

Al-Muluk al-Tawa'if: Arabic for "factional kings"; independent states that replaced the Spanish caliphate

Al-Murabitun: Arabic for "inhabitants of the *ribat*"; the "Almoravids", the Berber dynasty of North Africa

Mustafa Kemal: Kemal Atatürk; the founder and first president of the Republic of Turkey

Al-Musta'sim: last 'Abbasid caliph of Baghdad; killed by Hulagu Khan in 1258

Al-Mutawakkil III: last 'Abbasid "shadow caliph" of Cairo; taken to Constantinople by sultan Selim I

Mu'tazilite: school of philosophy believing the Qur'an to be "created"; doctrine supported by Al-Ma'mun

Al-Muwahhidun: Arabic for "the Unitarians" (the Almohads); second of the great Berber dynasties

Nadir Khan: Afshar Turkoman tribesman who drove out Afghans from Iran and later declared himself shah

Al-Nasir: sultan who reigned during the golden age of the Mamluks

Al-Nasir li Din Allah: Arabic for "defender of the faith of Allah"; title given to 'Abd ar-Rahman III on becoming caliph of Spain

Nasr II: the greatest ruler of the Samanid dynasty

Nasrids: the "Bani Nasr"; the last dynasty of Muslim Spain who ruled from Granada

Nicea (İznik): former Byzantine city in western Turkey which became Kilij Arslan's first capital

Nizam al-Mulk: influential Persian *wazir* of Great Seljuq state in Isfahan

Nizamiyah: colleges of *sunni* learning established throughout Seljuq lands by Nizam al-Mulk

Nuh II: last great Samanid ruler; his request for help from Sebuktigin caused the collapse of the Samanid dynasty

Nur ad-Din al-Zangi: ruler of northern Syria who successfully attacked the crusaders

Osman (Ghazi): founder of the Ottoman Empire; son of Ertoğrul

Osmanli: Turkish for "supporters of Osman"; Ottoman

Osmanlija: refined Turkish language spoken by educated elite in Ottoman times; Turkish with many Arabic and Persian influences

Oxus River: the *Amu Darya* River of Central Asia (in present-day Uzbekistan); once considered the border between the civilised and uncivilised worlds

Pahlavi: ancient pre-Islamic Persian language of the Sasanian Empire

Panipat: site north of Delhi where in 1526, the last ruler of the Delhi Sultanate was defeated by Babur in the First Battle of Panipat

Pope Urban II: Catholic leader who encouraged a crusade to capture Jerusalem from the Muslims in 1096

Qadi: Arabic for "judge"

Al-Qahirah: Arabic for the city of Cairo founded by the Fatimids in the late tenth century

Al-Qal'ah al-Hamra': Arabic for "red castle"; famous Alhambra Palace built by the Nasrids of Granada, Spain

Al-Qamr: Arabic for "moon"; name of the Fatimid caliph Al-Hakim's famous donkey

Qanat: Persian word for underground water channels used to irrigate many parts of Central Asia and Iran; often irreparably damaged by the Mongols

Qayrawan: old Islamic cultural capital in Tunisia; founded by 'Uqba ibn Nafi

Qizilbash: Turkish word for "red heads"; Turkoman tribesmen used by the Safavid Shah Isma'il to gain power

Al-Qubbat as-Sakhra: Arabic for the "Dome of the Rock"; sacred site in Holy Jerusalem

Al-Quds: Arabic word for Jerusalem, the third holiest city in Islam

Quraysh: Makkan tribe of the Prophet ﷺ

Qutb ad-Din Aybak: founder of the first dynasty of the Delhi Sultanate; the "Slave Dynasty"

Qutb Minar: tallest stone minaret in the world; built next to the Quwwat al-Islam Mosque in Delhi

Quwwat al-Islam: Arabic for "the might of Islam"; name of India's first great mosque

Rayhani: style of Arabic handwriting; used to write the giant Qur'ans commissioned by the Ilkhanid-Sultan, Uljaytu Khan

Reconquesta: Spanish for "Reconquesta"; the Spanish Christian attempt to reoccupy all of Muslim Spain

Ribat: Arabic for "religious fortress"; such forts were built as religious compounds by several North African Berber dynasties

Rio Salado: site of battle in 1340; the Muslim Nasrids were defeated by the Spanish Christians

Rudaki: first important poet of the modem Persian language; stayed at Samanid court in Bukhara

Rum: Arabic and Turkish word referring to the lands of the East Romans or Byzantines; later was used to mean "European"

Rumeli Hisari: Turkish for "European fortress"; stone fort built by the Ottoman sultan Mehmed II

Al-Sa'adah aal Muhammad: Arabic for "happiness is from the Family of Muhammad ﷺ"; the 'Abbasid revolutionary slogan

Safaviyah: Persian religious order whose name was used to designate the Safavid dynasty

Salah ad-Din: Kurdish liberator of Jerusalem and founder of the Ayyubid dynasty

Saman-Khoda: founder of the Samanid dynasty of Central Asia

Samanids: a break-away principality of the 'Abbasid state; capital city was Bukhara

Samarqand: city in Uzbekistan in Central Asia; capital of Timur's empire

Samarra': the new 'Abbasid capital city built 110 kilometres north of Baghdad by caliph Al-Mu'tasim

Sanhaja: a group of Berber tribes in Morocco

Sanskrit: ancient classical language of the Hindus of India; language learned by Al-Biruni

Saqaliba: Arabic for "Slavs"; captives from non-Muslim lands; became bodyguards of 'Abd ar-Rahman III

Saqr al-Quraysh: Arabic for "Falcon of the Quraysh"; name given to Spanish Umayyad caliph 'Abd ar-Rahman I

Sasanian: pre-Islamic Persian Empire; one of the two superpowers during the lifetime of the Prophet ﷺ

Sebuktigin: Turkish slave who founded the Ghaznavid dynasty

Selim I: great Ottoman sultan who conquered Egypt 1517 and ended Mamluk rule there

Selim III: Ottoman sultan who first introduced reforms like military academies with French instructors

Seljuq: leader of nomadic Turks who embraced Islam; his grandsons founded the Seljuq Empire

Seljuqs: nomadic Turkic people from Central Asia who partially reunified the 'Abbasid state

Seljuqs of Rum: longest-lasting of all the Seljuq states; their capital city was Konya

Shadow caliphate: continuation of the 'Abbasid caliphate in Cairo through relatives of the last caliph

Shah: Persian word for "king"

Shah Jahan: Mughal emperor remembered for the construction of the Taj Mahal

Shahnameh: "The Book of Kings"; the epic Persian poem written by Firdawsi for Mahmud of Ghazna

Shah Rukh: son of Timur; made Herat the new Timurid capital

Shamanism: religion practised by the pre-Islamic Turkic peoples of Asia; a worship of the natural world

Shi'ah: Arabic for "supporters of 'Ali " ; one of the two branches of Islam

Shirkuh: uncle of Salah ad-Din; became *wazir* in Fatimid court

Shir Shah Sur: powerful Afghan ruler defeated by the Mughal emperor Humayun in 1555

Sifr: Arabic word for "zero"; introduced into the West by the Arabs after they had borrowed it from India

Silk Road: ancient overland trading route that linked Chinese cities with seaports of the Mediterranean Sea

Sinan: the great architect (*mimar*) of the golden age of the Ottomans

Sirah: Arabic for "biography"; generally refers to biographies of the Prophet

Siyaset-nameh: "The Book of Good Government" written by the Seljuq *wazir* Nizam al-Mulk

Söğüt: name of Turkic group of nomads whose leader, Ertoğrul, initiated the Ottoman dynasty

Sufi: Arabic word for a Muslim mystic or dervish; from Arabic word for "wool"

Sulaiman I: great Ottoman sultan known as the Magnificent; reigned during the Ottoman golden age

Sultan: Arabic title of leadership first used by Mahmud of Ghazna

Sultan Husayn: Safavid king who caused the eventual downfall of his dynasty

Sultaniyah: second capital city of the Ilkhans of Iran; site of Uljaytu's famous mausoleum

Sunnah: Arabic for the "traditions and customs" of the Prophet

Sunni: Arabic for followers of the Prophet and his *sunnah*

Tabriz: city in northwest Iran; first capital of Ilkhans of Iran

Tahmasp I: son of Shah Isma'il; Safavid shah who introduced *mamluks* into his court and army

Taht-i Tavous: Persian for "peacock throne"; one of the great Mughal treasures carried off by Nadir Shah

Tamurt Wandalus: Berber for "land of the Vandals"; perhaps the origin of the Arabic word "Al-Andalus"

Tanka: type of silver coin in use throughout India and many parts of Central Asia in the Islamic period

Tanzimat: Turkish word for the period of reforms in the Ottoman Empire leading to real westernisation

Tariq ibn Ziyad: famous Berber commander of the Muslim invasion of Spain in 711

Tariqah: Arabic word for "path"; name given to Sufi religious orders

Tawhid: Arabic for the "oneness" of Allah; the concept of the Unity of Allah

Tengri: Mongolian name for the god worshipped by Jenghiz Khan; spirit (god) of the "Eternal Blue Sky"

Timur-i Lang: Turkic invader of Islamic lands; founder of Timurid dynasty; ruled from Samarqand

Tinmal: site of the Almohad *ribat* of Ibn Tumart in southern Morocco

Transoxiana: area in Central Asia north of the Oxus River

Tuaregs: Berber-speaking nomads of the Sahara Desert

Tughril Beg: leader of the Great Seljuqs who entered Baghdad in 1055

‘Ubayd Allah: founder of the Fatimid dynasty

‘Ulema: Arabic for the traditional Muslim scholars who interpreted Islamic Law

Uljaytu: great Ilkhanid sultan; built his magnificent tomb in the new Ilkhanid capital of Sultaniyah

Ulugh Beg: grandson of Timur-i Lang; important astronomer and mathematician

‘Umar: Companion of the Prophet ﷺ and second of the four "Rightly-Guided Caliphs"

‘Umar ibn ‘Abd al-‘Aziz: most respected of all Umayyad rulers; remembered as "‘Umar the Pious"

‘Ummah: Arabic for the "Muslim Community"

‘Uqba ibn Nafi: great Muslim commander who founded the city of Qayrawan in Tunisia

Urdu: national language of Pakistan; derived from Hindustani, but employs many Arabic and Persian words

Ustaz: Turkish word of Arabic origin meaning "head"; a master craftsman such as a master tile maker

Vega: Spanish word for "plain"; the famous fertile plain outside of Granada

Wa la Ghalib ‘ila Allah: Arabic for "there is no Victor but Allah"; the motto of the Nasrid dynasty of Spain

Al-Wadi al-Kabir: Arabic name for "the great river", i.e. the "Guadalquivir" that flows through Cordoba

Al-Walid: son of 'Abd al-Malik ibn Marwan; Umayyad ruler who built the Al-Aqsa' Mosque in Jerusalem

Wazir: Arabic for "minister of state"

Yazid: son of Mu'awiyah; second Umayyad caliph

Yeni cheri: Turkish for "new troops"; the Janissaries or slave soldiers of the Ottoman Empire

Zallaqah: important battle in 1086; won by the combined forces of Almoravid Berbers and Spanish Muslims

Zij-i Sultani: the "Catalogue of Stars"; the astronomical book written by the Timurid sultan, Ulugh Beg

Ziryab: Iraqi Arab who influenced the cultural habits of Muslims during the golden age of Cordoba

Zoroastrianism: the living Iranian religion founded by Zoroaster about three thousand years ago; teaches the worship of Ahura Mazda, the one uncreated Creator and universal deity; often incorrectly labelled the religion of "fire-worshippers": Zoroastrians, in fact, respect fire as a symbol of the energy of the Creator and use it only as a point of focus in their worship

SELECT BIBLIOGRAPHY

Arnold, Sir Thomas and Alfred Guillaume. *The Legacy of Islam*. Oxford: Oxford University Press, 1996.

Al-Azmeh, Aziz. *Ibn Khladun An Essay in Reinterpretation*. Budapest: Central European University Press, 2003.

Babur Shah. *The Baburnama*. (ed. trans. by Wheeler M. Thackston). New York: The Modern Library, 2002.

Barry, Michael. *Figurative Art in Medieval Islam and the Riddle of Bihzad of Heart (1465–1535)*. Paris: Flammarion, 2004.

Behrens-Abouseif, Doris. *Islamic Architecture in Cairo*. Cairo: The American University in Cairo Press, 1998.

Beny, Roloff and Seyyed Hossein Nasr. *Persia Bridge of Turquoise*. London: Thames and Hudson Ltd., 1975.

Blunt, Wilfred. *Isfahan Pearl of Persia*. London: Elek Books Limited, 1974.

Bosworth, Clifford Edmund. *The Islamic Dynasties*. Edinburgh: Edinburgh University Press, 1967.

Burckhardt, Titus. *Fez City of Islam*. Cambridge: The Islamic Texts Society, 1992.

---. *Moorish Culture in Spain*. Louisville, KY: Fons Vitae, 1999.

Clot, Andre. *Suleiman the Magnificent: The Man, His Life, His Epoch*. London: Al Saqi Books, 2005.

Dalrymple, William. *The Last Mughal: The Fall of a Dynasty: Delhi 1857*. London: Bloomsbury Publishing PLC, 2006.

Darke, Hubert. *The Book of Government or Rules for Kings: The Siyar al-Muluk or Siyyasat-nama of Nizam al-Mulk*. London: Curzon, 2002.

Degeorge, Gerard and Yves Porter. *The Art of the Islamic Tile*. Paris: Flammarion, 2002.

Dozy, Reinhart. *Spanish Islam a History of the Muslims of Spain*. (trans. by F. G. Stokes). New Delhi: Goodword Books, 2001.

Ecker, Heather. *Caliphs and Kings the Art and Influence of Islamic Spain*. Washington, D.C.: Smithsonian Institution, 2004.

Eraly, Abraham. *The Mughal Throne the Saga of India's Great Emperors*. London: Phoenix, 2004.

Esposito, John L. *The Oxford Encyclopedia of Islam*. Oxford: Oxford University Press, 1999.

Finkel, Caroline. *Osman's Dream the History of the Ottoman Empire*. New York: Basic Books, 2005.

Freely, John and Augusto Romano Burelli. *Sinan Architect of Suleyman the Magnificent and the Ottoman Golden Age*. London: Thames and Hudson Ltd., 1996.

Glasse, Cyrl. *The Concise Encyclopedia of Islam*. London: Stacey International, 1989.

Goodwin, Godfrey. *A History of Ottoman Architecture*. London: Thames and Hudson, Ltd., 1997.

Goodwin, Jason. *Lords of the Horizon a History of the Ottoman Empire*. New York: Picador, 1998.

Harvey, L.P. *Islamic Spain 1250 to 1500*. Chicago: The University of Chicago Press, 1992.

---. *Muslims in Spain 1500 to 1614*. Chicago: The University of Chicago Press, 2005.

Hillenbrand, Robert. *Islamic Architecture*. Edinburgh: University of Edinburgh, 1994.

Ibn Battutah. *The Travels of Ibn Battutah*. (trans. H.A.R. Gibb). New Delhi: Goodword Books, 2001.

Ibn Jubayr. *The Travels of Ibn Jubayr*. (trans. Roland Broadhurst). New Delhi: Goodword Books, 2001.

Ibn Khaldun. *The Muqaddimah*. (trans. Franz Rosenthal). Vol. 1. London: Routledge and Kegan Paul, 1967.

Ibn Tufayl, Abu Bakr Muhammad. *The Journey of the Soul [The Story of Hai bin Yaqzan]* (trans. by Dr. Riad Kocache). London: The Octagon Press, 1982.

India by Al-Biruni (ed. Qeyamuddin Ahmad), Delhi: National Book Trust, India, 1988.

Jacobs, Michael. *Alhambra*. New York: Rizzoli International Publications, Inc., 2000.

Kamen, Henry. *The Spanish Inquisition a Historical Revision*. New Haven: Yale University Press, 1998.

Lane-Poole, Stanley. *The Muslims of Spain*. New Delhi: Goodword Books, 2001.

---. *Saladin All-Powerful Sultan and Uniter of Islam*. New York: Cooper Square Press, 2002.

Lea, Henry Charles. *The Moriscos of Spain*. New Delhi: Goodword Books, 2001.

Levey, Michael. *The World of Ottoman Art*. London: Thames and Hudson Ltd., 1976.

Maalouf, Amin. *The Crusades Through Arab Eyes* (trans. Jon Rothschild). New York: Schocken Books Inc., 1985.

Mango, Andrew. *Atatürk the Biography of the Founder of Modern Turkey*. Woodstock, N.Y.: The Overlook Press, 2002.

Menocal, Maria Rosa. *Ornament of the World How Muslims, Jews, and Christians Created a Culture of Tolerance in Medieval Spain*. New York: Back Bay Books, 2002.

Michaud, Roland and Sabrina and Michael Barry. *Colour and Symbolism in Islamic Architecture Eight Centuries of the Tilemaker's Art*. London: Thames and Hudson Ltd., 1996.

Morgan, David. *The Mongols*. Malden, MA: Blackwell Publishing, 1990.

Necipoğlu, Gűlru. *The Age of Sinan Architectural Culture in the Ottoman Empire.* Princeton: Princeton University Press, 2005.

Nicolle, David. *Constantinople 1453 – The End of Byzantium.* Oxford: Osprey Publishing Ltd., 2000.

Nuseibeh, Said and Oleg Grabar. *The Dome of the Rock.* London: Thames and Hudson Ltd., 1996.

Phillips, Jonathan. *The Fourth Crusade and the Sack of Constantinople.* New York: Viking, 2004.

Rahman, Syed Azizur. *The Story of Islamic Spain.* New Delhi: Goodword Books, 2001.

Raymond, Andre. *Cairo City of History.* Cambridge, Mass.: Harvard University Press, 2000.

Roxburgh, David J. (ed). *Turks a Journey of a Thousand Years, 600–1600.* London: Royal Academy of Arts, 2005.

Schimmel, Annemarie. *The Empire of the Great Mughals.* London: Reaktion Books, 2004.

---. *Rumi's World The Life and Work of the Great Sufi Poet.* Boston: Shambhala, 2001.

Stierlin, Henri and Anne. *Splendors of an Islamic World.* London: Tauris Parke Books, 1997.

Weatherford, Jack. *Genghis Khan and the Making of the Modern World.* New York: Three Rivers Press, 2004.

INDEX